C000180191

MAKING A MARKET FOR A

This ethnographic study of the insurance industry performs an important and urgent task: it exposes the everyday practices by which global financial markets work. The authors bring wonderful clarity to difficult themes, from the structuring of financial deals to developing a macro-level theory of social practice that will be insightful for scholars adopting strategy-as-practice or practice approaches more broadly. This book will be a stimulating read for financial professionals, social scientists, regulators and policy makers alike.

Richard Whittington, Professor of Strategy, Said Business School, University of Oxford

This astonishingly thorough global ethnography, involving fieldwork in seventeen countries and over four hundred interviews, paints a fascinating picture of the practices of a unique, and hugely important industry.

Donald MacKenzie, Professor of Sociology, University of Edinburgh

Jarzabkowski, Bednarek and Spee succeed in the ambitious project of describing the global reinsurance market in terms of a set of interrelated practices. The book provides an original contribution to the social studies of markets and finance and is without a doubt one of the best available illustrations of the heuristic power of the practice approach. It is also a demonstration of how relational and practice-based approaches can tackle big questions and provide fresh and relevant insights. Above all, the book is testimony of the excellent intellectual skills and methodological prowess of the authors - a masterclass in how to study and describe in an accessible way a seemingly complex and almost intractable phenomenon. A notable achievement.

Davide Nicolini, Professor of Organization Studies, Warwick Business School

Despite ever worse natural and man-made disasters, somehow the money is found to cover gigantic losses and rebuild. Who insures the insurers and how do they do it? In this important contribution to the new sociology of financial markets Paula Jarzabkowski, Rebecca Bednarek and Paul Spee make the case for studying reinsurance as a neglected part of the global financial market. They track the agents through their yearly cycle of desk work, deal making, and global conference hopping. The losses are potentially so huge that no one company can cover then all – so this leads to collaborative deal-making and information sharing. The industry is cyclical and long term, and remarkably stable – up until now we are warned. It is detailed, mundane, almost boring arcane work carried out with the help of computer models but also requires finely tuned antennae to global events, social norms and financial acumen. It turns out second guessing God is all about detailed social and calculative practices and coordination.

Trevor Pinch, Goldwin Smith Professor of Science and Technology Studies, Cornell University

For hundreds of years we have traded variable cost - being risk - for fixed cost - being premium in our insurance world. Risk transfer, eventually leading to diversification of risk, is a mechanism that works as well today as ever. Today, we also start to think about risk differently with risk becoming a viable alternative asset class in a world of low interest rates. This book makes a significant contribution to a debate about an industry that is the oil in the engine of economic activity. It is a great piece of work.

Clement B Booth, Member of the Board of Management, Allianz SE

Making a Market for Acts of God is in the tradition of studies that ask how markets actually work. It is the richest ethnography yet on the process and practice of market making. Beyond that, it draws together earlier theories of market making to weave a thick description of the social nature of the markets.

Mitchel Y. Abolafia, Professor, University at Albany/SUNY,
Author of Making Markets: Restraint and Opportunism on Wall Street

In a very lively style, Paula, Rebecca and Paul zoom on every facet of our industry, analyzing codes, culture, norms and the complexity of each of them. They underline the value of the contextual and shared knowledge in the market which is an important contribution to the decision process when underwriting risks. They raise as well a series of concerns about the current changes in the reinsurance market as a shift toward converting insurance or reinsurance risks in the financial market or relying too much on models ignoring this contextual knowledge which has been so far so beneficial to our industry. The great value of this book is its complementary to the numerous technical and financial studies produced so far in our industry and its ethnographic approach of the market. Any one managing a company, a business, capital provider, underwriters, analysts should read this book. Everyone will recognize himself and its contribution to the value chain produced to mitigate these ACTS of GOD.

Michel Plecy, Former Deputy CEO of Partner RE Global
Member of boards of directors, Insurance companies of the Optimum Group

Making a Market for Acts of God

The Practice of Risk-Trading in the Global Reinsurance Industry

PAULA JARZABKOWSKI

REBECCA BEDNAREK

AND

PAUL SPEE

OXFORD

UNIVERSITY PRESS

OXFORD
UNIVERSITY PRESS

Great Clarendon Street, Oxford, OX2 6DP,
United Kingdom

Oxford University Press is a department of the University of Oxford.
It furthers the University's objective of excellence in research, scholarship,
and education by publishing worldwide. Oxford is a registered trade mark of
Oxford University Press in the UK and in certain other countries

© Paula Jarzabkowski, Rebecca Bednarek, and Paul Spee 2015

The moral rights of the authors have been asserted

First published 2015
First published in paperback 2017

All rights reserved. No part of this publication may be reproduced, stored in
a retrieval system, or transmitted, in any form or by any means, without the
prior permission in writing of Oxford University Press, or as expressly permitted
by law, by licence or under terms agreed with the appropriate reprographics
rights organization. Enquiries concerning reproduction outside the scope of the
above should be sent to the Rights Department, Oxford University Press, at the
address above

You must not circulate this work in any other form
and you must impose this same condition on any acquirer

Published in the United States of America by Oxford University Press
198 Madison Avenue, New York, NY 10016, United States of America

British Library Cataloguing in Publication Data
Data available

Library of Congress Cataloging in Publication Data
Data available

ISBN 978–0–19–966476–4 (Hbk.)
ISBN 978–0–19–878377–0 (Pbk.)

Cover image: © Shutterstock.com/hywards; © Rick Wilking/Reuters/Corbis.

Links to third party websites are provided by Oxford in good faith and
for information only. Oxford disclaims any responsibility for the materials
contained in any third party website referenced in this work.

Preface

WHO SHOULD READ THIS BOOK AND HOW SHOULD IT BE READ?

When we began this project we did not know much about reinsurance, the market that insures insurance companies. Insurance touched our lives in many ways: for example, policies on our homes and cars and professional indemnity as employees. We were also familiar with those "CNN events", the large-scale disasters, such as earthquakes, hurricanes, tsunamis, bushfire, and flood that are the very stuff in which reinsurance trades. Yet we were unaware that there was a market, reinsurance, that existed to help pay the insurance claims of people like us, as well as business, to rebuild after major disasters like Hurricane Katrina or the World Trade Center attacks. However, after more than three years of observing and interviewing people across the globe as they traded reinsurance, we now have unique insights into how this unusual market for disastrous events works.

Our aim is to bring this market to life for others. The data are very rich— we were there, sitting alongside the underwriters who traded through disasters such as earthquakes in Chile, Japan, and New Zealand; tornadoes in the United States; and other disasters around the globe, including floods, bushfires, oil spills, and acts of piracy. We will explain the workings of this socially and economically important market through our stories of these reinsurance professionals at work. We now outline who should read this book and how to read it.

WHO SHOULD READ THIS BOOK?

Those interested in natural and man-made disasters, from climate change to financial collapse. Reinsurance is a market that exists to provide cover for large-scale and unpredictable events from natural disasters, such as hurricanes, tornadoes, floods, fires, and earthquakes. Undoubtedly these types of disasters are increasing in both frequency and severity, with the cost of their losses mounting rapidly. Reinsurance also covers man-made disasters, such as environmental hazards, medical malpractice, and credit default. The financial collapse of 2008 made us all aware of systemic risks to society that are posed by such disasters in a world where markets are connected, and global companies or financial intuitions are deemed too big to fail. Reinsurance is part of society's safety net, picking up the pieces after disasters alongside government, aid organizations, and communities. A market that can function in this way should be of interest to anyone studying or managing these large social issues, whether natural or man-made.

Those interested in how financial markets work. Since the financial market collapse of 2008 there has been a wave of books explaining why these markets have not worked, from managerial hubris, to the physiological and psychological characteristics of the traders, to the inbuilt market mechanisms such as models that predispose failure. By contrast, our book shows how a global financial market **does** work. The reinsurance market has persisted since the late 1800s, consistently paying for disaster after disaster; we show how the collective risk-bearing practices of this market have enabled participants to survive shocks and continue to trade. Our study thus complements a growing vein of research in the social studies of finance, which examines social, cultural, and technological aspects of how market actors trade in financial risk. Reinsurance is a financial market with unique characteristics, worthy of study in its own right, not least because the unpredictable nature of the risks it trades in makes it less dependent on models than many other financial markets. Even so, it has many lessons to contribute to other markets.

Those interested in insurance and reinsurance risk. Any insurance and reinsurance professional will know more about their particular section of the market than a book like this could ever convey. For them, the value of this book is to show how their practice is connected to the global context and practices of the reinsurance industry. The book should provoke thought about the most sustainable and financially viable strategies for risk-transfer during a time of market upheaval.

Scholars interested in practice theory. Leading practice scholars have noted the immense potential of a practice lens for addressing big questions of importance to organizations and society. Yet thus far practice studies have been better at drilling into the (important) detail of everyday work; our study zooms out from these details to explain wider collective phenomena. Practice scholars should be interested in the specific analytical structure that we use to follow a global "nexus" of practices, as well as our analysis of particular practices such as "calculation". Our methods and approach will be of interest not only to those interested in market-making, but for practice scholars more broadly, including those studying technology, accounting, or strategy practice.

Those interested in global ethnography or ethnographies of markets. Finally, this book is emphatically ethnographic. We aim to make the market visible through ethnographic tales of the actual practice of the people within it. Thus we take readers on a global tour of the market, with stories ranging from flooding in Thailand to Credit & Surety risk in Continental Europe, to safeguarding high-value houses against bushfire in California. Along the way, we meet a range of underwriters and illuminate their collective practice, including John who analyzes risks to U.S. property, Ria, who examines bundles of risk in Pakistan, and Brent, who evaluates the risk to ships of all kinds and their passengers and cargo as they move from port to port. The theorizing within the book is located within this ethnographic storytelling. In addition, the global scope of this ethnographic study should help to extend the range of ethnographic methods.

HOW TO READ THIS BOOK

Some of our readers will wish to read from cover to cover; others will dip in and out of different sections according to their specific interests. The book is therefore constructed in several layers, which should help the reader to navigate the book and indeed the market.

Chapter 1 explains the framework of concepts that we use to structure the main empirical Chapters (2–5) of the book (see Table 1.1). Each chapter then takes readers through the broad principles of the market being addressed in that chapter, and shows how reinsurance traders, known as underwriters, enact those principles in their practice. The final two chapters tie these insights back into the theoretical framework, and emphasize our theoretical contribution to the study of market-making.

The **Reinsurance-as-Practice** sections in each chapter are slices of real life, where we draw directly on our ethnographic data to tell vivid stories of the (sometimes complex) practice of this market. Readers should be able to dip into these stories to gain a rich impression of the market, either within the narrative of the chapter, or separately from it.

Each chapter also has an inset **Buyer's Perspective** section. In these sections we clarify what is being bought and sold in the reinsurance market, by introducing Jane, the chief reinsurance buyer for GlobalInc, a leading insurance company. In showing the steps she takes to buy protection for her company from man-made and natural disasters, we answer such deceptively simple questions as "What is a reinsurance deal?" or "What is a reinsurance quote?"

Beyond developing the theoretical framework, Chapters 2–5 each also provide specific insight into particular phenomena, such as "market cycles" (Chapter 2) or "calculation" (Chapter 3), that speaks to other avenues of research. We briefly summarize some of these avenues in a section labeled **Further Theorizing** prior to the conclusion of each of these empirical chapters. These sections are chiefly aimed at scholars interested in that topic, and may be skipped by more general readers.

At the end of each chapter we provide a **Summary box** to remind the reader of the key points covered and reiterate our guiding theoretical structure.

Finally, while we have stripped out some of the technicality of reinsurance (a necessary step that will likely be noticeable to reinsurance professionals), a good deal of specific terminology is unavoidable. A comprehensive **glossary** is therefore provided, and we signify glossary terms in the text by bolding them and including an asterisk symbol the first time that they are used in any chapter; e.g. **line of business***. If you find a term puzzling, look to the glossary, where it should be explained.

Acknowledgments

We are grateful to the individual reinsurance professionals who gave their time and insight to this project, allowing us to share in their good times as well as the hard negotiations, the frustrations, and the late nights. We would never have understood the inner workings of the reinsurance market without this access, and the trust and generosity that went with it. We feel privileged and have fond memories of our time "in the field" with you all.

Special thanks are due to the Insurance Intellectual Capital Initiative (IICI), especially its chair, Bronek Masojada, who provided unstinting support, help with funding, access to contacts, constructive feedback, and guidance. We are also grateful to our Steering Group of Adrian Clark, James Illingworth, and Bill Rendall, who, with Bronek, coached, critiqued and reflected on our work over many years, and to Jane Curle, who made the meetings happen.

We thank the member organizations of the IICI: Amlin, Aon Benfield, Asia Capital Re, Hiscox, Liberty Syndicate Management, Lloyd's Tercentenary Foundation, the Society of Lloyd's, Validus, and the Worshipful Company of Insurers. In addition we are grateful to all the organizations that granted us access to conduct our project.

We appreciate the research funding received from different institutions, including the British Academy of Management; the Economic and Social Research Council, U.K.; the European Commission Marie Curie Fellowship; the IICI; and Aston Business School.

We thank our team members Dr. Laure Cabantous and Dr. Michael Smets with whom we collected data and shared experiences. You were critical in shaping our thinking and were, and are, invaluable teammates. In addition, we are very appreciative of the research assistance and data analysis received from Dr. Adriana Allocato, Dr. Gary Burke, and Stellar Luig.

Special thanks go to Professor Trevor Pinch, and to all colleagues in the Department of Science and Technology Studies at Cornell University, where the bulk of this book was written. We also offer thanks to Dr. Laure Cabantous, Dr. Matthew Hall, Professor Yuval Millo, Professor Mike Power, Professor Alex Preda, Dr. Michael Smets, and Dr. Mike Zundel for their comments on earlier drafts.

We are also grateful to Michel Plecy for turning his eyes to the authenticity for a reinsurance audience, and Nancy Osborn for providing feedback from a "lay audience" perspective. We are also indebted to Graham Topping for his feedback, critical eye, and for playing such an important role in whipping this book, and us, into shape.

x   *Acknowledgments*

Finally, we are thankful to our partners, Nick, James, and Alex respectively, for their understanding and support, both while we were immersed in conducting this ethnography and when we were obsessed with writing this book. It made all the difference.

We emphasize that the views expressed in this book are our own and do not reflect any authorization or endorsement by those we mention here. Additionally, while much that is good in the book is due to their help, any errors or oversights remain our own.

Contents

List of Reinsurance-as-Practice Empirical Illustrations

List of Buyer's Perspective Empirical Illustrations

List of Figures

List of Tables

1

Reinsurance

A Market for Acts of God

It's the unknown unknowns that we have to think about. By buying rein-surance we're transferring the risk of what we don't know, what we don't understand. And if we don't buy enough cover, then we could have some very nasty shocks.

(Interview with a senior executive in a large insurance company
explaining the purpose of reinsurance)

....

REINSURANCE-AS-PRACTICE 1A
Tōhoku Earthquake and Tsunami Shocks Japan . . . and its Reinsurers

On March 11, 2011 at 14:46 JST, the earth shook seventy kilometers (forty-three miles) off the Oshika Peninsula of Tōhoku in Japan.[1] Even in a country histori-cally well prepared for unstable ground, this magnitude nine earthquake was beyond anything anyone had predicted; it was the most powerful earthquake ever recorded to have hit Japan. The underwater shock generated powerful tsunami waves up to 40.5 meters high, and the devastation on land was hor-rific: 17,500 people died, 6,109 were injured, 2,848 went missing, and 340,000 people were displaced from the Tōhoku region. Beyond the human tragedy, this was also a physical disaster: 127,290 buildings collapsed, another 272,788 semi-collapsed, and a further 747,898 were partially damaged.[2] In addition, criti-cal infrastructure such as roads and railways was damaged, a dam collapsed and the nuclear power center at Fukushima went into meltdown, displacing thou-sands of employees and nearby residents, and creating an ongoing crisis with terrifying implications for the whole region.

[1] "Magnitude 9.03—Near the East Coast of Honshu, Japan." 2011. *United States Geological Survey (U.S.G.S.)*, April 5; http://www.webcitation.org/mainframe.php.

[2] National Police Agency of Japan. 2014. "Damage Situation and Police Countermeasures," February 10. http://www.npa.go.jp/archive/keibi/biki/higaijokyo_e.pdf; "The Great East Japan Earthquake." 2012. *World Bank*, May 9, Washington D.C.

In all, the World Bank estimated that the economic cost of the disaster was US$210 billion.[3] Even as the Japanese government and the Bank of Japan responded, aid and rescue teams flooded in from around the world to begin the massive task of recovery. Against this dramatic backdrop we focus on a market actor closely tied to such events: those reinsurance firms and their **underwriters*[4]** who insure the insurance firms, supporting insurers in paying the claims for their insured losses that are so critical for rebuilding after such disasters.

On March 11 in London, Simon,[5] a reinsurance underwriter in charge of the Japanese territory for his firm, was watching television before his tube ride into work when the breaking-news alert came in. His cup of coffee grew cold—forgotten as he watched in horror. As he rushed to the office, underwriting on the yearly reinsurance deals for Japan (which were currently being renewed) had ground to a halt. Simon spent the day following the live stream of news reports on his PC, and emailing his colleagues in Japan (**brokers*** and clients) with simple messages that they were in his thoughts. Around midday, he—almost symbolically—scrunched up the hard copy of a document on some "pricing" he had only just done for a Japanese deal, and tossed it in the bin. The careful calculations he had finalized so late last night in the office meant nothing now. Japan had changed overnight, and that included the work of underwriting Japanese insurance companies: providing reinsurance capital to help them bear the risk of major, often unpredictable, disasters, such as the earthquake that had just devastated Tōhoku. Simon winced as he considered that not only did he need to begin his pricing anew for any Japanese deal, he also needed to find out the losses his firm would have to pay from the Japanese deals they already covered. With all the uncertainty and chaos surrounding the event, it would be some time before he could get that kind of information. Today, therefore, he packed up relatively early. The late nights crunching the numbers and meetings with the executive team—in his own company as well his clients' firms—would be happening soon enough over the next weeks. Meanwhile, he grabbed his jacket and headed to a nearby bar to discuss the event with his colleagues, declaring, "This is what we are here for; to pay claims when the big one hits."

1.1. INTRODUCTION

This is a book about making a market for disasters such as the Tōhoku earthquake. Our approach is to analyze and explain this reinsurance market by

[3] Wharton Risk Management and Decision Processes Center. 2008. "Managing Large-Scale Risks in a New Era of Catastrophes: Insuring, Mitigating and Financing Recovery from Natural Disasters in the United States." Philadelphia, PA: The Wharton School, University of Pennsylvania; Swiss Re. 2012. "Natural catastrophes and man-made disasters in 2011: historic losses surface from record earthquakes and floods." Sigma Report, February.

[4] In this book, bold fonts with an asterisk are used the first time we use a specific reinsurance or theoretical term in any chapter, to denote that the meaning of the term may be looked up in the glossary.

[5] Pseudonyms for both individuals and firms are used throughout the book to preserve anonymity.

looking at the skilled professional **practice*** of reinsurance underwriters, like Simon, as they trade on risks, such as "Japanese Earthquake". The reinsurance market "insures insurance companies" for the risk that a major disaster might occur, resulting in multiple simultaneous or high magnitude claims that could cause insurance firms to collapse. As these **events*** are often unpredictable, and the damage and extent of loss they might cause is uncertain—those unknown unknowns in our opening quotation—we refer to this as a market for **Acts of God***. Our use of this term, while not strictly adhering to the legal definition, refers to the unpredictable and uncertain nature of such disasters, whether natural or man-made. For example, in recent years the reinsurance market has provided cover for natural disasters as diverse as hurricanes that devastated entire cities in the United States; earthquakes in Chile, New Zealand, and Japan; flooding in Australia and Thailand; and bushfires in California. At the same time it has paid out for man-made disasters, including terrorist attacks such as the World Trade Center in 2001; ongoing asbestos claims; piracy; environmental disasters, such as marine and oil rig spillage; and credit default. Trading in the probability of such disasters is fraught with unpredictability and uncertainty. In reinsurance there is never any way to predict **what** the next "big" one will be, **when** it will occur or **how much** it will cost. As one journalist puts it: "Reinsurers are ultimately responsible for every new thing that God can come up with."[6]

1.2. WHAT IS THIS MARKET?

Despite the highly visible "C.N.N. nature" of the large-scale events in which it trades, surprisingly little is known about the reinsurance market (Cummins and Trainar, 2009; Dupont-Courtade, 2013). We therefore briefly explain the parameters of this market.

The amount of **premium*** (revenue) received by reinsurers across the global market for the risk they take from insurance companies was \$233.6 billion in 2012.[7] This premium is received in return for reinsurance companies holding capital reserves to cover insured losses around the world that are growing in severity, frequency, and cost. For example, losses from catastrophic events have increased significantly from Hurricane Hugo in 1989, which, at \$4 billion of insured losses was the first event to cost more than \$1 billion;[8] to

---

[6] Greeley, B. 2011. "Sept. 11 Teaches Reinsurers about 'The God Clause'." *Bloomberg*, September 1. http://www.bloomberg.com/news/2011-09-01/sept-11-teaches-reinsurers-about-catastrophe-planning-the-god-clause-.html.

[7] "Global Reinsurance." 2013. *MarketLine Industry Profile*, October.

[8] Unless otherwise noted, all figures in the book are reported in United States Dollars.

events such as the World Trade Center in 2001, which incurred insured losses of approximately $35.5 billion to Hurricane Katrina in 2005, which cost some $46 billion in insured losses.[9]

These loss figures, while often U.S.-dominated because of the concentration of insured properties in high-risk regions, are not exclusively North American. Rather, 2011, which incurred losses from Australia, New Zealand, Japan and Thailand, was the second most expensive year for catastrophic loss on record, with an estimated insured loss of $116 billion.[10] Behind the magnitude of these ever increasing economic losses, there is enormous personal suffering and hardship as people attempt to rebuild properties, lives, and businesses. Reinsurance is thus a market that plays a critical social and economic role. It supports insurance companies to pay the claims that enable individuals, business, and society to get back on their feet after a disaster.

In Figure 1.1 we show the basic structure of the market, and its key players. As insurance companies take on the risk from a range of consumers—from domestic policyholders with home and car insurance, to businesses with everything from property to workers' compensation to business interruption insurance—an insurance firm carriers a portfolio of risks (Arrow A).

While these insurance companies have capital reserves to pay some claims on any of these risks, a big event, such as the Tōhoku earthquake above, or frequent smaller events, would result in claims that could exceed their capital reserves and cause insurers to collapse. Hence, insurance companies are called **cedents*** because they buy a reinsurance **deal*** that cedes away a specified portion of their portfolio of risk to reinsurers (Arrow B). These reinsurers receive a premium from their cedents in return for assuming a portion of risk, specified in a reinsurance deal. The reinsurers will be responsible for paying for the losses that have been specified in the deal if there is a disaster; therefore they must hold capital in reserve.

As this is a global market, with cedents transferring risks from different parts of the world to reinsurers who are also located in different capital hubs around the world, the market has an important third player: brokers (Arrow C). These brokers help cedents to structure a deal for transferring their risk, and then help them to find reinsurers who want to supply capital to such deals. We explain this process in more detail in Buyer's Perspective 1 in the text box.

---

[9] Wharton Risk Management and Decision Processes Center, 2008. "Managing Large-Scale Risks in a New Era of Catastrophes: Insuring, Mitigating and Financing Recovery from Natural Disasters in the United States." Philadelphia, PA: The Wharton School, University of Pennsylvania.

[10] "Natural Catastrophes and Man-Made Disasters in 2011: Historic Losses Surface from Record Earthquakes and Floods." 2012. *Swiss Re Sigma*, February.

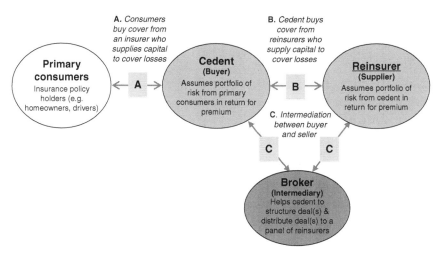

Fig. 1.1. An Overview of the Reinsurance Market

Our book focuses on the reinsurers in this market, in particular examining the underwriters who trade risks on behalf of their firms. While these risks are severe and unpredictable and the stakes for losses are high, reinsurance underwriters trade on such risks routinely, individually evaluating hundreds of risks each year as part of their everyday work. We make visible the skilled professional practice through which underwriters evaluate the probability of a disaster and the magnitude of any resultant loss, in order to charge a price for the risk being transferred to reinsurance firms. Always present in these **evaluations*** is the reinsurer's obligation to pay for any losses incurred on the deals they underwrite. In this book, we examine underwriting practice across risks as diverse as Indian Third Party Motor Liability, European **Credit & Surety***, and Californian Earthquake, showing how this practice generates a global market for Acts of God.

1.3. WHAT WE DID

From 2009 to 2012, we were granted extensive and unusual access to conduct a "fly-on-the-wall" ethnographic study of the global reinsurance market. As we were interested in how the market is generated within the everyday practice of underwriters evaluating and trading risk, we followed (Czarniawska, 2007) underwriters at work in the three main markets that channel reinsurance capital: Lloyd's of London, Bermuda, and Continental Europe. We also included the important Asia-Pacific market through fieldwork in Hong Kong, Japan, Singapore, and Australia. Across these markets, we shadowed and interviewed everyone from Chief Executive Officers to analysts in rein-surance, broking and insurance firms, and attended conferences, client meet-ings, and social activities with them. There were many social activities as this is an industry that has traditionally seen personal relationships as integral to big-money deals. Hence, we sipped champagne on sun-drenched ter-races in Monte Carlo, drank pints in watering holes on the square mile in London, downed shots on Christmas Eve in Bermuda, had leisurely lunches in Continental Europe, and danced at cabaret parties in Singapore. We also arrived early and sat late in offices, observing frustration, anger, exhilaration and stress, as underwriters conducted major financial transactions.

Reinsurance-as-Practice 1B gives a flavor of the rhythms of work in the reinsurance market, which we followed over three annual cycles. During this time, we experienced first-hand the market response to natural disasters, such as earthquakes in Chile, New Zealand and Japan, floods in Australia and Thailand, bushfires in Australia and California, and man-made disas-ters such as Deepwater Horizon, through the eyes of the people who under-write such events and pay for their losses. In total, we spent time across sixty-one separate offices in seventeen countries, conducting 935 observa-tions of underwriters and brokers at work and 382 interviews with stake-holders in all parts of the industry, as well as numerous other social and informal interactions (see Appendix A for further details). These rich data will be used to take the reader behind the scenes, showing how reinsurance underwriters trade in the complex, high-stakes deals that make a market for Acts of God.

....

REINSURANCE-AS-PRACTICE 1B
The Reinsurance Year: From Sipping Champagne to Allocating Capital

The reinsurance year begins in September with a three-day conference in Monte Carlo where key players from all over the world meet in a cluster of the most prestigious hotels around the main square. This is an important opportunity to mix with competitors, clients and brokers and get a sense of market conditions and trends.

We shadowed participants in Monte Carlo in September 2009. During the day we saw them dressed in chinos and polo shirts, drinking overpriced coffee, as we rushed alongside them through a tight schedule of meetings with brokers and clients, changing tables every thirty minutes in the Café de Paris and the main hotel venues. The evenings were more formal, starting with sipping champagne at cocktail parties, followed by dinners (in private dining rooms or on yachts for the inner circles), then serious drinking into the wee hours. At 8:00 a.m. the meetings began again.

While the setting is glamorous, these social activities are all business. Reinsurers talk about their risk-appetite and signal their expectation that prices will rise, while brokers and insurance clients talk prices down. Throughout these meetings people frequently check the hurricane tracker on their phones. September is the U.S. hurricane season and a bad storm could create huge losses that would reshape the market. There is no knowing when the next disaster might hit!

These conference activities are the beginning of a process that will culminate in the allocation of capital to specific reinsurance deals by particular renewal dates. Just as insurance policies renew annually, so do reinsurance deals, with the key renewal date being January 1. Hence, as the underwriters move from the September sun of Monte Carlo back to their desks in separate offices and firms around the world, the work becomes more analytic as the **renewal date*** approaches.

We followed the process by sitting with the underwriters at their desks, taking notes on the statistical data they received, learning how they analyzed specific deals in preparation for the looming January 1 renewal (see Chapters 3 and 4). Yet throughout the complex process of mathematical modeling, the social cues and information exchanged in the preceding months, such as at Monte Carlo, were not forgotten. Corridor chat and weekly meetings inside firms and gossip in the bars and restaurants around the various trading hubs focused on news of the market. Underwriters are continuously searching for information on that vital extra element of evaluating risk and making a market; how others in the market view these same deals on which they are all quoting. They are all keenly aware that no one knows the actual price of a deal until they have all provided their separate **quotes*** to the cedent and the cedent has issued a **consensus price*** based on those quotes (see Chapter 2). At that point, underwriters will need to make decisions about what share of the deal to take at that consensus price (see Chapter 5). Because the stakes are so high, the risk on any specific deal is spread across multiple reinsurers who each take different shares in that deal at the same consensus price.

Thus, as the world winds down for Christmas and New Year, underwriters (and the researchers shadowing them) enter into a heady last two weeks of negotiations and further analysis to finalize their share on deals. So we sat with underwriters at breakfast meetings, and joined in their late night takeaway curry and pizza as they did calculations at their desks. We winced as they screamed down phones, slamming the receiver back with frustration when they lost a share of a desired deal. We shared the elation as grown men jumped up and danced around the office in an embrace as the share on a deal came through. And we also looked forward to a rest, as the market was "put to bed" on New Year's Eve.

Typically, after a brief holiday in January, underwriters return to evaluating, pricing and placing capital on risk, focusing on the additional renewal dates of the first day of April, June and July. However, between the intensive analytic periods associated with these various renewal deadlines, reinsurers travel around the world seeing their clients, generating personal impressions about risks as they audit business practices, probe ownership and governance structures and look at the nuclear power plants, condominiums, residential homes and car yards that are being reinsured. They are consolidating existing relationships, forging new ones, and checking, over and over again, the exposure to perils and the potential for loss, in an effort to mitigate the unpredictability and uncertainty of the market in which they trade.

1.4. WHAT IS BEING TRADED?

The way that the reinsurance market trades in risks has some unique characteristics. Here we outline three key elements.

Unpredictability and uncertainty. There are many unpredictable and uncertain **perils/hazards*** that could hit an insurance company. Such perils need to be categorized as risks in order to be transferred to reinsurers. That is, cedents cannot simply transfer the probability of some unspecified peril occurring. Rather, as shown in Figure 1.2, particular types of perils, such as hurricanes, earthquakes, credit default, and so forth become categories of risk, according to the particular threat that they constitute to a cedent. For example, hurricanes and earthquakes constitute a risk to insured property, and are therefore classified as a particular type of risk, **Property Catastrophe*** risk. As particular perils are more likely in some regions than others—hurricane and earthquake are more likely in the United States; bushfire and flood in Australia—these risks might then be further classified by region as U.S. Property Catastrophe or Australian Property Catastrophe. Similarly the probability of credit default is classified as Credit & Surety risk, and the probability of marine cargo being lost due to hurricane, running aground, and so forth, will become **Marine*** risk. As cedents have multiple types of risks within their portfolio, they then buy separate reinsurance deals to cover them for each type of risk.

As shown in Figure 1.2, this deal will be structured in a particular way in order to be traded to the reinsurance market. When cedents buy a deal, they transfer the risk that they will have to pay for the losses occasioned by a specified type of event to the reinsurer. The reinsurer receives a premium, in return for which they have a legal obligation to pay for losses on such an event. Hence, the risk of a disaster is traded from the cedent to the reinsurer via a deal. Buyer's Perspective 1 explains how cedents develop a deal and put it to the reinsurance market.

Buyer's Perspective 1: What is a Reinsurance Deal and How does a Cedent Buy it?

Jane is the chief reinsurance buyer at GlobalInc, a global insurer domiciled in the United States. She is in charge of how much risk GlobalInc transfers to reinsurers, which she does by buying reinsurance deals. The reason GlobalInc buys reinsurance is to protect them from large, unpredictable events, such as a large hurricane, tornado or earthquake, or a major liability claim, where the resultant losses would be beyond the capital reserves of the firm. Jane will therefore buy one or more deals that cede some of GlobalInc's risk of such events to reinsurers. These legally binding deals will specify the (potential) losses being covered by the reinsurers in return for the premium they receive.

As reinsurance purchase is a complex balancing act between the cost of the cover (Jane does not want to pay too much) and the protection it provides, Jane works with a broker to help her structure the deals she wants to buy. She has the choice to buy a proportional (e.g. **quota share***) or a non-proportional (e.g. **excess-of-loss***) deal (see Figure 1.2). For GlobalInc's U.S. Property Catastrophe business, she prefers an excess-of-loss deal with an **attachment point*** of $100 million.[11] In this type of deal, the attachment point reflects the amount of loss that Jane believes GlobalInc can handle in-house, while all loss in excess of that $100 million will be transferred to reinsurers. As shown in Figure 1.2, the deal is structured in **layers*** according to the probability that an event that might cause damage within a particular band. Layer 1 will involve payment for any losses falling within a band of $100–$150 million, while Layer 2 is for losses in a band of $150–$300 million and Layer 3 is for losses in a band of $300–$600 million, with $600 million being the defined **limit*** of the total losses above which reinsurers no longer provide GlobalInc with cover (also see Buyers Perspective 3, Chapter 3). Jane is aware that she will have to pay more for Layer 1 protection than the higher layers, because it is more likely that one bad storm could cause a loss in that layer.

The broker then distributes the deal to the market for GlobalInc.[12] Jane wants to get a **panel*** of multiple reinsurers to cover her risk by each taking shares of the deal at the different layers, rather than trade it all to a single reinsurer. This is because she wants to be sure of a payout if there is a particularly severe event. If she spreads her risk across the global market, having twenty to thirty different reinsurers taking a share, then the chances of all of them defaulting are slender.

Jane then turns her attention to developing some of the other deals GlobalInc has in the market, including a Property Catastrophe deal in Europe (windstorm), a U.S. Motor Liability deal, and a U.S. MedMal (medical malpractice) deal.

"Over-the-counter" deals, designed by the buyers. As buyers tailor each deal to their specific demands, each deal is unique. That is, with reference to Buyer's Perspective 1, while other cedents might also buy a U.S. Property Catastrophe deal, none will have the exact same portfolio of properties in it as GlobalInc, nor be structured in exactly the same way. Furthermore, as shown in Figure 1.2, the probable events and risks upon which deals are based are vastly different. While two U.S. Property Catastrophe deals for the risk of windstorm might be somewhat comparable, they will be very different to a Chilean Property Catastrophe deal for the risk of earthquake and all of these will be vastly different to an Indian Third Party Motor Liability deal. This enormous variation in risks and deals—and the Acts of God that underpin them—raises a puzzle about how they

[11] Excess-of-loss deals that are structured into specified layers are the most common form of reinsurance deal for Property Catastrophe, particularly in developed markets or for larger cedents; Swiss Re, 2010. *The Essential Guide to Reinsurance.* Zurich: Swiss Re.

[12] While Jane has developed her deal with the help of a broker, some deals are developed on a "direct" basis with a particular reinsurer, particularly in the case of historic relationships with Continental European reinsurers (see Section 1.3). However, these deals are traded on the same basis to the wider market—they are developed by the cedent, in consultation with one reinsurance partner, and then distributed to a panel of reinsurers by a broker.

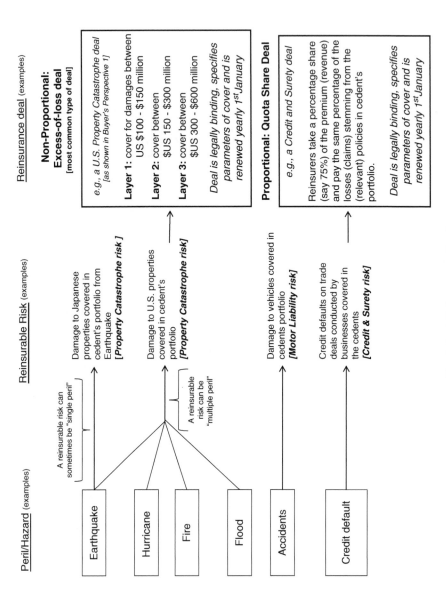

Peril/Hazard (examples)

Reinsurable Risk (examples)

Reinsurance deal (examples)

A reinsurable risk can sometimes be "single peril"

A reinsurable risk can be "multiple peril"

Earthquake

Hurricane

Fire

Flood

Accidents

Credit default

Damage to Japanese properties covered in cedent's portfolio from Earthquake
[Property Catastrophe risk]

Damage to U.S. properties covered in cedent's portfolio
[Property Catastrophe risk]

Damage to vehicles covered in cedents portfolio
[Motor Liability risk]

Credit defaults on trade deals conducted by businesses covered in the cedents
[Credit & Surety risk]

**Non-Proportional:
Excess-of-loss deal**
[most common type of deal]

e.g., a U.S. Property Catastrophe deal
[as shown in Buyer's Perspective 1]

Layer 1: cover for damages between US $100 - $150 million

Layer 2: cover between $US 150 - $300 million

Layer 3: cover between $US 300 - $600 million

Deal is legally binding, specifies parameters of cover and is renewed yearly 1st January

Proportional: Quota Share Deal

e.g., a Credit and Surety deal

Reinsurers take a percentage share (say 75%) of the premium (revenue) and pay the same percentage of the losses (claims) stemming from the (relevant) policies in cedent's portfolio.

Deal is legally binding, specifies parameters of cover and is renewed yearly 1st January

Fig. 1.2. A Reinsurance Deal

can all be traded across a panel of reinsurers within a global market. That is, how is it possible to have a global reinsurance market for these different deals that originate around the world, rather than a series of fragmented local markets for specific types of risk? In Chapters 3 and 4, we show the specific practice through which underwriters make these largely incomparable deals both comparable and tradable within a global market.

Collective risk bearing by competitors. While reinsurance is a competitive market, in which each firm is an independent profit-oriented company, no single firm takes all the risk on any deal. Rather, multiple reinsurers take shares of the same deal, so that if something catastrophic happens, no single firm pays all of the loss (Borch, 1962; Gugerli, 2013). This is because there are many deals in the market, often concentrated within a particular region, and some of these deals are very large. For example, Japanese company Zenkyoren's $10 billion catastrophe cover in 2014 is, reportedly, the largest deal in the world.[13] Hence, rather than a single reinsurer covering all the deals for Florida hurricanes, or covering the entire deal for a single cedent such as Zenkyoren, many different reinsurers each take shares of these various deals. Since it is impossible to know which deals will be hit, reinsurers have a better chance of survival if they all take a share in a deal, and all have to pay some, but not all, of any subsequent loss. Similarly, as shown in Buyer's Perspective 1, cedents have a better chance of being paid if they are not dependent on a single reinsurer, who might collapse if required to bear the entire loss of a big deal. Collective **risk-bearing*** is, thus, a way of hedging for the unpredictability of events and uncertainty about the value of loss by spreading risk across the players in the market. In effect, the reinsurance market is underpinned by a collective risk-bearing principle of "united we stand, divided we fall".

Perhaps most curiously, while reinsurers all provide different independent quotes for these deals, they ultimately all take shares on any particular deal at the same price (see Reinsurance-as-Practice 1B). This is known as a consensus price, a point we explain further in Chapter 2. The question is: how is such consensus achieved in a competitive market where firms are separately accountable to their own shareholders, have separate **security ratings*** (from agencies such as Standard & Poor's and Moody's), and are independently accountable to regulators? We address the relationship between individual competitive actions and collective risk-bearing in Chapters 2 and 5.

1.5. WHERE IS RISK TRADED? HUBS FOR GLOBAL CAPITAL ALLOCATION

Reinsurance risk originates and is traded from cedents around the world. Indeed, during our research we saw deals that originated from such vastly

---

[13] "News Review." 2014. *Insurance Linked*, March 24. http://insurancelinked.com/news-review-l-march-24-2014/.

different places as Pakistan, New Zealand, Romania, Germany, and the United States, and we will take you "around the world" to show how such deals are underwritten in this book. However, reinsurers located in three main reinsurance hubs supply the majority of the capital for these deals: London, Bermuda, and Continental Europe. These hubs developed for different purposes, which we briefly introduce here in order to provide some historical background to the reinsurance market (for a thorough historical treatment of the market; see Borscheid et al., 2013).

Lloyd's of London originated as an insurance market some 300 years ago in Edward Lloyd's coffee house, where mariners, ship owners and merchants gathered to strike deals to underwrite ships embarking on uncertain voyages (Herschaft, 2005; John, 1958). Lloyd's firms began writing reinsurance in the 1880s with a fire reinsurance policy on a book of North American risks (Kopf, 1929). Lloyd's members are underpinned by a central capital fund and share a common Lloyd's rating. While any specific reinsurance syndicate in Lloyd's may be relatively small in terms of global capital allocation, together they have impact, with Lloyd's comprising 6.6 per cent of the global reinsurance market by premium ceded in 2012.[14] The Lloyd's market is unique in being fully brokered, meaning that all business in Lloyd's must be traded via a Lloyd's accredited broker. Members of Lloyd's assemble daily to trade in the iconic Lloyd's building in London's Square Mile. As the only reinsurance market where brokers physically bring the deals to the reinsurers, the building sees a steady tread of feet to and from surrounding offices, all located at most a fifteen-minute walk from the underwriting floor. Hence, social interactions between brokers and reinsurers are more critical in this market than in any other (Smets et al., 2014). Yet this connectivity only characterizes one slice of the global reinsurance market. The other hubs operate on a very different model.

The largest and oldest dedicated reinsurers in the world originated in **Continental Europe**. They include the two biggest players, Munich Re and Swiss Re, who between them hold 33 per cent[15] of the global market by premium ceded. They were each founded in the mid-nineteenth century to service a domestic insurance customer base, within specific geographic Continental European locations that were not physically connected to each other (Kopf, 1929). Historically, and in contrast to Lloyd's, these dedicated reinsurers typically traded directly with their domestic cedents without a broker as intermediary.

As stand-alone large entities, continental reinsurers became particularly self-reliant in managing the premium they received from cedents to generate investment income and build capital reserves in case of a loss; in contrast

---

[14] "Global Reinsurance." 2013. *MarketLine Industry Profile*, October.
[15] "Global Reinsurance." 2013. *MarketLine Industry Profile*, October.

with Lloyd's with its common capital base. They also developed considerable individual expertise in risk evaluation, particularly by generating historical databases from their long-term relationships with cedents, which they developed into substantial analytical capabilities. As these reinsurers became the largest players in the world, they expanded globally from their original homes in places such as Zurich, Munich, and Hannover, setting up subsidiaries to access cedents and risks in other territories. Traditional Continental European reinsurers have very strong direct connections with their cedents, so enjoy deeper information exchanges than most brokered reinsurers. However, they are less able to access information about competitors than those in Lloyd's or Bermuda where close geographic proximity enables social relationships and gossip to flourish.

Bermuda is a small island off the east coast of the United States, with a regulatory structure that enables the rapid setup of business to capitalize on opportunities in the global market. The Bermudian reinsurance market has grown in waves, specifically in response to disaster events in the U.S. insurance market that generated increasing demand for reinsurance capital; and hence higher reinsurance premiums. The most recent waves followed the 2001 attack on the World Trade Center and the devastating 2005 hurricane season of Katrina, Rita and Wilma. As Bermuda is a market originating in response to a shortage in U.S. cover, Bermudian reinsurers have been focused on providing capital to U.S. risk, particularly Property Catastrophe, as opposed to other types of risk, such as **Casualty*** or Credit & Surety risk.

Bermuda's isolation, combined with the rapid development of new companies, has made Bermudian reinsurers very dependent on broking. They require brokers to act as a sales force to the insurance world, letting them know that Bermudian companies are a source of sound and viable capital, and to bring deals and cedents to the island. While each company operates separately (in comparison to Lloyd's), the relative isolation and small size of the island generates a degree of "physical" connection in the marketplace. All of the relevant companies are located on some ten streets within the Port of Hamilton, within walking distance of each other. Friday afternoons see the popular Harry's Bar on the waterfront full of reinsurers from rival firms having drinks and pumping each other for information. The island thus has a dense network of social interactions that facilitates peer-to-peer information sharing.

Summary: The global dispersion of reinsurance traders and risk. As we have shown, reinsurance is a socially and economically important financial market that trades in an unusual product—the risk of unpredictable disasters that originate around the globe. Because it is never possible to know when and where the next big event will hit or how big the loss will be, reinsurers dispersed globally have developed a practice of collective risk-bearing, taking shares in the various, vastly diverse deals that comprise the global market.

How they do this was the puzzle we set out to explore. Unlike other financial markets, they have no strong technological regime, such as a ticker or electronic exchange that provides a consistent point of contact for transactions anywhere in the world (e.g. Knorr Cetina and Bruegger, 2002a; 2002b; Preda, 2006). They have no singular model or algorithm with which to calculate risk in a common way (e.g. MacKenzie, 2006; Millo and MacKenzie, 2009). There is neither a strong regulatory regime enforcing the same practice (Fligstein and Mara-Drita, 1996), nor a normative regime arising from close proximity and everyday contact with each other (Baker, 1984; Zaloom, 2006). And yet these reinsurance underwriters, each in their different firms, in their different geographic hubs, working on very different types of deals, consistently, as part of their everyday practice, evaluate hundreds of reinsurance deals, generate a consensus price for each deal, and collectively share the risk of that deal with some of their competitors in the market. This book explains how this collective practice of the market emerges within the individual practice of the traders who underwrite reinsurance risk.

1.6. THEORIZING THE MARKET: ADVANCING A CONCEPT OF NESTED RELATIONALITY

A stream of work on the social studies of finance has begun to examine the complex social activities of market-making. Drawing from economic sociology as well as science and technology studies (Pinch and Swedberg, 2008), these studies start from the point that "prices are not abstract, given or spontaneously generating themselves, without any interference from human actors" (Preda, 2007: 519). They suggest that we examine how markets are made between participants as they interact "in specific settings under specific conditions." These specific settings and conditions, including rules, norms, spatial arrangements, technologies, and bodily orientations (Abolafia, 1996; Beunza and Stark, 2004; Knorr Cetina and Bruegger, 2002a; Preda, 2006; Zaloom, 2006) are the **practices** within which market-making activities such as pricing are possible. Our study of making a market for Acts of God is located within this view; that in their everyday work of participating in financial markets people engage in the practices that constitute the collective practice of the market.

The reinsurance market is particularly relevant to study as a global market because, as already outlined, risks that originate around the world are borne, collectively, across reinsurers in different firms in different geographic locations that comprise different national, cultural, historical and regulatory structures. We define a global market as one in which "patterns of relatedness and coordination . . . are global in scope" and in which "processes have global breadth," so comprising a "globally extended domain" within which market interactions and activities, such as those between buyers and suppliers, take place (Knorr Cetina and Bruegger, 2002a: 905).[16]

1.6.1. A Conceptual Framework: Relationality, Nested Relationality, and Relational Presence

Our book, thus, approaches markets through a social theory of practice.[17] Specifically, we draw upon the work of Theodore Schatzki (2001; 2002; 2006) to unpack the collective practices that make up a global market and ensure its coordination and functioning (see Table 1 for an overview of Schatzki's concepts adopted in this book). We will develop a layered conceptual framework of **relationality***, **nested relationality***, and **relational presence*** to explain how the collective practice of a market is accomplished in the practice of its participants.

First, we draw on the notion of **relationality**. A relational approach privileges the study of "relations and practices over the individual or organization" (Chia and Holt, 2006: 638; Cooper, 2005; Nicolini, 2013; Schatzki, 2002). That is, collective market practice can be studied in the relations among various market-making practices, such as the way that underwriters relate to each other (or an assumed collective "other") during the quoting on specific deals, described in Reinsurance-as-Practice 1B, in order to generate the collective practice of a consensus price. Empirically, therefore, we need to look beyond the separation of individual and market practice to how the two are entangled within and "actively constitute each other" (Cooper, 2005: 1,699). In this book we will tease out the relationality of work practice in global markets. We will show that people make the market function, from their various different financial hubs around the world, by relating the work that they are doing as they evaluate particular deals (such as that of GlobalInc in Buyer's Perspective 1), to the work that they assume others are doing on that same deal and other deals. For example, as we will show in Chapter 2, individual

---

[16] In this book we examine market-making from the perspective of the reinsurers who supply the capital to cover insurance risks. We do so advisedly because the relationship between these suppliers is critical in generating a consensus price at which multiple reinsurers are willing to transact. While many theories of markets examine how competition narrows the field, leading to a trading exchange between only a few parties, the collective risk-bearing nature of the reinsurance market examines how competition leads to an exchange, at a consensus price, between many suppliers; in our case a panel of reinsurers, with a single buyer, an insurer.

[17] While there are multiple practice theories, all with a largely consistent focus upon the way events and relatively stabilized social patterns unfold within the everyday practice of actors, in this book we draw primarily on Schatzki's theory of practice. For a more comprehensive overview of practice theory and of different practice theorists, refer to Knorr Cetina et al. (2000); Reckwitz (2002); Nicolini (2013).

underwriters all around the market, working on vastly different **risk-types***, engage in a very consistent practice of quoting. In doing so they participate in and perpetuate the collective market practices through which deals are quoted and consensus price emerges.

Second, we will show that this relationality involves multiple intercon-nected work practices that we term **nested relationality**. A global market is complex and so different aspects of the work of market-making are nested within each other. For example, we cannot just look at people's quoting prac-tice (see Chapter 2) or their calculative practice with statistical models (see Chapter 3). Each of these types of practice is critical but also partial in the col-lective practice of making a global market. Hence, we must understand each of these individual work practices, such as quoting or modeling, as they sit at the nexus of multiple other, interconnected work practices involved with eval-uating different types of risk (Chapter 4), or enacting the **risk-appetite*** of the different firms competing for a share of the various deals (see Chapter 5). That is, the work practices that comprise the market are nested within each other.

Third, we will develop a theory of **relational presence** to explain the inter-action between participants in a global market. In some markets, flickers on a trading ticker enable actors to respond electronically to the signals they receive from each other. Such **response presence** (e.g. Knorr Cetina and Bruegger, 2002a; Preda, 2006; 2009a) is not seen in reinsurance, where actors are not connected through such technology. Neither are they connected through a common space, such as the open outcry market to which Zaloom (2006: viii) refers, so viscerally, as a "flesh and bone" market, in which actors have an **embodied presence** with each other, literally, through their flail-ing arms, raised voices, and whole body gestures as they place bids (see also Baker, 1984; Goffman, 1967/2005). Rather, our actors are relationally present with each other through the common practices that underwriters enact, which constitute particular facets of market-making activity. For example, an underwriter on the GlobalInc deal will be relationally present with other underwriters that comprise the reinsurance panel for that same deal, even if not connected in real time, because they will use common quoting prac-tices for that deal. At the same time, these underwriters will be relationally present with underwriters on other U.S. Property Catastrophe deals because they will use similar calculative practices to evaluate such deals. And these underwriters will be relationally present with underwriters on different risk-types, such as Credit & Surety risk (see Figure 1.2) through the risk-appetites of their firms. Hence, any one underwriter will be relationally present with other underwriters as each one performs their individual practice, at a nexus of the multiple nested relationalities that comprise the market. This notion of relational presence therefore contrasts with the concepts of embodied and response presence in existing explanations of coordination in financial mar-kets (Knorr Cetina and Bruegger, 2002a). In summary, throughout this book we will develop the empirical basis for our conceptual framework of relationality, nested relationality, and relational presence within which a global market is able to function.

1.6.2. Sites of Market-Making Activity

In each chapter we zoom in on a specific **site*** of market-making activity (Schatzki, 2002; 2005), using rich ethnographic stories to explain its particular work practices. We then zoom out to show how those individually enacted work practices relationally construct collective market practice (Nicolini, 2009).

In common parlance "site" means a specific place, such as Bermuda or London, or even a particular firm. However, reinsurance deals are not written by a single firm, or in a single geographic region, but rather through the collective practice by which competitors take shares in deals at a consensus price. Hence, we take the practice concept of site, which goes beyond location, space, or time. Instead it incorporates the way that these elements come together as people interact over any specific activity of market making, such as the activity of quoting deals to establish a consensus price. We therefore conceptualize the reinsurance market as composed of multiple sites of market-making activity, in which "things exist and events happen" (Schatzki, 2002: 63). Further, these sites are themselves **practices** (such as evaluation) within which activities (such as modeling) happen (Schatzki, 2005: 468). Specifically, we examine the practice of making the market within the following sites.

The process of evaluating and quoting deals. A market does not exist per se, except in so much as the actors within it trade something. In reinsurance, underwriters trade deals that transfer risk from cedents to reinsurers (see Section 1.2 and Figure 1.2). This trading involves specific activity in evaluating and quoting these deals in order to establish a consensus price at which they may be traded. Different reinsurers then take a share of these deals, based on their evaluation. This activity takes place within the individual work practices of actors across the global market. We therefore conceptualize the activities of evaluating and quoting deals as two particular sites of collective market-making activity, which we explain in Chapters 2 and 3.

Specific risk-types. As shown in Figure 1.2, there are many types of very different reinsurance risks from U.S. Property Catastrophe, to Marine, to Credit & Surety. Each of these risk-types constitutes a very different site of market-making activity, involving particular calculative practices that are specific to that risk-type. Underwriters make their career in evaluating a particular risk-type, so becoming skilled professionals in the calculative practices that are germane to that risk-type. These underwriters are the ones that generate the collective market practice of the consensus price for deals within that risk-type, and make the decisions about taking shares of those deals. We therefore consider specific risk-types as particular sites of market-making activity that we explain in Chapter 4.

The risk-appetite of the firm. While underwriters do the work of evaluating and quoting on deals, the firms in which they work are the actual risk-carriers that hold the capital to pay out on losses. These firms have different appetites for the various risk-types, such as Property Catastrophe, Casualty, Marine, and so forth; and different deals. This variable risk-appetite shapes which types of underwriters that firms employ, and how hard these underwriters compete for a share of different risk-types and deals. Hence, the risk-appetite of a firm is not a concrete "thing" but rather is enacted in a dynamic and fluid process (Power, 2009) by underwriters throughout the year, according to their success in competing for and gaining shares of those deals that are particularly attractive to their firm. The practice of enacting risk-appetite is absolutely critical in determining which specific firms comprise the collective market that is bearing risk on any particular deal. We explore how risk-appetite shapes competition between firms in Chapter 5.

While we focus our ethnographic eye on a different site in each chapter, none of these exists in isolation. Rather, they "can only be studied relationally, and they can only be understood as part of a nexus of connections" (Nicolini, 2013: 229). Therefore, in Chapter 6, we draw together the nested relationality within and between sites. We thereby show how the reinsurance market has been able to function collectively as a global market in providing for disaster after disaster, even as disasters continue to increase in frequency and severity year-on-year. Yet we sound a note of caution, pointing to the particular combinations (the nested relationality) that might be implicated in financial crises that spiral throughout a global system. We propose that an understanding of nested relationality is a first step in potential damage control for the alarming changes in practice we see emerging in this industry, which have parallels with crises in other financial industries (see also Chapter 7).

1.6.3. Building on Existing Theory

An aim of this book is make our theorizing accessible through our ethnographic tales of the field (Van Maanen, 2011). We therefore weave theoretical concepts into the narrative of each chapter, using many rich illustrations of Reinsurance-as-Practice to make our conceptual points and develop our framework of nested relationality and relational presence. In doing so, our book also draws upon and speaks to existing bodies of theory, to which it both owes a debt and also makes a contribution. We allude briefly to these here, as well as developing further theorizing points within each chapter.

First, our study is located within the general practice turn in management and organization theory (Feldman and Orlikowski, 2011; Nicolini, 2013), which has gained considerable momentum over the last two decades in fields as diverse a strategy-as-practice (see Jarzabkowski, 2005; Jarzabkowski et al., 2007; Jarzabkowski and Spee, 2009; Johnson et al., 2003; Vaara and Whittington, 2012; Whittington, 2006); technology-in-practice (see Leonardi and Barley, 2010; Orlikowski, 2001; 2007; Orlikowski and Scott, 2008); and accounting-in-practice (see Hopwood and Miller, 1994; Ahrens and Chapman, 2007; Faure and Rouleau, 2011; Mikes, 2009; Whittington, 2011). In particular, our study is relevant to those scholars who increasingly posit a practice approach as a way to examine how work is accomplished within a bundle of practices (Chia and Holt, 2006; Pickering, 1995; Schatzki, 2002; 2006) in which technologies, spatial arrangements, materials, bodies, motivations, and emotions come together. We provide an empirically-substantiated framework for applying practice theory to the complex issues of markets and show how scholars may zoom in on the details of an individual underwriter's work practice, even as that practice is revelatory of the collective practice of the market (Nicolini, 2013).

Second, our work is linked to a growing tradition of ethnographic work in social studies of finance that shows how financial markets actually work (e.g. Abolafia, 1996; Beunza et al., 2006; Beunza and Stark, 2012; Çalışkan, 2010; Knorr Cetina and Bruegger, 2002a; Mackenzie, 2006; Millo and Mackenzie, 2009; Preda, 2009b). We draw from these studies in three key aspects of market-making: the concept of value/evaluation; stabilizing the "work" of the market within collective practice; and making the market within a bundle of material, social, cultural and calculative practices.

The concept of **value** is at the heart of any market. It covers a broad spectrum of "goods" from the aesthetic to the financial to the domestic (e.g. Antal et al., 2015; Heuts and Mol, 2013; Pinch, 2015). Yet value is a somewhat problematic concept on at least two fronts. Firstly, there is the concept of value, which, in a market economy, is typically associated with economic value and the metrics associated with price (Aspers, 2009; Swedberg, 1994). Some authors have criticized this singular concept of value, drawing attention to the disputability and multiplicity of concepts of value, such as exchange value, use value, or semantic value among others (e.g. Helgesson and Muniesa, 2013; Lamont, 2012). There are thus calls to conceptualize value more broadly, particularly examining the intangible aspects of value which are not easily converted into a price, score, or ranking (Antal et al., 2015). Secondly, there is a distinction between value, which is the worth attributed to some "good" (e.g. a score or a price) and evaluation, that emphasizes the process through which any attribution of worth is constructed (Lamont, 2012; Stark, 2009; Vatin, 2013). For example, the scores given to a wine to express its value are abstract representations that provide little insight into the professional practice of evaluating that wine by a recognized expert (Hennion, 2015). Hence we need to understand how concepts of value encode the professional practice of evaluation through which they are generated (Lamont, 2012). For the purposes of this book, we adopt these distinctions, considering the price attributed to reinsurance risk to contain a complex set of concepts about its value that do not reside simply in whether a deal has a lower or higher **rate of return***; but, rather, capture and express the professional practice of evaluating risk that is the everyday work of reinsurance underwriters (see Chapters 3 and 4).

These concepts of value and evaluation are central to the **marketization*** of reinsurance risk, in which it is critical to attribute economic value to unpredictable risk in order to trade it as a financial object. As we shall show in Chapters 3 and 4, the process of evaluation is complex, incorporating many concepts that extend our understanding of the calculative practices through which financial objects are traded (Çalışkan and Callon, 2010; Callon and Muniesa, 2005) such as the localized knowledge of the underwriter and his/her skill in evoking the underlying risks to give meaning to the prices being constructed. It is therefore important to distinguish between the economic value that is constructed in some "objective" measure such as price, which may appear singular, and the multiplicity of values attributed within the evaluation process that leads to price (Helgesson and Muniesa, 2013).

Sociological studies of markets also draw attention to the critical role of social interactions and normative rules of market participation in stabilizing the work of the market. For example, some studies have examined how dense social networks that are characterized by repeat transactions make defectors who do not conform highly visible, so that they can be sanctioned (Granovetter, 1985; White, 2001). Others have examined how actors sustain the collective practice of the market within their own actions. Abolafia (1996) and Baker (1984) are seminal works in this field for social studies of finance, showing how individual opportunism and collective restraint are practiced on trading floors. They note how market actors enact a dense social web of normative obligations to trade, such as being prepared to offer prices on difficult deals, in order to keep the market liquid (see also Beckert, 2009; Zaloom, 2006). Of course, social interaction is not a control in itself, since it can also generate spirals and mania (Abolafia and Kilduff, 1988), or reproduce hubris and false confidence (Ho, 2009). It is imperative to study the social structure of markets as they both produce market stability (Abolafia, 1996), but can also produce the cultures and practices of unsustainable financial markets (Ho, 2009). We examine these issues of producing collective market practice particularly in Chapters 2 and 5, and focus on potentially destabilizing elements in Chapter 6.

Finally, social studies of finance open our eyes to the tools and technologies of trading, illuminating a rich vein of objects to examine in the practice of market making (Muniesa et al., 2007). Studies have shown that the quantitative technologies for trading, the financial models, are not simply "black boxes" within which price is constructed, but are influential calculative devices that shape the market (Callon, 1998). For example, in the trading of financial derivatives, the Black-Scholes-Merton pricing model was not simply a tool at the service of traders: it actually shaped the practice of the market, as trading began to reflect the pricing patterns determined by the model (MacKenzie, 2006; Millo and MacKenzie, 2009).

These tools and technologies form part of the socio-material bundle involved in trading (Beunza et al., 2006). For example, Schatzki (2002) provides a detailed example of the rich bundle of practices involved in day trading, including scanning screens, looking up newspapers, talking to traders at other desks, talking to the screen, monitoring flickers of color on screen, watching a particular graphic, using different keyboard and mouse functions, and moving around the work station. These practices are not incidental but, as Preda (2006; 2009a; 2009b) shows, central to the work of calculation: they enable the trader to participate in and construct the market (see also Knorr Cetina and Bruegger, 2002a; 2002b). Indeed, these specific arrangements influence price-making, for example the specific spatial arrangements of trading floors, combined with the use of tools and technologies, shapes the way traders see opportunity and attribute value in arbitrage markets (Beunza and Stark, 2004). Such studies thus draw attention to trading tools and technologies and the way that they enact the market (Mackenzie and Millo, 2003; Millo and Mackenzie, 2009). We examine how such tools and technologies are used in the practice of evaluation in Chapters 3 and 4.

1.7. BOOK STRUCTURE

We now provide an overview of the structure of this book (see also Table 1.1). In each chapter, we build the components of our theory of nested relationality by "zooming in" (Nicolini, 2009) upon a specific set of relational practices that are enacted within the activity of that particular site. We then "zoom out" (Nicolini, 2009) to explain how these relational practices enable the coordination of activity that characterizes that particular aspect of the market.

Each of the empirical chapters (Chapters 2 to 5) is built around a set of core concepts within practice theory that involves the **general understandings*** that shape activity within that particular site and the **practical understandings*** through which they are enacted and the way that these are coordinated across a global market (Schatzki, 2002; see Table 1.1). Using Knorr

Table 1.1. The Kaleidoscope of the Reinsurance Market

	Empirical dynamic of market functioning	Turning the kaleidoscope: Site	General understanding	Coordinating practices	Practical understanding
Definitions	n/a	Sites "are where things exist and events happen" (Schatzki, 2002, 63).	General understandings are "a sense of how to participate in a community gathering" (Schatzki, 2002, 86).	Dynamic social practices that are enacted in organizing the activities of interdependent actors (Jarzabkowski et al., 2012).	Practical understandings are "complexes of know-hows regarding the actions constituting the practice" (Schatzki, 2006, 1864).
Chapter 2	How reinsurers bear unpredictable and uncertain risk collectively at a consensus price.	2.2 *Quoting on deals* as a site for market-making.	2.3 Collective risk-bearing rests on *consensus pricing* of deals. *Market cycles* stabilize the flow of capital.	2.4 Quoting and trading around a specific *renewal date* coordinates the actions of market actors.	2.5–6 *Renewing business* and *process for quoting* enact the consensus and cyclical features of the market.
Chapter 3	How varied risks stemming from different perils can be traded as deals.	3.2 *Evaluating deals* as a site for market making.	3.3 *Marketization* of risk pertains to an understanding that supports that risks can be calculated.	3.4 Working with *calculative devices* in the form of vendor models connect individual underwriters in the calculation of varied deals.	3.5 *Technicalizing and contextualizing* render deals comparable as tradable objects in a financial market.
Chapter 4	How varied risk-types can be traded as deals when there is little information and no vendor models.	4.2 Evaluative practices enacted within different risk-types.	4.3 Marketization persists despite difficulties of calculation/quantification of the deals pertaining to certain risk-types.	4.4 *Epistemic cultures* inform how underwriters on particular risk-types are connected in the knowledgeable practices of evaluating deals of that risk-type.	4.5 Different ways of *blending* technicalizing and contextualizing within epistemic cultures depending on risk-types.
Chapter 5	How firms (variably) compete amidst consensus as they allocate capital to different risk-types and deals.	5.2 Enacting the *firm's risk-appetite* as a site for market-making.	5.3 Competing to shape the consensus price of deals and for a share of them.	5.4 Firm *risk-appetite*, filters which firms are connected in sharing risk on any particular deal.	5.5 Firm risk-appetite enacted through diversification, relationship longevity, and capital availability, all of which varies between firms on any particular deal.
Chapter 6	How the market functions within nested relationality, and how current changes are altering these relations with harmful consequences.	Drawing together the nested relationality within and between sites.	Nested relationality is relationality between the bundle of sites and practices outlined in previous chapters.		

Cetina's (1999) metaphor of a kaleidoscope, we think of each chapter as a turn of the kaleidoscope that brings the particular practices within that site under reflection. In each chapter, we illustrate our points empirically with rich ethnographic tales that we label as Reinsurance-as-Practice in order to show how this aspect of the market works in practice. The aim is to bring the practice of the market to life and provide empirical weight for our concept of nested relationality. The structure follows the "sites" of practice we described in Section 1.6.2.

In Chapter 2, we turn the kaleidoscope to focus on how consensus price and **market cycles*** are enacted within the process of quoting and renewing deals. We illustrate this process through a rich example of Reinsurance-as-Practice which follows the catastrophic Thai floods in 2011 and their impact on the market cycle.

In Chapter 3 we explain the marketization of reinsurance risk, turning the threat of perils into tradable deals through the increasing pervasiveness of statistical **models***. We illustrate the practices of technicalizing and contextualizing deals with a Reinsurance-as-Practice example of an underwriter, John, evaluating U.S. Property Catastrophe deals for risks such as hurricane damage within the Gulf of Mexico.

In Chapter 4 we turn the kaleidoscope to focus on variation in risk-types. We explain that large swathes of the risk covered by the reinsurance industry are considered "un-modelable" and come with very little statistical information. We show that such risks can be evaluated and traded by different groups of dedicated reinsurance experts with specific knowledge of the calculative practices for that risk-type. Their varied practices are illustrated with a series of Reinsurance-as-Practice examples of evaluating different risk-types, including Credit & Surety, Marine and Property Catastrophe risks, from different regions including Spain, India, and Pakistan.

Chapter 5 brings into focus variation in the way firms compete to shape the consensus price and to gain shares in particular deals according to their risk- appetite. We bring this theme of competition alive with a Reinsurance-as-Practice example of underwriters in four different firms around the world, each competing for the same deal on a different basis, according to the variation in their risk-appetite.

In Chapter 6 we explain how the market is enacted within a nested relationality between sites and practices. This chapter will show that nested relationality both enables the market to function, but is also fragile, in that the entire nest depends on the complex interweaving of a series of specific practices in particular sites. When some of these practices shift, for whatever reason, they shift the entire set of relationships within which the market is made. We will explain some rapidly escalating threats to the current nested relationality. In particular, we will suggest that these changes are shifting the reinsurance market from a market for Acts of God to a market for financially tradable commodities, with potentially serious consequences for its viability.

We conclude, in Chapter 7, with summarizing reflections, where we draw some parallels to other financial markets and suggest some practical and theoretical lessons arising from our exploration of reinsurance as a market for Acts of God.

2

United We Stand, Divided We Fall

Bearing Risk Collectively

2.1. INTRODUCTION

This chapter explains how actors make a market that trades risk from insurance companies to reinsurance companies. In this first turn of the kaleidoscope, we bring into focus the **relationality***[1] between the practice of reinsurance underwriters acting competitively for their firms and the collective practice of the market in sharing risk for reinsurance deals. We will show how these underwriters, even as they are dispersed around the globe, enact similar practices for **quoting*** on deals and for taking a share of these deals at a **consensus price***, meaning that a single price will be agreed for all reinsurers taking a share of any particular deal across the market. These collective practices for quoting and trading, while not regulated, constitute strong normative obligations that are a powerful stabilizing force, constraining the competitive impulse for opportunistic trading and pricing wars. Even as they compete for their own profitability, reinsurers are keenly aware that in this market for Acts of God, unpredictable events, such as the Tōhoku earthquake, or the attack on the World Trade Center, can hit at any time and bring down a firm that acts in isolation, or even cause the market to collapse. Hence, despite pricing risk individually in their different firms around the world, often without any direct interaction, they bear risk collectively as a market. This chapter explains how such collective practice is enacted.

The chapter is structured as follows. First, we highlight the quoting of deals as a specific **site*** in which to examine the relationality between individual practice and collective market practice. Second, we explain two **general**

---

[1] In this book, bold fonts with an asterisk are used the first time we use a specific reinsurance or theoretical term in any chapter (apart from a few of the most common terms which we highlight in Chapter 1 only) to denote that the meaning of the term may be looked up in the glossary.

about the collective risk-bearing practice of the market: the
ιg of deals, and fluctuation between high-priced (hard) and
.) **market cycles***. We will show how these two general under-
ɟ to stabilize the flow of capital in the market. Third, we will
deals are renewed annually on a pre-specified **renewal date***,
to coordinate the quoting practices of competitors around the
ɪaking the market for that deal. Fourth, we reveal two **practical
undeɪɔ.. ᴅings*** that underwriters enact in their everyday work: the practice
of renewing business and the practice of quoting deals. We use the story of
the Thai floods in 2011 as a way to bring them to life and show how consensus
pricing and market cycles happen in practice. We also direct reader's attention to the Buyer's Perspective 2, where we explain how Jane, reinsurance
buyer for GlobalInc, generates a consensus price from the quotes she receives.

Buyer's Perspective 2: What is a Quote; and How does the Cedent Select a Consensus Price?

For each deal that she has in the market, Jane, the senior reinsurance buyer at
GlobalInc, receives an array of **quotes*** from a selection of reinsurers. These
quotes indicate:

- The **quoted price*** at which each reinsurer is willing to take a share of the
  deal; and
- The percentage share of the deal they wish to take at that quoted price. A higher
  share means a higher amount of premium for the reinsurer for assuming a
  correspondingly higher share of the risk.

Jane expects variation in the quoted prices she receives, as well as different shares
to be offered, as the different reinsurance underwriters will have different views on
the deal. For example, those who see the deal as a bigger risk will ask for a greater
premium for their capital so their quotes will be higher. She will assess these quotes
not only on the price, but also based on her view of the quoting reinsurers, such
as her assessment of their security ratings, reputation, claims handling, and how
much **capacity*** (the size of the share) they are willing to offer to cover the risk.

Based on these quotes it is now up to Jane to select the one that will form the
consensus price. This price will be offered to all reinsurers in return for their
coverage of this deal. By selecting a quote as the consensus price, Jane is stating
how much GlobalInc is willing to pay for this reinsurance cover; it is then up to
the reinsurers to decide whether they wish to take a share of the deal at that price.

For GlobalInc's U.S. **Property Catastrophe*** deal (see Buyer's Perspective
1) Jane compares fifteen quotes. She faces the conundrum of keeping the reinsurance bill to a minimum, but also agreeing to a price that will be sufficiently
attractive to the panel of quoting reinsurers so that she can be sure the deal will
get full cover for potential losses. As each reinsurer takes a share of the deal,
which can vary from 2.5 percent or less up to 30 percent, selecting a cheap quote

as the consensus price may mean that some reinsurers will not take a share of the deal, and Jane risks not getting 100 percent cover or **full placement***. Thus, selecting a quote is a balancing act for Jane between not overspending on reinsurance while getting a full placement to protect GlobalInc.

In conversation with the **broker***, Jane favors the third lowest quote. It is received from Security Re, a long-term partner of GlobalInc that has taken a share on this deal for several years. Security Re has a high Standard and Poor's **security rating***, so Jane has confidence that they have the financial strength to withstand any big events. They have quickly paid the claims for losses in the past, enabling GlobalInc to also respond quickly to any event, and thereby to retain policyholders. Security Re's quote is therefore selected as the consensus price and Jane makes a decision that she would also like them to take the share they have offered. She decides what shares she will offer the other quoting reinsurers, if they would like to take the deal at the consensus price and asks the broker to now take these offers to the quoting reinsurers as well as showing the deal at the consensus price to some additional reinsurers, in case she cannot get full placement from her quoting panel. For Security Re, their quote now becomes binding, and they will be required to provide capital at the price and share that they offered. Other quoting reinsurers have another chance to review the price and decide on whether they want the share they have been offered at that price. Those reinsurers that **do** take a share at the consensus price will become GlobalInc's reinsurance **panel***. Jane awaits the responses from reinsurers, and hopes that the deal will get 100 percent coverage.

2.2. QUOTING DEALS AS A SITE OF MARKET-MAKING ACTIVITY

The quoting of deals is one particular site within which the activity of the market is enacted (Schatzki, 2002). There are thousands of reinsurance deals in the market, each of which needs to be quoted in order for a consensus price to be established at which a reinsurer can take a share of that deal. Buyer's Perspective 2 explains the process by which a **cedent*** wishing to purchase cover against, say, the risk of damage from Japanese earthquakes, establishes this consensus price and offers shares on the deal to a panel of reinsurers. When the contract for these shares of the deal comes into effect on the renewal date, the market for that deal will thus be "made" alongside many other deals that also renew on that date. Since there cannot be a market per se, except through this process, the activity of quoting deals is a critical site within which the market is made.

However, because of the unpredictability of the risk, and uncertainty over the value of any loss, establishing the market for each deal can be quite fraught. This is illustrated in Reinsurance-as-Practice 2A, which builds from our opening story in Chapter 1 (Reinsurance-as-Practice 1A) by outlining the turmoil over quoting Japanese deals following the Tōhoku earthquake. The example briefly illustrates the concepts we elaborate in this chapter, such as market cycles, consensus price, renewing business, and the impetus that the renewal date gives to the quoting process.

....

REINSURANCE-AS-PRACTICE 2A

Tōhoku Earthquake and Tsunami Occur Mid-Renewal

The main renewal date for Japanese reinsurance business is April 1, meaning that March is the month in which reinsurers around the world quote on Japanese deals. In 2011 it was "business as usual" until the Tōhoku earthquake and tsunami hit on March 11, after many underwriters had provided their quotes for the forthcoming year's cover. Prior to this, as most Japanese firms had suffered relatively few losses in the preceding decade, the region was in a "soft cycle," with low prices paid to reinsurers. We had heard frequent complaints about the soft cycle on Japanese business during the previous 2010 renewal. As one underwriter grumbled to Paula: "With most of the Japanese business the prices are down about 20 percent." Hence, most quotes made prior to the earthquake in 2011 reflected this ongoing soft cycle: they were cheap! Suddenly, in the middle of this soft market, a catastrophic event occurred that was outside any modeled predictions: "No seismologist had ever thought a quake of such magnitude could strike the region."[2] Underwriters were aware that their 2011 quotes would not reflect the actual losses they were about to suffer through paying out on their existing cover of those deals: "It's not something you want to explain to your boss," one underwriter fretted, "that you've just given away a cheap quote while the company pays out millions!"

As Japan searched for survivors among the wreckage, and fears rose over nuclear contamination from the Fukushima power plant, the reinsurance industry was in turmoil. Reports began to filter in that emphasized the size of the loss. For example, senior Moody's Tokyo analyst Kenjo Kawada noted that he expected these losses to harm credit ratings "for the property and casualty sector in Japan and reinsurers globally."[3] However, the extent and scope of these losses was a long way from being established.

Looking to the renewal date in less than three weeks, uncertainty was rife. Normally, after a catastrophic event with major loss payments, underwriters could expect to get higher prices on deals and would have quoted accordingly. Underwriters who had already submitted their quotes at soft market prices wondered if it would be necessary to abide by those low quotes. Yet Japanese cedents, who placed great emphasis on long-term business relationships, were sending strong signals that they did not expect to be penalized by higher reinsurance prices at a time of disaster.

Paula joined Tim and two other international property-catastrophe underwriters at a bar near Lloyd's of London one evening following the event, as they

[2] O'Brien, S. 2013. "Japan's Tohoku Earthquake: A Force of Change." *Insurance Insight*, May 16.
[3] Ruquet, M. 2011. "Moody's: Japan Quake Hits Commercial P&C Hardest," *Property Casualty 360*, March 21. http://www.propertycasualty360.com/2011/03/21/moodys-japan-qu ake-hits-commercial-pc-hardest.

discussed a very strategically worded press release from Takashi Oka, reinsurance buyer at leading Japanese cedent Tokio Marine. Oka had stated that the April 1, 2011 renewals would be "a real test to see who stands out as our true partners for the years to come." His statement seemed a warning not to be opportunistic in raising prices, as he further went on to suggest that some reinsurers might be "trying to take advantage of the situation to try to harden the market more than necessary." His press interview, re-asserting that he valued reinsurers' "commitment to the relationship" with his company, seemed to indicate that he expected reinsurers to stand by their existing quotes this year.[4] Over pints of beer, the underwriters mused that they had been underwriting these Japanese deals for many years. They did not want their actions in April 2011 to affect their share of deals the following year. As Tim noted, 2012 should be a much more lucrative market to compensate for the losses they would be paying and "the Japanese reward loyalty". Hence, while they had already quoted, they felt it made competitive sense to maintain their capital commitment this renewal at the pre-Tōhoku, soft market prices. If they did, they could expect to be rewarded when the benefits of price rises came next year. Indeed, Tim pointed out that loyalty now might enable them to jump ahead of their rivals in the following year. Plus, Tim commented as he finished the last of his beer, "We have no idea what the size of the loss to us is yet; next year I'll know at least!"

Around the global market, rumor and gossip were rife, as underwriters attempted to assess both the loss and the likely behavior of their competitors, as the April 1 renewal deadline came ever closer. Yet, despite so much uncertainty, the eventual renewal was described by media commentators as "orderly".[5] Given that the Japanese earthquake eventually cost the (re)insurance industry $37.5 billion,[6] what enabled this order given such market disarray? We shed light on that question in this chapter.

. . . .

2.3. GENERAL UNDERSTANDINGS: CONSENSUS PRICING AND MARKET CYCLES

Collective risk-bearing is critical in making a market for Acts of God (Borscheid et al., 2013). The magnitude of events such as the 2001 terrorist attack on the World Trade Center, which cost the industry $32 billion, dwarfs the capital reserves of even the world's strongest reinsurers. The capital to cover such deals is therefore spread across a panel of reinsurers that can be anything from five to more than sixty depending on the size of the deal. The reinsurance market thus bears risk collectively through multiple individual

---

[4] "Reinsurers Face Real Test at April Renewal," 2011. *Insurance Day*, March 17.
[5] Willis Re. 2011. "Press Release: Tohoku Won't Turn the Soft Market Tide," March 31. www.willisre.com/Media_Room.
[6] "Counting the Costs Of 2011." 2012. *The Insurance Insider*, January.

reinsurers each taking shares on different deals. No single reinsurer assumes all the risk on a deal or region; so after an event, none will pay all of the losses and this helps the market to function in the context of the uncertainty of such costly events. Yet this collective practice is particularly remarkable in the reinsurance industry because, as one broker explained: "Our market is in contrast to direct negotiations face to face or in contrast to the commodities exchange, where the price is seen by everyone else" (Interview, Broker, London).

Such collective practice is grounded in general understandings, which are "a sense of how to participate in a community gathering; for instance, in a religious ceremony" (Schatzki, 2002: 86–88). That is, general understandings are a collective practice that are meaningful for the members of a particular community, such as the reinsurance community, albeit that they may appear strange to outsiders. General understandings about how to participate in the reinsurance market play a critical role in collective risk bearing, because they provide a basis for globally dispersed underwriters, who are not in direct contact, to engage in collective practice (Schatzki, 2001; 2002). We now explain two general understandings: consensus pricing and market cycles, that members of the reinsurance community—underwriters, cedents and brokers—engage in as part of the collective risk-bearing practice of this market. While we explain the two separately in order to show how they work, consensus pricing and market cycles are, in practice, closely entwined in enabling collective risk-bearing, as we will show.

2.3.1. Consensus Pricing

Reinsurance deals are traded at a consensus price, meaning that a price is reached amongst dispersed competitors and **all** interested reinsurers place capital on that deal at that same price.[7] We illustrate this process for deriving a consensus price in Figure 2.1 as reinsurers move from quoting to accepting shares of the deal at the consensus price. As the figure shows, each cedent develops the risk cover they want to buy into a deal specifically tailored to their needs, which is then sent to a panel of reinsurers globally (see Buyer's Perspective 1). At any moment, there are thousands of such tailored deals in the market (Figure 2.1, A). Underwriters then quote individually on deals, meaning they assess and price the deal (Figure 2.1, B), which they submit to the cedent as an independent quote: "Reinsurers don't talk to each other and say 'Right, we've got ABC coming round, we're giving a 10 percent cut or a 10 percent increase.' Everybody forms their own opinion" (Interview, Broker,

---

[7] Mango, D. 2007. "Reinsurance Market Microstructure: Pricing Risk," *International Actuarial Association*. http://www.actuaries.org/ASTIN/Colloquia/Orlando/Papers/Mango2.pdf

London). Given the uncertainty over the value of any potential loss, all parties consider this general understanding of consensus pricing as a central way to evaluate what a deal is worth.

As explained in Buyer's Perspective 2, the cedent considers these independently formed quotes and selects one quote as the consensus price at which the deal will be offered to all reinsurers (Figure 2.1, C). Importantly, the consensus price is not necessarily the lowest quoted price, but rather, is the price that the cedent believes will provide an adequate financial incentive to ensure that a diverse panel of reinsurers will bear the risk. Taking the lowest quote might narrow their panel of reinsurers, or create a **shortfall*** in which they cannot attract enough capital to sufficiently cover their deal, as this reinsurance buyer at a leading cedent explains:

> We want to place the deal 100 percent. So we are trying to match the best price with the best security—and then we are happy. I remember a couple of quotes, they were very attractive price-wise but other reinsurers would never be in a position to meet the terms and conditions being offered on those quotes. So even if I chose such a quote, I would never be successful placing 100 percent of the deal on those conditions. (Cedent, Continental Europe, Interview)

While quoting generates a range of potential prices for a deal, once the cedent has established the price, there is a general understanding that all reinsurers wishing to take a share of that deal will do so at the same price (Figure 2.1, D). So, regardless of whether an underwriter's quote has been higher or lower than the eventual consensus price, or indeed regardless of any variation in the reputation or quality of the firms, there is no room to individually renegotiate the price of that deal.[8] Of course, reinsurers do not have to agree with the consensus price. If it is too far out of line with their quote or they are dissatisfied with it as a price for the risk they will incur, they can choose not to take a share of the deal (see Chapter 5, Reinsurance-as-Practice 5D). However, once enough reinsurers have taken a share at the consensus price that the deal is fully placed, it is put under contract to those reinsurers who receive premium in exchange for the risk cover they provide (Figure 2.1, E). Underwriters thus act **independently** to quote the deal, and yet are **interdependent** in taking shares of it at the consensus price, meaning that the risk of payout for claims is borne collectively across the entire panel of reinsurers.

Consensus price and collective risk-bearing. This consensus price is critical for collective risk-bearing. Without price consistency, risk is not shared collectively as some players stand to win or lose more from an event. Reinsurers invest the premium they are paid for deals to generate both profit and also accrue capital reserves with which to pay claims. If some reinsurers covered the deal at a lower

---

[8] There are some private deals in the industry, which are fully placed between only one cedent and reinsurer, or a limited panel, and so do not go through this same consensus pricing. However, the typical process for deals is consensus pricing.

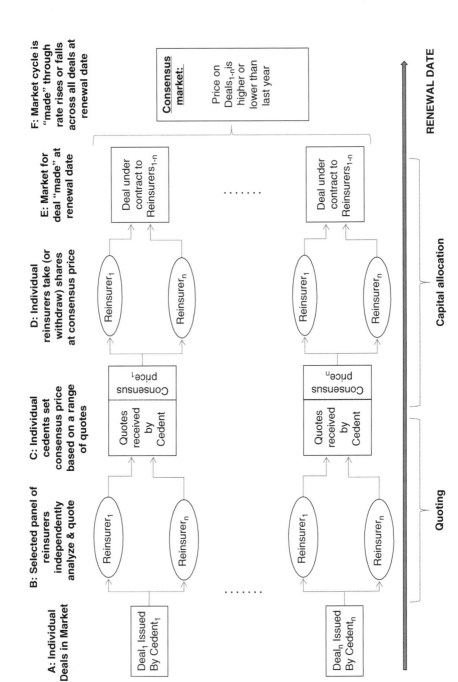

Fig. 2.1. Process of Establishing Consensus Price on Deals

price than others, when an event occurs those reinsurers would have less premium from that deal to invest in capital reserves. Hence, they would be more heavily penalized than those who got the higher price. They might, therefore, also be more likely to default on paying the losses. Buyers also enact the general understanding that consensus pricing is a good way to bear collective risk based on normative assumptions about security and fairness:

> I look at [reinsurance] as a partnership. Everyone should be treated fairly and equally. I always feel that if I give something to one partner I've got to offer the same deal to everyone else. I don't have differing terms on a deal for different reinsurers, so I don't have to worry about a loss; is someone going to pay or not pay? Everyone's in the same boat with me. (Interview, Cedent, United States)

This general understanding about consensus pricing is central to the collective risk-bearing function of the market. Through it, participants reduce their individual uncertainty about, and exposure to, unpredictable risk, sharing it collectively with their competitors.

2.3.2. Market Cycles

The cyclical nature of the reinsurance market, shifting between hard (high-priced) cycles and soft (low-priced) cycles is another general understanding that underpins collective risk-bearing amongst competitors. Practically, cycles occur when reinsurers have to pay for a big loss. When these payouts are very large, reinsurers' capital is depleted, lowering the global capital supply to the industry and driving up reinsurance prices on all deals globally; the cost of their capital has increased. That is, after major or sustained events that deplete their reserves, underwriters push up prices for most deals significantly to reflect actual or collectively presumed capital scarcity, so causing a hard market in which reinsurers receive higher prices. For example, prices for the global property catastrophe market increased by 65 percent following Hurricane Andrew in 1992.[9] This association between price rises on deals, and the overall effect on the market cycle is reflected in Figure 2.1, F. There is thus a **general understanding** that the reinsurance market is cyclical (Cummins and Outreville, 1987; Niehaus and Terry, 1993), shifting between hard and soft cycles in order to stabilize the long-term flow of capital between buyers and suppliers.

---

[9] Rates for the global property catastrophe market increased by 24 percent following the World Trade Center attacks in 2011 and 32 percent following the 2005 hurricane season in the United States, which included Katrina, Rita, and Wilma (Klein, C. 2009. "World Catastrophe Reinsurance Market 2009: A Changing Property-Catastrophe Reinsurance Industry." *Guy Carpenter*, September 21. http://www.gccapitalideas.com/2009/09/21/world-catastrophe-reinsurance-market-2009-a-changing-property-catastrophe-reinsurance-industry/).

Such cycles, which are triggered by changes in capital supply and demand arising from severe events, such as the Tōhoku earthquake and tsunami, are one key way that the reinsurance market copes with unanticipated events. For example, during one informal lunch, Paula was part of a conversation in which the CEO of a reinsurance firm, a broker, and an underwriter discussed whether the 2011 Thai floods would generate a hard market:

CEO: An event like this has to affect the whole market. It's like throwing a rock into a pond; the closer you are to where the rock lands the bigger the effect will be, the further out you are the less affected . . . but you're still affected. Some cedents are going to say, "What's this got to do with us, here in America or in Europe?" You have to remind them that all losses have to be paid from the same wallet; **it's a capital event.**

BROKER: That's right, and it depends on the size of rock too and the unexpected nature of it.

UW: The level of the water in the pond, is **what stage the market is at.**

CEO: How full the pond is, how big the rock is, how close you are, but also how unexpected the rock is; all has an impact.

BROKER: That's true. There's a sort of chain effect going on at the moment. It started with earthquakes in Christchurch, the Australian floods, then the earthquake and tsunami in Japan. Now this. What's, where's the next one? That generally scares people. **It could turn the market.** (Observation, Reinsurer and Broker, London)

As described in this metaphor, events such as the Thai floods generate a ripple effect that spreads through the global capital supply from the epicenter where the event occurred. Price hardening is dependent on how full the pond is (the level of capital available globally) the size of the rock (a big loss-making event that displaces capital), how unexpected it is (capital suppliers' uncertainty about whether they might have unexpectedly large payouts) and proximity to the splash (a ripple effect on pricing across regions in a globally-connected market). Based on these factors an event might result in a small ripple effect on capital supply, causing hardening of the market just in the immediate region or have a big ripple effect on global capital supply, causing a hard market around the world, such as occurred with the 2001 attack on the World Trade Center or the three Hurricanes—Katrina, Rita, and Wilma—in 2005. Even when there is not a global hard market, the market may have cycles that are particular to events and regions. For example, while Japanese deals had been in a soft cycle prior to the Tōhoku earthquake and tsunami, reinsurers anticipated that a hard cycle would follow it to compensate for what were expected to be very large payouts (see Reinsurance-as-Practice 2A).[10]

---

[10] Hard markets do not continue indefinitely. They are characterized by price rises on deals, meaning that reinsurers get more premium in return for the capital they hold in reserve on those deals. These price rises attract new market entrants chasing the increased rates after

Market cycles are not simply an economic function. They are also social constructions of an event and its potential effect on price. The flow of capital is shaped by complex social interactions around its availability (e.g. Abolafia and Kilduff, 1988). As shown in Reinsurance-as-Practice 2A, after an event underwriters take part in gossip and examine news reports about who is affected, how badly, and how the potential losses might affect pricing. In doing so, they construct a view about the potential availability of capital. In the Tōhoku example, as the earthquake occurred only three weeks before the renewal date, reinsurers had to allocate capital to deals before they knew the extent to which the event had depleted capital reserves. They therefore made decisions based on their socially mediated view of the potential for market hardening. The practice of underwriters in quoting a higher price, or withdrawing from a particular deal helps to shape the collective capital flows in the market. Hence, analyzing the social construction of market cycles furthers our understanding of how information (Aspers, 2009) constitutes pricing data (Preda, 2007). Market cycles shift our focus from relatively passive treatments of information; instead we must examine the dynamic production and consumption of the information used to construct price fluctuations (Beunza and Stark, 2004; Hardie and Mackenzie, 2007). We will illustrate such information flows in Section 2.6, through the pricing of reinsurance deals in the wake of the Thai floods.

Reinsurance market cycles support collective risk-bearing by stabilizing longer-term capital flows in a market where the extent of losses on unpredictable risks is unknown until after the fact. Because it is difficult to know what the price of a deal should be, after a number of loss-free years its price decreases, in a manner similar to a "no-claims" discount on a domestic insurance policy. As deals are typically renewed with a largely similar panel of reinsurers each year, during these loss-free years, reinsurers are able to accumulate the premium from the deal because they do not pay claims. Hence, even in a soft cycle, reinsurers may make money. Premium accumulation during loss-free years enables reinsurers to generate capital reserves that are sufficient to pay for expected losses. However, when a major event occurs where losses are beyond anything predicted, reinsurers expect to restock those capital reserves from the subsequent hard market cycle. Hence, as indicated in the Tōhoku example (Reinsurance-as-Practice 2A), reinsurers do not desert deals in the low-priced cycles, but rather stay with them in anticipation

severe events. For example, Bermuda became a prominent hub for reinsurance capital because its relatively light regulatory regime enabled the rapid establishment of the "class of 2001" and the "class of 2005", meaning firms that flocked to the island to set up reinsurance divisions to capture the rate increases following the World Trade Center in 2001 and Hurricanes Katrina, Rita, and Wilma in 2005. These Bermudian reinsurers boosted the supply of global capital during a time of scarcity, particularly for loss-affected U.S. property catastrophe business, so progressively "softening" the market as the cost of capital adjusted to the increase in supply.

of superior returns in hard cycles: "The price of those covers, once they're impacted, will then go up to get renewed. The market wants the payback!" (Interview, Broker, London).

Thus, reinsurance cycles stabilize the flow of capital throughout both loss-free and loss-impacted years, neither of which can be anticipated. For individual reinsurers, remaining with a deal throughout the cycle makes competitive sense in terms of smoothing the capital impact of events upon the firm's reserves. Furthermore, the "ripple" effect of cycles allows the financial shock of large unpredictable events to be spread throughout the market through global rate rises, thus making these events coverable. For instance, it was accepted after the terrorist attacks on the World Trade Center that the loss-affected deals alone could not adequately "payback" on those losses through rate rises. Instead the notion of a ripple meant that the cost-burden was spread more broadly across all deals in the market, so supporting ongoing stability in the face of such costly and unpredictable events. Cycles thus enable risk-bearing in the midst of uncertainty, since individual reinsurers participate on deals with their competitors over the long term, paying collectively for losses and collectively benefiting from pushing rates up after an event.

2.4. COORDINATING THROUGH THE RENEWAL DATE

These general understandings of consensus pricing and market cycles are complex to coordinate across a global market. As shown in Figure 2.1, individual reinsurers around the world must tender a quote on each of the thousands of deals in the market, based on their perception of whether the market for that deal is hard or soft, which will be influenced by both specific losses that have occurred on that deal and any other losses within the wider market. Cedents must then establish the consensus price on their specific deals based on the range of quotes that they have received, their perception of whether their own deal has had losses that warrant a hardening of price, and other global market factors such as major disasters that might affect the cost of capital and so generate a harder market cycle. The consensus price on each of these deals is then returned to the panel of reinsurers around the globe and shares on each deal are allocated to those reinsurers who still wish to take part at that price. The renewal date, which is a particular feature of the reinsurance market, is one key means of coordinating such individual practice across multiple reinsurers, cedents, and their brokers on thousands of deals around the world.

The market for each deal closes on a specific day, known as the renewal date, at which that deal needs to be under contract to a panel of reinsurers who will cover the losses incurred until the next renewal, typically one year away. If the deal does not have a full panel of reinsurers signed by the date it is similar to the lapse in an insurance policy; if something goes wrong, losses will not be covered. Reinsurers who want to be part of the deal must negotiate their share in the period leading up to that date. Actions around the world are thus made in relation to the renewal date and this is critical in coordinating the closure of deals. For example, when the Tōhoku earthquake occurred on March 11, the impending renewal generated a form of order amidst the uncertainty, as individual reinsurers had three weeks to make decisions and allocate capital to deals for the April 1 renewal date.

The policy for a deal is typically for one year. There are five main renewal dates[11] and the market for each deal is made on its specific renewal date. Following each of the main renewal dates, the major broking firms release their analysis of the market cycle, which reflects the **rate*** rises or decreases on all the deals around the world. That is, as deals typically renew each year, their prices may be aggregated and compared across years. For example, by the end of 2010, the global market was softening, according to analysis by Aon Benfield: "The January 2011 renewals softened at the high end of the rate of change,"[12] meaning that despite some minor price fluctuations on some deals and regions, the overall market cycle in 2010 had been softening and this continued at the renewal date.

These pre-specified renewal dates give the reinsurance market a "punctuated" character, as they provide a focal point that orients individual practice. While the activities of market-making are continuous, these dates specify moments at which the market that is "made" can be appraised. This is different to many other financial markets, where deals are being traded continuously, such as the electronic securities and currency exchanges studied by others (e.g. Beunza and Stark, 2004; Knorr Cetina and Bruegger, 2002a; Zaloom, 2006). In electronic markets (Beunza and Stark, 2004; Knorr Cetina and Bruegger, 2002b; Preda, 2009a) both the participants and the price on unfolding trades are being made moment-by-moment. By contrast, the punctuated nature of the reinsurance market has more in common with (and potential lessons for) syndicated markets, in which multiple actors are coordinated around a particular trade, such as a syndicated loan on a specified date (Hallak and Schure, 2011). We illustrate this coordinating role of the renewal date in Reinsurance-as-Practice 2B, using the example of the Thai floods.

---

[11] January 1 (the largest renewal date); April 1; June 1; July 1; October 1.
[12] Aon Benfield. 2011. "Reinsurance Market Outlook: Partnership Renewed." January. Chicago: Aon Benfield.

2.5. PRACTICAL UNDERSTANDINGS: RENEWING
DEALS THROUGH THE QUOTING PROCESS

We use Schatzki's (2006: 1,864) concept of **practical understandings***, defined as "complexes of know-hows regarding the actions constituting the practice" to explain how general understandings about the market are enacted within people's actions. Practical understandings are the informed, but mundane or "everyday" actions through which individual underwriters around the world enact the collective practice of consensus pricing and market cycles. We explain two practical understandings: 1) enacting a widespread industry quoting process and 2) renewing business. In enacting these practical understandings in their everyday work, underwriters construct their individual practice on any deal in relation to the consensus price and the particular stage of the market cycle.

2.5.1. Enacting the Quoting Process

Consensus pricing is enacted within a widespread practical understanding about the process for quoting deals. We always observed the same basic process for quoting on deals across different competing underwriters in multiple firms and regions, which we initially found surprising. That is, whether it was a Vietnamese deal being underwritten in Singapore, a Russian deal in Zurich, or a U.S. deal in Bermuda, the same basic process, and constituent activities, of receiving the deal, analyzing it, quoting, receiving the consensus price and signing shares to place capital, were consistent (see Figure 2.1). The outcome of this consistent quoting process, enacted upon each deal by multiple actors dispersed across the market, is a consensus price on each of those deals.

The quoting process provides the basis for collective market practice. While each reinsurer quotes independently, this is not a purely private **evaluation***, as brokers and cedents see all quotes on a particular deal, and competitors hear rumors, as well as observe which reinsurer sets the eventual consensus price in the preceding year. The rule of thumb is that, while they cannot be sure what others are quoting, most reinsurers want to quote on the high side, in order to nudge the consensus price up from the previous year. However, there are negative implications if a quote is too misaligned with those of others. For instance, if underwriters quote too high, so that they are out of the range, they risk being left off the deal by the cedent when the consensus price is established, because the alternative is losing face by accepting the business at a significantly lower price than they indicated it was worth, which weakens their reputation (see Baker, 1984; Zaloom, 2006). Similarly, if they quote too low, they may lower the price for the market as a whole, or look inexperienced in judging risk. As one underwriter explained: "We do the technical part of arriving at a price but also we try to think about the market cycle and the market price. And how realistic is the price. If the market price is too high compared to what we've quoted, then you're not credible anymore" (Interview, Reinsurer, **Account Executive***, Continental Europe). Underwriters are therefore constantly trying to position their quotes relative to those of others and to their perceptions of the market cycle, by seeking information about the actions of their competitors (Aspers, 2009; Beunza and Stark, 2004; Hardie and Mackenzie, 2007; White, 1981).

Enacting the quoting process is a critical competitive behavior that is also theoretically important in market-making. It not only canvasses individual views on deals, but also shapes mutual social orientations (Aspers, 2009; Beckert, 2009), as individuals observe the quoting behavior of their competitors in the process of generating prices (Baker, 1984). Individual practice is thus associated with, and tempered by, anticipated collective market practice. As other studies show, there are social norms around quoting that help to stabilize collective market practice. In particular, market-makers—those reinsurers whose moves influence the behavior of others—are expected to quote, and also to conduct trades at their quoted price (Abolafia, 1996; Baker, 1984). That is, actors cannot use their quoting activities opportunistically to inflate or depress prices without intention to fulfill those quotes. Reciprocally, quoting is universally considered an important "service" that reinsurers provide to a cedent in order to be considered for a significant share on a deal. Reinsurers who do not quote may later be allowed to take a small share at the consensus price, to fill out coverage of the deal, but they are generally regarded as peripheral. Furthermore, those actors who quote, even on difficult or unfavorable deals, are able to gain greater access to good deals. Hence, the social norms associated with quoting have a stabilizing influence, as they ensure that leaders will help to make the price by quoting, and that they will abide by those quotes.

Brokers are particularly important in reinforcing these norms. Other than for the largest reinsurers (such as Swiss Re and Munich Re) most deals are channeled through brokers who are able to ignore or bypass quotes from people who are perceived to have contravened the social norms of the market. For example, brokers may not bring attractive deals to reinsurers who are not willing to provide quotes on a range of deals (Baker, 1984; Smets et al., 2014; Zaloom, 2006). Similarly, brokers will actively seek out those reinsurers who are known to be influential, or market leaders, because if their quote is accepted as the consensus price, others in the market will likely follow in accepting that price because those reinsurers have a good reputation for evaluating deals (Baker, 1984; Salamat and Burton, 2008). Importantly, brokers also spread news, gossip and other information that diffuses these normative expectations across the market (Aspers, 2009; White, 1981; 1995).

2.5.2. The Practice of Renewing Business

Reinsurance is largely a renewal business. Deals are renewed annually and reinsurers typically remain on their existing portfolio of deals over many years. For example, on January 1, 2013, leading reinsurer Hanover Re, renewed 91 percent of their existing non-life book of deals.[13] Supporting a deal with capital over many years, and across hard and soft cycles, is a characteristic of the business relationship between cedents and reinsurers, even as the deals themselves may be restructured, and the share that the reinsurer takes may vary across years. While not a written rule, this practical understanding persists even when deals make relatively low returns during soft cycles.

The practice of renewing business through placing capital at the consensus price (Figure 2.1) is at least partially based in two forms of competitive value that accrue to long-term relationships in such an uncertain market. First, renewed deals constitute a deep social base of information about a client that has an innate value beyond its price in any given year. Access to information is critical to financial markets (Aspers, 2009; Beunza and Stark, 2004). This is particularly pertinent in reinsurance, where the statistical probability of events and their potential to generate loss is so uncertain that information gleaned about a deal, cedent or region is critical for evaluating the risk a reinsurer is taking (see Chapters 3 and 4). Coming off a deal will disrupt the flow of information that supports such **evaluation***. Hence, even where underwriters might reduce their share of a deal to a "watching line" during a soft cycle, meaning taking a very small share of it, renewing deals is a firmly ingrained business practice. By renewing deals, underwriters continue to participate in the information flows that are critical in constructing consensus price.

Second, as shown in the Tōhoku earthquake example, where Tim and his fellow underwriters had remained with Japanese deals through the soft cycle, such reinsurers are better placed competitively to receive shares of the deal when the market hardens, thus reaping returns from higher prices (Reinsurance-as-Practice 2A). Long-term relationships provide them with a tacit economic benefit based on a principle of reciprocity or payback following a loss. Expectations of reciprocity in other financial markets have also been noted, where those who support less favorable deals are rewarded with better access to more favorable deals (e.g. Baker, 1984). Similarly, while there is no formal rule, reinsurers expect cedents not to "shop around" after a loss for a cheaper price, but to give shares on higher-rate deals to those reinsurers who paid the loss. Thus, the everyday practice of renewing business is sound competitive practice. An underwriter who had just moved to a new

---

[13] "January 1, 2013 Non-Life Treaty Renewals." 2013. Hannover Re, February. http://www.hannover-re.com/resources/cc/generic/ir-presentations/results/pres130204.pdf.

reinsurance firm explained to us that he could not get on a deal because of the cedent's loyalty to renewal business:

> I know these guys very well personally but we are not on the deal despite the fact that we could quote cheaper. They said: "Our reinsurers, our long-term panel, have lost so much money." He's right; they lost a lot of money and he wants to try to give some payback. And he said if somebody is voluntarily going away then you are on it! But they won't just take the cheaper price. (Observation, Reinsurer, Underwriter, Continental Europe)

The renewal date provides a temporal rhythm that helps to coordinate fluctuations in price on renewal business across hard and soft cycles. Once a year reinsurers re-evaluate renewing deals, at which they can consider the returns on a particular deal as a long-term investment. As one CEO said, with a shrug, about some currently lower return **casualty*** business: "You're in there for the next twenty-five years and you're always going to get your margin over time" (Interview, Reinsurer, Executive, Continental Europe). Renewing business thus sustains market cycles. Because cedents provide payback to their loyal reinsurers through price rises on deals after a loss, rather than taking on capital from alternative sources at lower rates, the market hardens. By contrast, if cedents shopped around, while reinsurers dipped in and out of deals opportunistically according to price, there would be fewer incentives for reinsurers to take deals in soft cycles or for cedents to provide higher prices that make hard cycles. Thus, renewing business in a soft cycle makes competitive sense: "Is it still profitable for us? No. . . . but it's continuity-driven. We cannot say goodbye because we will never step in this business again, we will never get it back!" (Interview, Reinsurer, Executive, Continental Europe). Hence, renewing business is an important way of coordinating individual practice with the collective practice of market cycles.

While there is undoubtedly an economic consideration in renewing business there is also a tacit social premise to this practice that goes beyond the particular advantage to a firm. The social structure of the market exercises normative controls over individual tendencies to opportunism that could destabilize the market (Abolafia, 1996; Barker, 1984; Beckert, 2009). In reinsurance, an underwriter has a social obligation to act for the "good of the market" by participating in renewal business and, if withdrawing from a deal, to do so slowly with clear signals, so that the cedent can replace the capital through other reinsurers.

By participating in the social norms of renewing business, actors counteract the opportunism of moving on and off deals that might destabilize long-term capital flows (Abolafia, 1996). Violation of this norm attracts sanctions, such as cedents declining to give particular reinsurers shares of their deals. As one underwriter stated: "Reinsurers do understand that it's a very small market and that very fast there will be a rumor going around, their reputation is very easily lost" (Interview, Reinsurer, Underwriter, Continental

Europe). Interestingly, such sanctions apply even to the largest players who might be considered, because of their superior capital base, to be able to act more opportunistically. However, because these large players provide such a significant proportion of the capital on a deal, they are expected to act even more consistently as market-makers (Abolafia, 1996; Baker, 1984), in order not to disrupt the capital on deals too suddenly. For example, in an interview at the Monte Carlo Rendezvous in 2009, David Huckstepp, **Chief Underwriting Officer*** of a leading Lloyd's firm, commented on the announcement that Swiss Re would be withdrawing from **Credit & Surety*** business:

> Pulling out is ultimately a bad thing to do. Reinsurers are there to provide stability to clients by paying claims and offering some capacity next year so they can keep going . . . It is the ultimate disservice to clients to run away. To change the book of business gradually is fine, but to leave them in the lurch goes down extremely badly with clients. They will question the value of placing business.[14]

This violation of the practice of renewing business was the subject of much industry news and gossip. It was considered damaging not only to the collective practice of the market, but also to the competitive advantage of that firm. Indeed, even two years later, one underwriter explained to Paula:

> It's more the loyalty in terms of the capacity. They [large cedents] had a very difficult time when Swiss Re was pulling out of the market . . . Swiss Re said, "We are withdrawing from Credit & Surety." It was after a big loss they'd made. These cedents were very nervous. They found new capacity for their deals, only for Swiss Re to say a few years later, "We made the wrong decision. We will renew our shares; don't worry about it." And this is the loyalty of the [cedents], they said "I'm sorry, we talked to all these people and these people offered us their help, so no way that we are going to let them down." (Interview, Reinsurer, Underwriter, Continental Europe)

Renewing business is thus both a competitive individual practice in order to gain a favorable share of deals, and also a collective market practice for stabilizing capital across market cycles.

2.6. THE THAI FLOODS: COORDINATING CONSENSUS PRICING AND MARKET CYCLES

We now explore how these general and practical understandings enact the market through the example of how reinsurers responded to the Thai floods leading up to the January 1 renewal date at the end of 2011 (see Table 2.1). Throughout 2010, the global reinsurance market was in a soft cycle, meaning

---

[14] "Reinsurers Accused of Picking up Bad Habits from Retro Market." 2009. *Reactions*, November 20.

Table 2.1. Timeline of the Thai Floods

	Renewal activities	Key events
Late July 2011		Ayutthaya and other provinces in the northeast and central Thailand **start** flooding, spreading into Bangkok and the southeast.
October 28	**September–October** Pre-submission: Renewal conferences & meeting clients	Flooding referred to as "Thai Floods" **first mentioned by research participants.**
October 31		**Industry conference** (Singapore) where Thai floods are the main topic of conversation.
Early November	**November–December** Submission & Quoting	Initial industry-wide loss estimates released via newsletters and reports. It is apparent that losses will not be contained only to Thai deals, but have spread into global supply chains.
November 18		Large **Japanese** cedents release company-specific loss forecasts, emerging as the most affected insurance companies.
Late November		A number of smaller (re)insurance companies withdraw from renewal activities in Thailand or go into run-off in expectation of huge payouts, **reducing the available pool of capital.**
December 6		Swiss Re the first large reinsurer to provide loss estimates, Munich Re (largest reinsurer in the world) quickly follows.
Mid–Late December		Broker reports and media statements suggest that there is sufficient capital and that price rises will be relatively localized.
January 1, 2012	**Renewal deadline**	Deals are finalized, locking-in capital, although accurate loss estimates are still not available because the floodwaters have not yet receded.
Mid-January	**Post-renewal**	Flooding in all areas finished.
Late-January		Revised loss estimates from large heavily-exposed Japanese cedents increase threefold from initial ones, indicating uncertainty of information reinsurers had to work with prior to the January 1 renewal date.

prices were low. Yet in the first quarter of 2011, floods in Australia and earthquakes in New Zealand and Japan caused severe losses, triggering some of the largest ever payouts outside the United States and reducing reinsurers' capital reserves. Executives of leading reinsurers expected that another capital event in the near future would, therefore, shift prices upwards. The Thai floods that began in July 2011, intensifying throughout the latter half of the year, started to look like such a capital event in the busy lead up to the January 1, 2012 renewal.

In illustrating how underwriters constructed the impact of the Thai flood during the renewal process, we shall explain the ripple effect of an event in raising specific deal prices and hardening local or even global market cycles (see Section 2.3.2). Participants initially constructed the event within their varied individual practice, as one that would collectively generate a hard market for all deals globally. However, by the renewal date, the market had collectively settled on significant local hardening, reported as 500–1,000 percent[15] rate increases on deals in Thailand and the surrounding regions, but only minor rate rises for deals in the rest of the world.

How does individual practice enact such collective market practice? Our Thai floods example shows how actors distributed around the global market produce and consume information (Aspers, 2009; Beunza and Stark, 2004; Knorr Cetina and Bruegger, 2002a), such as gossip, loss reports, media and analyst statements, site visits, client and peer interactions, and internal analyses. This enables them to orient towards each other in their individual quoting on specific deals, so shaping the consensus price that emerges on each deal, as well as how these deals shape the overall market cycle. We provide empirical weight to our concept of **relationality***—a pattern of connection between two or more things—by showing how individual practice on deals is coordinated with and produces the collective practice of the market in response to the Thai floods. We depict this activity in Figure 2.2. Our ethnographic story is built around six interrelated and overlapping actions that underwriters enact:

- Positioning their quotes in relation to effects of the event on competitors (Relationality A)
- Enacting expectations about rates rises in renewing loss-affected deals (Relationality B)
- Relating quotes on specific deals to the wider market for deals (Relationality C)
- Relating quotes on specific deals to the emerging stage of the market cycle (Relationality D)
- Relating quotes on deals to the renewal deadline (Relationality E)
- Relating pricing cycle to upcoming renewal (Relationality F).

[15] "Berkshire Hathaway Lured by Thai Cat Opportunities." 2012. *Insurance Insider*, January.

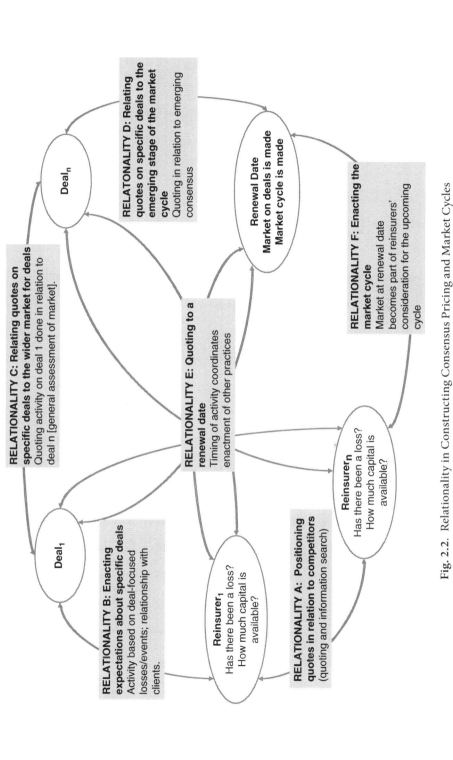

Fig. 2.2. Relationality in Constructing Consensus Pricing and Market Cycles

The example illustrates how general understandings of consensus pricing and market cycles are enacted within the everyday practice of quoting and renewing deals by a specific renewal date.

....

REINSURANCE-AS-PRACTICE 2B
The Thai Floods

The Thai floods: setting the scene. In the last week of October 2011, Paula joined the 800-plus delegates gathered in the opulent air-conditioned Marina Bay Sands complex for the Singapore International Reinsurance Conference (SIRC). During the conference alarming news began to appear that seven major industrial parks just north of Bangkok were under water, with flood waters still rising. The conference was abuzz with gossip, as reinsurers from around the world began to recognize the seriousness of the flood, and to pump their competitors, cedents and brokers attending the conference for information. It became the main topic of conversation. As one broker emphasized to his clients during a conference meeting: "It's by far the largest loss in the Asian market ever, **ever**." The media quickly began to release reports on the information emerging during the conference, with Rebecca, who was shadowing underwriters in Zurich, emailing updates to Paula in Singapore, as they both observed similar conversations taking place around releases such as this one by Aon Benfield:

> The event is likely to be the costliest natural disaster in Southeast Asia. While the overall insured loss has yet to be realized due to the ongoing nature of the situation, there is a potential for substantial losses to cedents from different sectors like property, automotive and agriculture.[16]

The event was a shock; models had not predicted it, as flooding was not regarded as a critical risk in Thailand. As the renewal period progressed, many reinsurers continued to be surprised by the significant claims they might have to pay, even on deals not specifically located in Thailand, as the flooding had disrupted global supply chains that they reinsured.[17]

As reinsurers began recognizing the possible impact of the floods, they discussed the potential for far-reaching rate rises. They knew, however, that its effect on the price of deals was not guaranteed. For instance, during December, Fred, a leading broker in the Asia-Pacific region, was holding a meeting with a leading reinsurer who had flown into Singapore to discuss the floods, said, "But exciting times though, how good does it get? I mean we've been waiting for a market like this for ages!" The reinsurer responded that they would need to wait and see: "Well, the market isn't really developed yet apparently; it's still developing."

The market was "developing" throughout the renewals, as underwriters globally were aware that the amount of capital depleted from the market might not

---

[16] Aon Benfield. 2011. "Thailand Floods: An Event Update." October, Singapore: Aon Benfield.

[17] Guy Carpenter. 2012. "Thailand Flood 2011: Executive Summary." October 28. http://www.gccapitalideas.com/2012/10/28/thailand-flood-2011-executive-summary/.

become apparent until well after the January 1 renewal date. As the following statement from Lloyd's acknowledged: "Claims from flooding on this scale are always complex and will develop over time as the waters recede and loss adjusters gain access to the affected areas."[18] Indeed, as we observed the renewal unfold, estimated losses to the reinsurance industry remained unclear, with reports varying from $4–30 billion.

The market cycle was thus not simply an economic function of calculating costs and attributing price rises. Rather, reinsurers were **constructing** the effects of the event, through their collective actions in quoting and renewing deals amidst this uncertainty. Below we tease apart the interdependent and overlapping actions being enacted within the renewal process, to show how, in relation to one another, they shaped the consensus pricing that emerged by the renewal date.

Relationality A: Positioning quotes in relation to effects of the event on reinsurance competitors. As individual underwriters tried to form a view on a deal's potential consensus price, they paid close, almost obsessive, attention to any source of information that provided insight into how their competitors were impacted by and reacting to Thai floods. Underwriters kept an ear open for any gossip, and hungrily scanned loss releases made by companies, statements in the media and analyst reports (Figure 2.2, Relationality A). They were, of course, not only seeking but also actively producing information, so shaping each other's quoting practice through their various individual responses to the Thai floods.

While the extent of damage could not be accurately gauged (the floodwaters did not recede until mid-January) cedents and reinsurers were still required by ratings agencies and regulatory authorities to make loss reports. Within reinsurance firms, we started to hear anxious comments such as, "When are we going to release our statement to the market?" and "We don't want to release the wrong figures." They were uttered fretfully during meetings and in water cooler conversations; they were also peppered through the email correspondence. By late November some reinsurers began to generate information and place it in the public domain. There was a flurry of excitement in the firms we were shadowing, as underwriters avidly consumed releases in the reinsurance press, such as French firm, Caisse Centrale de Reassurance (CCR) announcing its withdrawal from Thailand: "The floods triggered a couple of withdrawals from loss-affected Asian markets, including French state reinsurer CCR and today's announcement that Asian-focused Lloyd's syndicate 1965 was going into run-off."[19]

Underwriters discussed such information, trying to work out how they should use it to inform their quoting. While run-off meant that some firms' capital reserves were so badly affected that could no longer accept new business and would have to manage the winding down of their existing business, it would take more than the predicaments of these relatively minor players to turn the market from soft to hard. As one underwriter, Henry, reflected to his colleagues the morning he received the announcement about CCR, "CCR is very small in the market; this won't have a big impact on rates." Information about other market

---

[18] "Mitsui Sumitomo Accounts for Half of Japanese Big Three's ¥260bn Thai Losses." 2011. *Insurance Insider*, November 18.

[19] "Thai Treaty Re-Think to Pose Fac Market Opportunity." 2011. *Insurance Insider*, November 30.

actors was vital. In order to push prices up on renewal business, they needed some indication of what others might be likely to do on these same deals, which would be influenced by how badly they had been hit.

Reinsurers were concerned that the picture remained so unclear well into December. As the renewal progressed, releases and press statements from the bigger reinsurers—those market-makers who would be more influential—and commentary on how those players were going to react remained ambiguous. On the one hand, Munich Re **might** be pushing for broad-scale rate rises: "Munich Re implied that it would push hard for higher prices and tighter terms and conditions to compensate itself for its losses. It said that Thailand was 'a wake-up call'.[20] Underwriters eagerly digested news that these bigger players were badly hit. For example, after a meeting a group of busy underwriters lingered to swap stories regarding their competitors' misfortunes. One underwriter, Franz, gleefully relayed gossip from his talk the previous day with Mega Re underwriters saying that, "Mega Re and others are going to take a huge hit from Thailand. Super Re bust; Eastern Re bust." Franz's gossip—and indeed the above media statement—suggested that the Thai floods might have impacted enough players to be a market-hardening event.

On the other hand, many reinsurers were stating publicly that, despite losses, their capital reserves remained strong. For example, Victor Peignet, CEO of SCOR Global P&C, was reported as saying that "the (re)insurer had managed to withstand the impact of the brutal sequence of catastrophic events." Whilst acknowledging that these events would likely impact other reinsurers around the globe, "the widespread consequences of the Thai floods and other catastrophes also bear witness to the increasing interconnections at work in our globalized economy. Thanks to its strong ERM policy, SCOR is well prepared to cope with both the deals and opportunities related to this evolving environment."[21]

Others also expressed reservations as to whether the loss reports being released by some major reinsurers made broad rate rises possible. For instance, one underwriter whispered conspiratorially to Rebecca that he believed some of the major reinsurers were deliberately not helping to push rates up with their loss estimates. "So disappointing," he said, shaking his head. "They [major reinsurer] traditionally low-ball their initial estimation so they look good." Such (perceived) tactics from the largest players did not instill confidence that widespread rate rises would ensue. Would the understated nature of these estimates downplay the losses and hamper efforts to push collectively for rate increases?

Amid general uncertainty about the size of the actual loss, the relationality between individual and collective actions was fraught with tension. However, there was a further tension between reinsurers' competitive actions and their efforts to act collectively to enact rate rises. Reinsurers wanted a collective response, in which they had all taken a loss, would all bear the burden, and could all therefore expect a rate rise. As one underwriter explained to a client when discussing renewal business over the phone: "It is the biggest loss in the region **ever**. It is what it is: we're **all** in it—**everyone**! Only a fraction [of the loss] remains local. Ninety-five percent goes to us—the international reinsurance market."

---

[20] "Munich Re Forcasts Net Thai Loss of $670 Mn." 2011. *Insurance Insider*, December 6.
[21] "SCOR Estimates EUR140 Mn Thai Loss." 2011. *Insurance Insider*, December 16.

Yet, individually reinsurers wanted to appear stronger than their competitors. They did not want clients to think that their capital was uncertain, or that they could not be relied on to pay future losses, which would weaken their competitive position or standing in the market. For instance, during a client meeting a cedent asked an underwriter whether the Thai floods had hit them. Christophe, the underwriter, quickly replied, "It's not major for us. We are certainly not the company most affected by this. We will be impacted but compared to our competitors we are far away." In this way, Christophe asserted his company's "strong" position, as did many others, allaying any rumors that their capital was eroded, which might spark downgrading by security analysts or cause their clients to lose confidence in them. Yet in doing so, they downplayed the impact of the event and thus the potential for broad-based rate rises.

Relationality B: Enacting expectations about rate rises in renewing loss-affected deals. Reinsurers also sought information on which specific deals were affected (Figure 2.2, Relationality B). Knowledge of the specific losses was critical in positioning their quotes appropriately on those loss-affected deals. The main concern everyone was discussing during the renewal was that global supply chains had been disrupted, meaning that losses would not be restricted simply to Thai cedents and deals. Rather, the floods might affect many of the other deals that they were renewing; but which ones and to what degree? Even if the market did not harden more broadly, reinsurers could at least expect payback though rate rises on any loss-affected deals; but first they needed to evaluate the extent of those losses. Underwriters sifted through information from a variety of sources, including loss reports, analyst commentary and social interaction with clients and brokers. Every few days, cedents brought out new loss reports regarding their specific deals that fueled media articles and analyst commentary, such as "Mitsui Sumitomo account for half of Japan big three's Y260bn Thai loss."[22] Yet these loss reports were known to be uncertain and likely to change.

Reinsurers thus also tried to get more specific information about losses on their renewing deals by making site visits to the loss-affected area and through client meetings. During a meeting in Europe, a senior manager reported back on his recent information-gathering trip to Thailand, summarizing the information he had gained to his team and explaining, "We are still having discussion with our most important clients and getting numbers. These numbers are still confidential; not yet released." However, it remained an ongoing battle. For example, at the Zurich subsidiary of the same firm, Peter was frustrated after the third phone call with a cedent about Thailand that week: "It's hard to get some information [about Thai losses] from these guys [cedents] anyway, over the phone. You have to see them, go to the pub with them, and have a drink." Indeed, underwriters delayed quoting in the hopes that further information would develop. During one meeting a senior manager explained his strategy to his colleagues: "He [cedent] is not giving me any of his Thai losses so I am in the process of stopping the quotation process for all of their deals." As this shows, underwriters saw efforts to gain deal-specific loss information as critical in enabling them to quote.

[22] "Mitsui Sumitomo Accounts for Half of Japanese Big Three's ¥260bn Thai Losses." 2011. *Insurance Insider*, November 18.

As the renewal deadline approached, underwriters began also to shape the consensus market for specific deals through their quotes, which they explained as being about "sending signals" or "testing" the market. For example Simon, a Property Catastrophe underwriter, outlined to colleagues his plan to tell a cedent with whom he had a few deals that he would increase the price on one of their Thai flood-exposed deals: "I am planning on going back to them first on [Deal 1]. We want to test if our 50 percent price increase is accepted." He and many other underwriters around the market were testing cedents' receptivity to rate rises.

As this section suggests, reinsurers both collected news about specific deals to inform their quoting, and also sent messages that rates on loss-affected deals were expected to rise. This individual practice, enacted simultaneously by many reinsurers across the market, began to shape the collective market for specific deals (see Figure 2.2, Relationality B).

Relationality C. Relating quotes on specific deals to the wider market for deals in general. Actions on any particular deal need to be considered in relation to what is happening with other deals in the market (Figure 2.2, Relationality C). Hence, underwriters focused not only on the specific loss-affected deals described above, but also on how the losses were being felt in the reinsurance market more generally. The Thai floods might mean that a deal in Thailand, or in nearby Indonesia, Malaysia, or Vietnam, which might have similar flood-prone conditions, would have rate rises; despite not having been impacted by this specific flood. Further, other deals around the world totally disconnected from Thailand could also rise in price if losses depleted reinsurance capital generally. Thus, as one manager told his team: "This is a message I have for you for the renewal: even countries which are not going to be really impacted by the Thailand events, we should see improvement in the price."

Reinsurers indicated through actions such as their media statements, and phone calls and emails to clients and brokers that even in loss-free areas, rates would be likely to rise. For example, during a client meeting in Singapore a broker had strong words with the client: "Obviously you'll also have flood perils in Indonesia, and so what we're seeing out of Thailand will be relevant . . . previously Indonesia has been dismissed in terms of flood perils. But we are now seeing that flood can be a problem in such regions. So rates will have to rise. Reinsurers can't be expected to just lie on the railroad tracks and get run over." Such shaping of expectations occurred on deals in Asian regions with similar characteristics, such as the one in Indonesia above, but also with deals with no link to the floods. For example, a reinsurer talked to a client about renewing their deal: "We thought that while the global market has had quite a lot of hits that it wouldn't affect your region, but now with the Thai floods and the implications of that, it's apparent that pricing hardening must be part of this market too, so you can't expect a softer market, which we'd initially expected." Even as underwriters tried to extend the ripple effect of the Thai floods by preparing cedents for rate rises outside the loss-affected region, reinsurers were alert for news about competitors (as discussed above) that they might turn to their advantage: "The issues around the Thai Floods are important for us. As companies like [Competitor X] readjust; we can potentially see pricing opportunities further afield." In this way, Relationality A and C are closely entwined, as signs of reduction in competitors' capital availability would indicate the potential to push rates up on other deals, not just those that were loss-affected.

For example, in examining a Malaysian deal, one senior manager queried his colleagues: "Is there an opportunity for us on this deal? Many of our competitors will be in trouble because of Thailand." By relating any particular deal to other deals that they were also renewing, and relating these actions to rumors about what their competitors were doing, reinsurers were thus participating in the potential for a collective rate rise on all deals across the market (Figure 2.2, Relationality C).

Relationality D and E. Relating price to the emerging market cycle and the imminent renewal date. As the renewal date drew still closer without accurate loss information, reinsurers needed to move on with finalizing specific deals (Figure 2.2, Relationality D). In doing so, underwriters tried to work out the optimum timing to present their quotes (Figure 2.2, Relationality E). Their practice focused on finalizing the quote in relation to the current cycle, a process simultaneously enacting that market cycle as either hard or soft.

When it came to quoting reinsurers remained torn. There were indications that collective practice was turning the market, and they could afford to quote high: "My feeling about the floods is that the global market will continue to harden. Let's be aggressive in our quoting." But disturbing rumors were also coming in that some big, influential players were already quoting and not putting prices up as anticipated: "It has only been [Large Reinsurer] who is quoting . . . they are quoting as if Thailand had not happened." This reflected the ongoing tension between individual and collective market practice. If each individual quoted higher, this would have collective benefits of increasing the consensus price on any particular deal. However, individual underwriters wanted to quote in ways that might give them advantage over their competitors and enable them to access more business. For instance, regarding one large reinsurer rumored to be quoting low, an underwriter concluded, "I think they know that they can hold out longer than smaller players in a soft cycle due to their financial strength so they are deliberately keeping the market soft and waiting for their competitors to exit so they have more business and profit!" Consensus pricing thus involves competitive moves in which bigger or stronger players have great influence in shaping the market.

As the consensus price on some initial deals began to filter through to reinsurers, a clearer picture of the effect on the overall market began to emerge. Prices on deals in the loss-affected region and its immediate surroundings were indeed rising. For example, during a return trip to Singapore, Paula joined a meeting where a reinsurance executive outlined that "as far as I can tell the Philippines, Malaysia, and Indonesia are all starting to see some upwards pressure. But I'm not convinced there's a lot for us there." The broker agreed: "I think the biggest impact is directly on Thai business at the moment. And everything else is a bit of a . . . [tapers off]." As this suggests, the effect of the Thai floods was largely region-specific and did not spread, even to the wider Asian region. As one underwriter summarized, with obvious regret: "You just have pockets of success. For example, in China it was not affected, so prices don't go up much. You know, on the contrary they said, 'Hey my market is OK, so why should I suffer like the rest of the market?' . . . In China they don't care about Thailand's flood." As the renewal deadline approached, this realization reverberated amongst reinsurers; they would not be able to insist on broad rate rises. Broker reports in late December reflected the emerging picture: "There has been no overall change in market pricing."[23] At this point, it was only two weeks before the renewal date. Underwriters needed to act or they would be left out of the market (Figure 2.2, Relationality E).

Individual practice began to conform to the collective market practice that they were all constructing in response to the Thai floods. In order to renew business, underwriters needed to adjust their prices on deals they had not yet quoted and renew their shares on deals at a lower consensus price than they might have quoted. As one underwriter noted in a heated discussion with his manager: "If we continue to play tough with pricing negotiation, I want to highlight the danger—we might not have business for our staff. Is it the plan that we are not going to renew a lot of business? We have to be clear that this—we risk losing all this business!" Reinsurers consequently sought to renew deals in relation to the current market cycle. Curtailing their initial impulses to push for rate rises, reinsurers either reduced quotes that had not yet been submitted, or prepared to accept a lower consensus price than they had quoted: "We quoted quite aggressively to the market, but we saw that the rest of the market started to get afraid. And we were close to overdoing it and losing in the end . . . Rather than maintaining a share on anything."

While individual reinsurers saw the relatively lower consensus pricing as an outcome of others' actions—their competitors were "the market" who got afraid—they had in fact constructed this market collectively through their actions. Initially, there had been quite bullish statements like, "Get rape and pillage prices. Try for some significant improvements and be prepared to walk away," meaning that reinsurers would not renew business if they could not get their prices. However, this became a more moderate, renewal-oriented approach as January 1 approached: "We have lost so much in Asia-Pacific this year. We have to do something. I'm going out to the market, I'm telling the broker: 'The renewal cannot be on the expiring [previous year] terms.' However, I will meet with them halfway." Indeed, despite disappointment, we rarely saw a reinsurer fail to renew a deal. In this way, deal by deal, underwriters related their individual practice to that of their competitors, adjusting to the collective market but also enacting it through those adjustments.

Post renewal: Relating the stage of the market cycle to the next renewal date. An isolated reinsurer cannot turn the market from soft to hard. Rather, reinsurers heed what competitors are doing on deals within loss-affected regions and beyond, both to jockey for competitive advantage, and also to generate parameters for their own quoting. Reinsurers were aware that their practice was inter-related with that of their competitors. Their various individual actions were relational in constructing the consensus pricing on any specific deal, as well as the overall market cycle.

On January 1, 2012 the market on specific deals was "made", so enacting a moment in the market cycle. Prices on loss-affected deals and some surrounding regions had increased significantly: "Stratospheric rate increases have marked Thailand out as the hardest market in the world."[24] However, such increases were not sufficient to trigger a broad hard market cycle in territories

---

[23] "Cats Created "Two-Speed" Insurance Market—Marsh." 2011. *Reactions*, December.
[24] "Renewals." 2012. *Reinsurance Magazine*, February.

further removed from the event. By enacting their practical understandings of the quoting process and of renewing business, market participants had tried to shape rate rises; but they also heeded each other's competitive actions, as they eventually settled for a localized ripple in the market cycle.

Of course, the market was only "made" temporarily. Immediately after the renewal, reinsurers began considering how the current market cycle would impact forthcoming renewals (Figure 2.2, Relationality F). As the reinsurance media noted: "A gloomy interpretation could easily be put on the rate increases achieved on January 1. However, most reinsurers are sanguine, as they perceive the market is well positioned to build on the gains of the last six months at 2012's next key renewal date.[25] Reinsurers were already looking towards the next renewal on April 1, 2012, when most Japanese deals renewed. The Japanese had been badly hit by both Tōhoku and then by the floods in Thailand, where they held much of their manufacturing plant. Surely the consensus prices would go up then?

2.7. RELATIONALITY BETWEEN INDIVIDUAL PRACTICE, CONSENSUS PRICE, AND MARKET CYCLE

Our observation of the renewals following the Thai floods brings the relationality between individual competitive practice, consensus price on deals, and the market cycle into sharp relief. It is important to recognize that even without an event, quoting deals and shaping the market cycle would have followed the same relational process. That is, individual practice would still have both shaped and been shaped by the consensus price emerging on specific deals, and these prices would have shaped and been shaped by the emerging market cycle, as illustrated in Reinsurance-as-Practice 2B. It shows how the collective practice of a consensus price can emerge from individual practice in quoting and renewing deals, and how a collective market cycle emerges from the consensus prices formed on multiple deals. In doing so, it develops the foundation of our theory of **relational presence*** between dispersed market actors. That is, how actors neither connected in real time physically (Baker, 1984) nor electronically (Knorr Cetina and Bruegger, 2002a; 2000b; Mackenzie, 2004) are able to interact relationally across the market through their common quoting practice. We now further explain our conceptual model of the relationalities through which different elements of the market are coordinated within collective practice.

[25] "January Renewals Buoy Cat Underwriters Ahead of 1.4." 2012. *Insurance Insider*, January 11.

First, as shown in Figure 2.2 (Reinsurer$_{1-n}$) the practice of any individual is always enacted in relation to the temporal rhythms of the market. That is, actors begin any renewal period with reference to the preceding year's consensus price and their current understanding of the market cycle. Similarly, the particular point in the market cycle that is enacted at the end of any renewal period constitutes a reference point for the next renewal (Relationality F). Hence, the circular nature of our conceptual model reflects how the rate movements at any specific renewal reflect a moment of hardening or softening of the market through which its longer-term capital flows are enacted. In this process, market-making is continuous so that at any particular moment participants are both acting retrospectively upon previous price and cycle, and prospectively upon anticipated future price and cycle (Pettigrew, 1990; Weick, 2001).

Second, individual reinsurers act in relation to what their competitors are doing (Figure 2.2, Relationality A). They thus produce and consume information about how any losses may affect their competitors, which could lower their capital availability. While all actions shape the dense relationality between reinsurers, larger players who may be considered market-makers (Abolafia, 2001; Baker, 1984), are particularly influential in shaping collective practice, as illustrated by the attention paid by other reinsurers to the actions of Munich Re, Swiss Re, and SCOR in our example.

Third, markets are made within the trading of specific deals (Figure 2.2, Relationality B). Hence, individual reinsurers consider how long they have been renewing a specific deal, their relationship with the client, their history of losses on that deal and so forth (see also Chapter 3). As reinsurance is predominantly a renewal business, their actions are relational to their specific experience of that deal.[26] Individual underwriters are also considering competitors' relationships with a particular deal, particularly how others may quote, which in turns shapes their own quoting of that deal. At the same time, the temporal pull of the renewal date coordinates their individual practice on deals, including competitive considerations of when to quote (Figure 2.2 Relationality E). Hence, the consensus price emerging on any deal is relationally constructed in the interactions between reinsurers, deals and the impending renewal date, even as they quote independently upon each deal.

Fourth, individual deals are not quoted in isolation. Rather, their quoting by underwriters is done in relation to other deals and this is critical in shaping both the specific price on any particular deal (Figure 2.2, Relationality C) and,

---

[26] See, for example: "January 1, 2013 Non-Life Treaty Renewals." 2013. Hannover Re, February. http://www.hannover-re.com/resources/cc/generic/ir-presentations/results/pres130204.pdf; SCOR Global P&C. 2013. "Robust January Renewals with Selective Growth and Satisfactory Price Increases." SCOR. http://www.scor.com/images/stories/pdf/Inverstors/financial-reporting/presentation/pcrenewals_2013.pdf.

as a consequence, the market cycle for all deals (Figure 2.2, Relationality D). In particular, underwriters will quote in relation to other similar deals, such as those in proximity to a loss-affected region, as shown in our example of the spillover from Thai deals to Southeast Asian regions with similar characteristics. They also consider whether they might raise quotes on other deals not affected by any loss, because they perceive that their competitors' capital availability has been squeezed, so driving up their cost of capital. While actors cannot **know** the extent to which capital is affected, as this is emerging throughout the renewal period, they shape these capital flows through their quoting of all the deals on which they are involved.

Fifth, the renewal date acts as a powerful coordinating mechanism for these densely interwoven relational practices between individual reinsurers, particular deals, and across deals, at points within the market cycle. Specifically, the renewal date (Relationality E) requires actors to "show their hand" by quoting, so that their practice becomes part of the emerging consensus price for each deal. As the consensus price on any particular deal is established, all participants within the market for that deal then know this price, which in turn shapes quoting practice on deals that are still in progress. As the renewal date comes ever closer, more deals are "made" and, in the process, the hardening or softening of the market cycle is constructed.

Finally, as our recursive arrow back to reinsurers shows (Figure 2.2, Relationality F), the market cycle that is made at the renewal date then becomes a temporal marker in the unfolding process of constructing the market. As reinsurers consider their deals for the next renewal date, they reference the market cycle and the rates achieved at the prior renewal date.

2.8. FURTHER THEORIZING

In addition to developing the building blocks of relational presence and relationality that are the basis for the conceptual framework advanced in this book, this chapter also speaks to some other theoretical areas on making markets. In particular, we provide deep practice-based insights into how capital flow and pricing cycles are stabilized in the context of unpredictable risk.[27]

Our study contributes to research on how **social norms** stabilize the market by exercising **restraint** over opportunistic trading behavior from self-interested market actors (e.g. Abolafia, 1996; 2010a; Baker, 1984; Beckert,

---

[27] In relation to pricing cycles, the role of the "renewal date" is of theoretical interest in unpacking the temporality of markets. In particular, the renewal date is a unique form of market temporality that contrasts with existing studies of financial markets (e.g. Knorr Cetina and Bruegger, 2000; Knorr Cetina and Preda, 2007; Miyazaki, 2003).

2009, Granovetter, 1985). The general understanding within the reinsurance market that sharing risk at a consensus price is a means of protecting both buyers and sellers against the unpredictability of events constitutes a powerful restraint on opportunistic pricing. Namely, there is no gain from outbidding competitors.[28] Indeed, our relational approach shows how the interplay between opportunism (our individual actors' interest in pushing the market prices high in response to an event such as the Thai floods) and restraint (modifying their practice to conform to that of the collective market) is continuously unfolding. Most studies assume that self-regulation comes into effect when opportunism begins to tip the balance, so generating a swing back to restraint (e.g. Abolafia, 1996; 2010a; 2010b), often in order to avoid the external regulation that comes with excessive opportunism and crisis (Abolafia and Kilduff, 1988; Fligstein, 1996; Fligstein and Goldstein, 2010). By contrast, our relational explanation shows that the collective construction of restraint in the everyday practice of individuals constitutes a more continuous stabilizing of the market that suppresses such swings between opportunism and restraint.

Our theorizing of relationality shows how collective practice is exercised across a global market, rather than being grounded in the scrutiny and control of a few powerful "market makers" or in a network of personal relationships (e.g. Abolafia, 1996; Baker, 1984; Zaloom, 2006). While powerful actors, such as the biggest reinsurers, are undoubtedly influential, they neither dictate the price nor are they immune to the sanctions of the market (see also Chapter 5). Rather, the collective practice of sharing risk on deals means that all actors participate in the normative perpetuation of the market, such as expectations about renewing business, and the profound notions of reciprocity and payback between cedent and reinsurer that underpin the market cycle. Thus, as we showed in Section 2.5.2, a relatively small player in the London market may criticize the actions of a market leader (in this case Swiss Re's exit from the Credit & Surety market) where that leader contravenes norms, while the leader's own reputation and status in that particular aspect of the market is harmed. Importantly, our theory of relationality shows how these stabilizing norms can be exercised collectively within the practice of a global market, even where actors are not able to maintain close scrutiny of each other.

Finally, in demonstrating how collective practice stabilizes the market, we have also shown how market cycles are constructed. There has been little work extrapolating from what people do in their trading practice to how this practice constructs market cycles. Our study shows that pricing cycles and capital flows are not simply economic functions of supply and demand, but are constructed within the practice of dispersed actors not connected in

---

[28] This issue of how competition occurs in this market is examined in Chapter 5.

real time as they respond to events, withholding or committing their capital according to their relational construction of the market cycle.

In doing so, we are able to show the somewhat counterintuitive dynamic whereby market cycles can be an important stabilizing source of continuity in capital flow. In many markets, wide price fluctuation is evidence of mania, hype and opportunism (e.g. Abolafia and Kilduff, 1988), as for example with the bubbles and collapse that characterize housing markets (Abolafia, 2010; Zuckerman, 2010; 2012). That is, price fluctuations cause discontinuity as they disrupt the flow of capital. However, we offer a theorization of market cycles as a **source** of stability and as a means for managing the persistent uncertainty of risk-trading. In the reinsurance market the practice of cycling between hard and soft cycles is grounded in a continuous balance of opportunism and restraint to ensure long-term capital flows. As shown, social norms in this market dictate that prices reduce when there is no loss, which restrains opportunism on the part of the seller of capital who rarely abandons the buyer, while prices increase after a loss, which retrains opportunism on the part of buyers, who do not "shop around" to find cheaper prices but rather pay back those suppliers who have suffered losses. This is not a formal obligation, but is underpinned by profound understandings amongst all parties about the stabilizing value of long-term trading relationships in a context where the risk of loss, and thus of its appropriate price, is so uncertain.

In summary, our detailed investigation of the normative nature of this market demonstrates not only how market cycles are constructed, but how they can be stabilizing mechanisms to ensure the flow of capital across time. Future research might delve deeper into the way that markets collectively self-regulate within the individual practice of traders, how that constitutes a stabilizing force, and when and why that gets out of balance (see also Chapter 6).

2.9. CONCLUSION

In this chapter we have explained the relationality among individual practice, consensus price on specific deals and market cycles, within which the collective risk-bearing practice of a market for Acts of God is organized (Figure 2.2). We have shown that the relationality among the bundle of practices involved is coordinated within a pre-specified renewal date at which the consensus price for specific deals is made, and on which the stage of the market cycle is also "made" at a moment in time. Finally, we have shown how the **general understandings** of consensus price and market cycles within the reinsurance market are enacted within the **practical understandings** of a well-defined quoting process for renewing business through which underwriters enact their everyday work. In doing so, the chapter shows how the collective practice of a global market can be coordinated through relational practices amongst dispersed actors, rather than the embodied face-to-face or electronic screen interactions or connectivity between actors that characterize studies of other markets (e.g. see Baker, 1984; Knorr Cetina and Bruegger, 2002a; Mackenzie, 2004; Zaloom, 2006).

The chapter has thus exposed some of the principles of collective risk-bearing through which actors' work constructs and mitigates the uncertainty of a market for Acts of God. Yet it also raises several puzzles. We provided glimpses into two very different types of event, the Tōhoku earthquake and tsunami (Reinsurance-as-Practice 2A), and the Thai floods (Reinsurance-as-Practice 2B). How can such vastly different and incommensurable risks be reconciled into something comparable and tradable within a consistent, industry-wide quoting process? More broadly, how are the prices and quotes we discuss in this chapter actually calculated? Chapter 3 will explore this problem by taking a further turn of the kaleidoscope to examine the role of modeling and other forms of judgment in evaluating deals.

Summary

In this chapter we have:

- Shown how the **quoting of deals** is a fundamental site for market making activity.
- Shown how the **general understandings** of **consensus price**, in which all reinsurers on a deal take shares at the same price, and **market cycles**, in which prices for deals fluctuate, are integral to making this market. In particular, they create a context of collective risk-bearing that mitigates the uncertainty of pricing risk for unpredictable events. We emphasized the importance of these general understandings in coping with disaster through the story of the Tōhoku earthquake in Reinsurance-as-Practice 2A.
- Shown how the **renewal date** coordinates the individual practice of market actors to establish a consensus price for any particular deal in relation to multiple deals being renewed at that date.
- Shown how underwriters enact the consensus price and market cycles through two practical understandings of the **process for quoting deals** and the normative practice of **renewing deals** over **long-term relationships**. In our explanation of underwriters' responses to the Thai Floods in Reinsurance-as-Practice 2B, we illustrated how these practical understandings construct both the consensus price on deals, and fluctuations in the market cycle, at any particular renewal date.

3

Transforming Disasters into Tradable Deals

3.1. INTRODUCTION

As we have seen in previous chapters, reinsurance covers the insured claims arising from large-scale man-made and natural disasters. For instance Hurricane Katrina in 2005 incurred approximately $46 billion in insured losses.[1] It is difficult to value such unpredictable and vastly different disasters, ranging from bushfires to asbestos claims, and trade them within a market, given that their potential losses are often unknowable in advance. For example, how can the risk of a hurricane be calculated and compared with that of an earthquake, or terrorist attack? And yet the creation of such comparability is the purpose and practice of the reinsurance market. In this chapter, we address the practice through which varied risks are converted into comparable objects to be traded within a financial market.

The chapter is structured as follows. First, we turn the kaleidoscope to focus upon the evaluation of U.S. **Property Catastrophe***[2] deals as the specific **site*** of market-making practice in this chapter (see Chapter 4 for other types of risks). Second, we explain marketization (Çalışkan and Callon, 2009; 2010) as a **general understanding*** that potential disasters can be identified and traded as reinsurance **deals***. That is, in order for the threat of disasters to be traded in a market, they are turned into deals that can be evaluated. Third, in order to be traded as comparable financial objects, such deals must be subject to financial calculations that lead to a numerical

---

[1] Wharton Risk Management and Decision Processes Center, 2008. *Managing Large-Scale Risks in a New Era of Catastrophes: Insuring, Mitigating and Financing Recovery from Natural Disasters in the United States.* Philadelphia, PA: The Wharton School, University of Pennsylvania.

[2] In this book, bold fonts with an asterisk are used the first time we use a specific reinsurance or theoretical term in any chapter, to denote that the meaning of the term may be looked up in the glossary.

outcome; a specific value or **price***. We therefore propose that the wide-spread use of common statistical **models*** constitutes a coordinating prac-tice through which individual actors are connected in the calculation of Property Catastrophe deals (Beunza and Stark, 2012; Millo and MacKenzie, 2009). Fourth, we explain the **practical understandings*** within which deal evaluation is enacted, and which result in a price at which reinsurers and insurers are willing to exchange the risk of a disaster. Specifically, we refer to two widespread calculative practices (Çalışkan and Callon, 2009; 2010) that we term technicalizing and contextualizing of deals. Taken together, these practices render deals comparable as tradable objects in a financial market. Given this focus on calculation, we focus on the process through which underwriters generate a **quote*** for a deal.

Empirically, we zoom in on the practice of an underwriter, John, evaluating U.S. Property Catastrophe deals that cover dwellings in locations as diverse as Florida, Texas, California, and the Midwest, with disasters varying from bush-fire to hurricane, to provide rich ethnographic observations of these concep-tual points. We set the scene by shadowing John as he meets cedents on a busy day at a major industry conference, the 2009 PCI (Property Casualty Insurance Association America) annual conference in Florida. At PCI, reinsurers get the most up-to-date information from cedents and brokers as the renewal sea-son gets into swing. John's journey through the conference illustrates first, that the risks he considers are hugely varied: from earthquake and forest-fire in California, to windstorm threat to multimillion dollar coastal houses in Florida, to residential and rural housing throughout the state of New York. And second, that John and the other participants discuss all these "risks" as tradable objects. There is a deep general understanding that such risks are marketable.

....

REINSURANCE-AS-PRACTICE 3A
Evaluating U.S. Property Catastrophe deals—Collecting Information at an Industry Conference

October 26, 2009. On the flight to Orlando, John, a U.S. Property underwriter for Bermuda Re, takes a final look at his diary of nineteen appointments for the three-day annual PCI conference. Only minutes after landing, John is engaged in a flurry of meetings with **Chief Risk Officers*** and **Chief Underwriting Officers*** of U.S. Property insurers. On this particular morning, Paula is shadowing him through his meetings.

FloTex. Running a little late for his first meeting (10:02 a.m.), John checks the floor map to identify FloTex in the maze of more than eighty round tables set up in the ballroom. When he arrives at Table 59, Mick (FloTex Chief Risk Officer) has already placed an information pack on the table. John is familiar with the FloTex deal, which he has been renewing for about eight years. After some brief pleas-antries, they discuss the pack, focusing on FloTex's exposure throughout the Gulf of Mexico, from Texas to Florida. Many of FloTex's insured properties sit within this "Hurricane Alley" and had above-average losses from Hurricanes Ivan and Wilma. Mick brings John up to date with the exposure management for 2010–2011. John makes notes about their plans to scale back policies for zip codes that have sustained large losses in the last five years. Over the next three years, Mick expects the exposure to drop by 10 to 15 percent, particularly in Texas, which he plans on supplementing with growth in premium from writing insurance policies further inland. However, Mick hints that he wants a rate reduction for the reinsurance cover, as he has minimized some of his exposure. John does not comment on this but he raises his concern about a recent visit to FloTex's headquarters and tour of their key exposures, that showed how some of the commercial properties in FloTex's portfolio, particularly some large warehouses, were old and less well equipped to resist hurricanes than he had assumed. "That's likely to push my quoted rate up by a few points to bring it in line with my treatment of other similar portfolios in Texas," he admits. After some further discussion of the structure of the deal, the hour is up and John rises as they exchange a few final pleasantries.

BlingCo. Next (11:03 a.m.), John heads over to Table 23 to meet Charlotte from BlingCo. BlingCo insures homes of high-net-worth individuals in California. Charlotte reminds John of BlingCo's definition of high net worth; it requires policyholders to pay more than $50,000 a year for their policy, which includes the house and contents, such as fine art. The deal renews on June 1, almost a year from now. Charlotte introduces the latest techniques to prevent damage from bushfires as a way to reduce potential claims for BlingCo. "Every second year, we offer policyholders the opportunity to paint their homes with paint including a 'non-burning' component at no extra charge." An internal review by BlingCo's claims team identified that prevention, especially for high-net-worth individuals, avoids huge bills for burnt content where proof of purchase is difficult. She outlines that, in addition, BlingCo has appraisers who regularly visit policyholders to re-assess the property and content value, particularly for policies exceeding $10 million, so she feels confident about the accuracy of the insured values in the deal. BlingCo is a very attractive deal in the market due to its low frequency of losses, its prudent underwriting, its immediate adjustment of claims, and quick payment. Emphasizing that the deal has been loss-free for the past six years, Charlotte indicates her expectation of a steep rate reduction given the 10 percent in reduced value of homes and valuable goods, such as fine art, as a result of the recent financial crisis. John concludes the meeting by saying that he will look at the figures "once the submission is on my desk" although he cautions, "I already thought the rate was on the cheap side."

CrossNation. (12:00 a.m. to 1:30 p.m.), John heads to a private room for lunch with representatives from CrossNation, one of the largest insurers in the United States. CrossNation, which operates in forty-eight states, renews a Property deal (excluding flood), which has a total insured value of $2.1 billion, on January 1. After a brief catch-up on life in Bermuda, Chris, CrossNation's reinsurance buyer, introduces their growth plan for the next three years. To illustrate CrossNation's operations, Chris pulls out a map that demonstrates the different exposures across forty-eight of the fifty states (excluding Alaska and Hawaii). For example, green shows the least exposure to windstorm damage compared to magenta at the other end of the scale. Most of the business is underwritten in Florida, Texas, and New York, with some significant Midwest tornado exposure. The Florida portion of the deal pushes the price up significantly in comparison to some other deals John will see at this conference. Based on a rigorous review of policies, CrossNation has reduced the exposure to hurricanes in the southeast by not renewing policies of residential homes in certain zip codes. John chuckles, "To me it doesn't change the fact that you are one of my more heavily Florida-exposed deals." Thus, he expects them to "pay" for that. He also points out that they had been particularly impacted by tornadoes last year, whereas some of their nationwide competitors had been comparatively less affected due to their different concentration of commercial property in the Midwest. "Expect the rate to move upward," he warns the CrossNation team. However, as the lunch comes to a close, John affirms the importance of the business relationship between Bermuda Re and CrossNation.

On his way to the next meeting, John tells Paula that he had always seen CrossNation as a safe pair of hands in areas like Florida and the Midwest, given their history of prudent underwriting.

After the day's meetings, John catches up, over drinks, with brokers and a few underwriters from competing reinsurers. For almost an hour, the group discusses the impact of recent Florida legislative changes on the rates insurers are allowed to charge. Given the pressure on insurers, who suffered losses from Gustav in 2008, they expect many Floridian insurers will struggle to remain solvent, although bigger multi-state players like CrossNation will not be impacted.

Following the PCI conference Paula follows many of the reinsurers and some cedents to Bermuda, where she will shadow cedent meetings, observe preliminary underwriting, and attend the big rugby match sponsored by the reinsurance companies. She writes up her notes on the seventeen deals (twelve renewals, five new) she has seen, which range from earthquake and bushfire in California to windstorm in Florida, to tornado across the Midwest. She wonders how these vastly different deals will be evaluated and compared by underwriters and this is the puzzle addressed in this chapter. Fieldnotes provide insight: Paula notices that John, and the other underwriters the team shadowed in Bermuda, London, and Continental Europe, were not only interested in collecting quantitative information about property values. For example, the cedent's tight control over loss was central to John's discussion with BlingCo, as well as to his remarks about CrossNation.

3.2. EVALUATING DEALS AS SITE OF MARKET-MAKING

As there is no regulated or pre-specified scale or minimum price at which a deal should trade (Aspers, 2009), and the value of any loss that might occur from a peril is highly uncertain, evaluation is a central process in making price in this market (Preda, 2007). Hence, this chapter examines the practice of evaluating deals as a site of market-making activity, focusing specifically on how deals are evaluated and rendered comparable for trading as financial objects.

Making deals tradable involves two important elements. First, no two deals are alike because of variation in both the underlying perils and the portfolio of properties that they cover; for example, a Florida residential property deal to cover risk of hurricane, or a Californian commercial property deal to cover risk of earthquake. Hence, for an underwriter to evaluate these deals, and place capital on them, they must be rendered comparable as financial objects (Callon and Muniesa, 2005; Huault and Rainelli-Weiss, 2011; MacKenzie, 2009) with relative rates of risk and return. That is, for any particular reinsurer, there must be some consistent basis on which the quoted price can be calculated across different deals, despite the specific and tailored nature of each deal. Second, because multiple reinsurers across the market will bear collective risk on any particular deal at a **consensus price*** these reinsurers need a consistent approach to evaluating deals. A consistent evaluation process means that, even if they arrive at different prices, they have done so on a broadly consistent basis. Hence, the evaluation of deals is an important site in which the everyday practice of underwriters is relationally connected to the market practice of collective risk-bearing on deals.

In this chapter, we focus specifically on the evaluation process for U.S. Property Catastrophe deals. Property Catastrophe is the dominant **risk-type***, accounting for 39 percent of the premium in the global reinsurance market.[3] North American Property Catastrophe deals are deemed the most calculable because the detailed information on insured dwellings provides a consistent basis for estimations of possible losses. For these deals, information is available by zip code and even by street and house number, enabling them to be evaluated in terms of their exposure to a specified peril, such as a fault line in San Francisco. This rich information has enabled the development of statistical models about the probability of an event and a highly analytic approach to deal evaluation, making U.S. property risks the most standardized in the world. They are thus a good starting point to drill down into calculative practices in this market (Callon and Muniesa, 2005; Millo and MacKenzie, 2009; 2009). Nonetheless, as our ethnographic tales of John, a U.S. Property Catastrophe underwriter, will show, significant work must be done to price and compare even these highly modelable deals.

---

[3] "Global Reinsurance," 2013. *Marketline Industry Profile*, October.

Buyer's Perspective 3: How Does the Cedent Present the Deal to the Quoting Panel?

Jane has invited a **panel*** of reinsurers to quote on GlobalInc's U.S. Property Catastrophe deal (see Buyer's Perspective 1). Those reinsurers need information about the insured dwellings in order to calculate the risk they are being asked to share. GlobalInc passes on the data it collects on each property it insures, which come to gigabytes of raw data in total, including building codes, geographical coordinates (e.g. zip codes), and so forth. These data can be used to inform the reinsurers' assessment of their exposure to loss in the case of a catastrophic event. Moreover, GlobalInc has already run the exposure data through existing **models*** such as RMS, in conjunction with their broker, in order to both inform them about their own risk, as well as providing the results to reinsurers; although Jane knows that the reinsurers will want to do their own modeling of the risk.

In addition, GlobalInc provides an overview (in the form of spreadsheets) on all losses it has suffered on these dwellings in the past. This provides a loss history on a specific deal. Jane has held meetings with all of her most important reinsurers over the past twelve months, at which she explained the losses in the preceding year, as well as telling them about GlobalInc's strategic plans going forward. These meetings, combined with the loss history and other data she sends via her broker, are particularly important for those reinsurers who are renewing the deal. It will help them to go beyond the pure modeled results in evaluating their relationship with GlobalInc and consider whether this deal is in payback for losses, which they will then factor into the quoted price that they will return to Jane after their evaluation.

3.3. GENERAL UNDERSTANDING: MARKETIZATION

The growth of the reinsurance industry over the last 150 years (Borscheid, et al., 2013) is based on a general understanding that risk can be managed and transferred via market mechanisms. This understanding is termed "marketization" (Çalışkan and Callon, 2009) and refers to the growth of modern capitalist markets, in which parties compete for the opportunity to exchange goods or products for profit (Swedberg, 1994; Weber, 1922/1968). From this perspective, if things—even unpredictable and intangible things, such as risks (or securities or futures)—can be calculated and compared, they can be traded in a market (Çalışkan and Callon, 2009; Callon and Muniesa, 2005). Thus, the market and its calculative practice are relationally entwined; it is through the practice of calculating things that the market for them is made (Çalışkan and Callon, 2010; MacKenzie, 2006). The price for a reinsurance deal rests on the ability to evaluate the risk that is transferred from the cedent to multiple reinsurers. The transaction, meaning the transfer of risk from cedent to reinsurer, thus requires a process of calculation so that a price for these risks can be established. In this process of evaluating a deal the marketization of risk is enacted and made possible.

Due to the unpredictability of events, and the uncertainty of any loss, it is difficult to evaluate the cost of supplying capital to reinsurance deals and thus the price that may be charged. For example, in loss-free years, reinsurers know that the premium and investments from that premium remain undisturbed; yet the cost of loss-affected years cannot be known in advance and typically exceeds the premium a reinsurer earned within one year multiple times. However, the purpose of a reinsurance market is to value these risks, so that the liability to pay for them may be transferred from cedents to reinsurers, in return for a premium. Making a market thus depends on a general understanding that unpredictable disasters may be evaluated as particular deals using standardized calculative practices that render them comparable for the purposes of trading within a market (Çalışkan and Callon, 2010).[4]

While each deal is unique in terms of its underlying data and the risks it covers, a central tenet of marketization is that all deals will be delineated in a largely consistent way through specific parameters and boundaries (see Figure 3.1). This means that Deal A and Deal B share certain characteristics regarding how they are presented to reinsurers, despite differences in the underlying physical characteristics; for example, commercial or residential properties, and peril; or covering earthquake or windstorm. Furthermore, any one particular deal is presented in the same way to all reinsurers who are going to evaluate it. Thus, all reinsurers start from the same basis in their calculations.

Typically, deals for U.S. Property Catastrophe are submitted to reinsurers with a data pack comprising both a document with details of the deal, and a file containing detailed data on the insured dwellings. This data pack delineates the deal by specifying the nature and territory of the risk to be covered, so distinguishing between bushfires, earthquakes, and terrorism, and the particular region of cover. For example, in Reinsurance-as-Practice 3A, we saw John discussing a FloTex deal for "windstorm", BlingCo's Californian deal covering "forest fire and earthquake" events, or the CrossNation Property Catastrophe deal "excluding flood". This specification is a critical step in calculating deals as it makes the risk identifiable and creates boundaries of inclusion and exclusion. The data pack includes a large amount of information on the specific policies in the deal, including everything from structural aspects of the insured properties, such as roofing and building materials; insured values; zip code location, and so forth; banded in different ways in order to support statistical modeling. It also includes information about the

---

[4] It is not necessarily taken for granted that a market for reinsurance exists/should exist. Rather, this market must be made (Jaffee and Russell, 1997).

Table 3.1. Sample of Data Categories in a Data Pack

Buildings: Tabular data on the following			
Total insured value buildings (TIV)	Buildings values categorized by zip code	Year dwellings were built	Buildings values by county
Buildings values by distance to the underlying risk (e.g. fault line)	Buildings values split in residential and commercial	Structural components of buildings (e.g. roof shape, roof type, building materials)	Buildings classified by various bands that cut the data in different ways: value, building code, zone, etc.
Loss history: Tabular data on the following			
Loss ratio (*losses as a percentage of premium*)	Incurred losses (past 5–10 years)		Outstanding claims
Deal structure			
Attachment point, number of layers, and which risks they include/exclude			
Modeling			
Modeled outputs according to AIR, RMS, and/or EQECAT per layer			

history of losses and claims on this deal. Table 3.1 provides a sample of the type of information provided in a data pack, which may extend to forty or more pages of data.

The structure of the deal is often presented as a diagram to accompany the tabled data and is usually structured into "layers" to help clearly define the exposure (Boyer and Nyce, 2013; Ladoucette and Teugels, 2006). Figure 3.1 shows a simplified depiction of the FloTex deal, which John discussed with the cedent at the PCI conference above, and which has a typical structure for a U.S. Property Catastrophe deal. FloTex is purchasing an **excess-of-loss*** cover[5] for windstorm, with an attachment point of $20 million, meaning once losses hit $20 million the reinsurance cover starts. FloTex will pay any losses it incurs up to $20 million, transferring any loss that exceeds this amount to reinsurers. As shown in Figure 3.1, losses above $20 million are structured into layers, differentiated according to the potential severity of loss. In this case, Layer 1 covers losses from $20–$40 million. This is the most likely layer to occasion a loss, because it is the least severe; a moderate windstorm might trigger a payment in this layer, while Layer 4, which is triggered by losses

---

[5] The data pack will also specify the contractual nature and structure of the deal, which falls into two main types. First, proportional deals are those in which the reinsurer takes a proportional share in the profits and losses of the cedent's entire portfolio; second, non-proportional deals are typically those on an excess-of-loss basis, meaning that the reinsurer agrees to pay a set amount when a loss exceeds particular thresholds, which are set in layers (see Chapter 1, Figure 1.2). Most U.S. Property Deals are excess-of-loss deals, which is why we focus on them in this chapter.

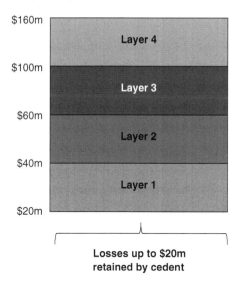

Fig. 3.1. Structure of an Excess-of-Loss Reinsurance Deal

above $100 million, is only likely to occur on a major windstorm that hits at the heart of the FloTex portfolio, damaging many of its properties. Because each layer represents a different level of risk, each will be priced separately, and reinsurers will quote and take separate shares on each of these layers. Other excess-of-loss deals, such as for CrossNation or BlingCo, follow the same convention, identifying an attachment point and differentiating the risk of potential losses into layers.[6]

While the underlying perils (tornado, earthquake, etc.) are incommensurable, the specification of deals within these standardized parameters enables them to be evaluated comparably and traded as financial objects. This very specific delineation of a deal structure is fundamental to the marketization of risk. It renders risk viable for trading by transforming it into a deal that can be calculated and priced by the multiple participants within the marketplace. Hence, even though underwriters are physically remote, working in different firms globally, those who quote on a deal gain access to the same type of information, structured in the same way, and at the same time. For instance, when John receives a data pack on CrossNation, his competitors are receiving the exact same data pack through which to evaluate the same deal. Thus the method for structuring deals establishes the foundation for competing reinsurers to evaluate these deals individually, and decide which

---

[6] These structures may be more complex, including specific layers for windstorm, or earthquake, or including not only "vertical" cover for loss according to severity, but also "sideways" cover for loss arising from many frequent small claims, as opposed to one large event. However, the principles are largely the same as our depiction.

deals to place capital on separately, while bearing risk collectively on the same basis. Common calculative practices and devices, such as a similar set of modeling tools, are important in making deals comparable (Beunza and Stark, 2012; Callon and Muniesa, 2005; MacKenzie and Millo, 2003; Millo and MacKenzie, 2009). In addition, when underwriters use a consistent and widespread model to evaluate deals, they participate in a process that is widely regarded as legitimate for calculating the probability of a disaster, which further legitimates the model, and also the prices that they might derive in using such models (see Millo and MacKenzie, 2009). In short, the marketization of risk has led to the development of statistical models that quantify risks, and their continuous and widespread use reinforces the general understanding that risks are calculable, comparable and thus tradable. We discuss these models in the next section.

3.4. COORDINATING THE MARKET: MODELS AS CALCULATIVE DEVICES

In the reinsurance industry, statistical models for analyzing the probability of an event, drawing upon seismology, meteorology, engineering and actuarial science, originated in the late 1980s. Third-party firms, henceforth "vendors", license these models to insurers, broking houses and reinsurers. **Vendor models*** developed into industry standards following Hurricane Andrew in 1992, which brought major devastation to Florida and the Gulf of Mexico. At the time, it was the costliest hurricane in North America, bankrupting some insurance companies and depleting capital reserves of reinsurers. The devastation—both in terms of physical infrastructure and capital—demanded more reliable predictions of windstorms in order to create appropriate and sufficient insurance and reinsurance covers. This gave impetus to the rise of vendor models (e.g. RMS, AIR, EQECAT) that have expanded from providing probabilities of windstorm in the U.S. to statistical calculation of other types of risks in other territories (see Table 3.2). "While they [vendor models] were released in the late 1980s, there wasn't wide use of any of the models until after Hurricane Andrew in 1992. And then reinsurers, everyone just started buying them." (Interview, Reinsurer, Underwriter, Bermuda). Hurricane Andrew thus "changed the game" in reinsurance risk analysis, shifting evaluation towards more sophisticated analytic techniques seen as appropriate to a finance industry (Borscheid et al., 2013; Grossi and Kunreuther, 2005).

These models are complex calculative devices that contain information about the underlying risk, such as probabilities of events that help to mitigate perceptions about their unpredictability. They are updated regularly with fine-grained zip code data that specifies where properties are, the building

Table 3.2. Vendor Models

Vendor model	Description
AIR	• Founded: 1987 • Perils: windstorms; earthquakes; flooding; terrorism; longevity • Territories: U.S.; Central America; Europe; Australia; Japan • Version release (Catradar): 2013
RMS	• Founded: 1988 • Perils: hurricanes; earthquakes; flooding; terrorism; longevity • Territories: U.S.; Europe; Australia; Japan • Version release: 13 (2013)
EQECAT	• Founded: 1994 • Perils: hurricanes; earthquakes; flooding • Territories: U.S.; Europe; Australia; Japan • Version release: RQE v14 (released 2013)

codes on their structural features, and the latest geological or meteorological information on the probability of particular types of events occurring. As one manager explains: "Models are constantly refined, with two updates a year, which the vendors are duty-bound to provide us with, which fine-tune or make adjustments each year. In this way the model is constantly enhanced" (Interview, Reinsurer, Underwriter, Bermuda). Because these vendor models have become embedded as standard calculative devices, it has become unthinkable to evaluate a North American catastrophe deal without them; indeed one CEO noted, following an industry presentation by Paula, that failing to use models would be "negligent". That is, the widespread use of vendor models gives not only underwriters but also their wider stakeholders confidence in the calculation process for evaluating risk: "The investors who are investing in our industry [reinsurance], they're saying 'in your industry using the vendor tools [models] makes sense', and they're the tools of preferred use at the moment." (Interview, Broker, London). Vendor models are thus an industry standard that provides legitimation to the evaluation process, so further perpetuating their own legitimacy.[7]

The ability to compare and trade deals in a market is aided by a common set of statistical models to evaluate risk (Callon and Muniesa, 2005; Millo and MacKenzie, 2009). We therefore conceptualize these vendor models as coordinating practices for the marketization of risk. They provide a consistent, industry-wide method of calculation for evaluating North American property deals, based on a set of parameters and formulae devised from

---

[7] Some of the larger reinsurers—such as Swiss Re, Munich Re, and Partner Re among others—develop their own sophisticated models and catastrophe simulations internally. These are important in their evaluative process. However, regardless of whether they have these internal models, they will also use and run the vendor models as well.

meteorological, geological, engineering, and actuarial science (Grossi and Kunreuther, 2005). Hence buyers, suppliers, and their intermediaries all apply the same parameters, embedded in the models, in order to identify the extent of a deal's exposure to a particular risk (e.g. how many houses of a particular value and building code specification are in the likely path of a tornado), the probability of that risk happening, also referred to as **return period***, and its potential severity (e.g. a one-in-fifty, one-in-250 or even a one-in-1,000-year probability of a tornado that could cause that level of damage). As vendor models structure the data on deals in a consistent way, they coordinate the presentation of these inherently different things as if they were all similar things. For example, regardless of the specific risk and deal specification, the data pack on every U.S. property deal includes its modeled output, calculated using one of these models.

Models estimate probability by reconstructing past events. For example, they build on information about the most destructive hurricanes, such as Andrew, Katrina, and Wilma, to determine probable hurricane paths and their potential damages. Second, a model can run tens of thousands of scenarios in order to identify what might happen in any plausible way that nature may strike. The vendor models thus impose definitions and set boundaries on what might happen, based on worst-case scenarios derived from past destruction. As records of past destruction are relatively recent, such scenarios also involve statistical extrapolations, particularly for longer return periods such as an event that might occur once in a thousand years. Based on the information provided on specific deals, models can calculate probable losses. In particular, the scenarios can be applied to the structure of the deal (see Figure 3.1), so that the model specifies that Layer 1 may correspond to a one-in-fifty year event, while Layer 4 may be a one-in-500 event (an event of this size is less likely to occur than the one represented by Layer 1). Based on the specific insured values included in the data pack, the models can then project a financial value for the loss sustained under each scenario.

Vendor models coordinate the marketization of deals in two ways. First, they ensure that different deals are all rendered calculable in the same way, using the same core calculative devices (Çalışkan and Callon, 2009; Millo and MacKenzie, 2009). Second, they ensure all underwriters on the same deal, wherever they are located, work to the same basic calculative criteria. As one executive reflects: "That business [Property Catastrophe] is probably more highly modeled than anything else. It's highly modeled for various reasons. One, it is modeled by third parties, so it creates an even playing field to all players on the market" (Interview, Executive, Continental Europe). These models thus connect the calculative practice of globally dispersed underwriters. Specifically, as we will show, while the precise calculative practices of individual underwriters in using these models may vary, they all begin with the same set of models and assumptions, which have also been used by the cedent and their broker to structure the information in the deal.

Marketization and its associated models are savage masters—they push forward in a single direction. The drive to increase modelability of deals means that Property Catastrophe underwriters receive, year after year, ever more granular data, and request ever-increasingly detailed information.[8] In particular, following an event the modeling companies will appraise the reliability of the modeled predictions for such an event and update the model. Similarly, both cedents and reinsurers will run the actual losses they received against the model to see how well the predictions align. This continuous updating of vendor models underpins the drive towards increased information, which in turn underpins the general understanding that these risks are calculable, all of which in turn reinforces the centrality of the vendor model. For example, when starting out as an underwriter fifteen years ago, John received floppy disks of data, whereas he now looks at gigabytes of data that are provided on USB sticks or can be downloaded from websites. The rise of vendor models has been intrinsically linked to an increase in detailed statistical data: models are both dependent on and shape the production and consumption of data (see MacKenzie, 2006; Millo and MacKenzie, 2009).

In summary, the use of vendor models builds on the general understanding that unpredictable risk can be calculated as tradable deals, and these deals can be compared with other deals for the purposes of capital placement. However, models, in and of themselves, do not enact this marketization of risk, except within the calculative practice of underwriters (Beunza et al., 2006; McFall, 2011; Preda, 2009b). We therefore now examine the practical understandings through which models are used in everyday practice.

3.5. PRACTICAL UNDERSTANDING: PRACTICING DEAL EVALUATION

Models do not "do" anything! Rather, their calculative properties are enacted within the everyday practice of evaluating deals, which is the focus of this section. Calculation requires that entities, such as deals, be put through common calculative devices, such as a spreadsheet or a model, which transforms them into a numerical outcome (Callon et al., 2007; Callon and Muniesa, 2005; Muniesa et al., 2007). This numerical outcome is critical in detaching that entity from its particular physical or material basis and constructing it as

---

[8] Mawk, K. 2008. "Data Quality Matters." *Global Insurance Intelligence*, December 18. http://www.globalreinsurance.com/lines-and-risks/data-quality-matters/1375999.article.

Table 3.3. Practical Understandings of Technicalizing and Contextualizing

	Calculative practice	Actions
Technicalizing	Modeling	Quantifying and enumerating a deal through vendor models available for specific territories and risk-types.
	Rating	Interpreting and refining the modeled output numerically within the rating sheet (spreadsheet), including accounting for deal-specific issues, such as changes to exposure, to weight the modeled output.
Contextualizing	Evoking the physical characteristics	Drawing on knowledge of the insured object (e.g. how a specific property behaves) and risk-type (e.g. the landfall and path of hurricanes) to understand characteristics of the deal.
	Incorporating the cedent relationship	Knowledge of the cedent's operations comprises soft factors such as claims handling, the quality of information and the reciprocity of relationship.
	Incorporating market dynamics	Using knowledge of the market cycle and rumors to inform capital placement decision.

a tradable object;[9] that is, it is a thing that may be traded for a specific price within a market. The deal evaluation process serves this calculative purpose in the reinsurance market, transforming deals into comparable and tradable objects. We distinguish between two overlapping practical understandings that are central to this practice of calculation, **technicalizing** and **contextualizing** (see Table 3.3), which comprise multiple everyday practices that are integral to the work of evaluating deals (Schatzki, 2002). We now introduce the technicalizing of U.S. Property Catastrophe deals; then illustrate that process through a rich ethnographic narrative of an underwriter evaluating specific deals.

3.5.1. Technicalizing

Technicalizing is a knowledgeable practice enacted through an underwriter's know-how in using vendor models, which includes understanding their strengths and weaknesses in evaluating deals. Technicalizing is comprised of two calculative practices: i) modeling, and ii) rating, that culminate in a **technical rate** for a deal. The technical rate is the calculated value of the deal,

---

[9] That is, the entity is no longer defined by its raw materials or their function or purpose per se—such as a shoe being defined by its function in protecting feet from rough surfaces—but by its value as a tradable commodity, which may be bought or sold.

in return for the degree of risk taken; but it is not the price at which a deal is quoted or at which it trades. Rather, the quoted price of a deal is enacted within a broader range of calculative practices which we will call "contextualizing", explored in section 3.4.2 below.

Modeling draws on an underwriter's knowhow in using vendor models, such as RMS and AIR. In the example we describe below, the underwriter, John, is analyzing U.S. Property Catastrophe deals. For each deal, a model will generate results that indicate the potential losses from predefined scenarios, such as exposure of the particular properties to the path of windstorms, and the probable maximum loss (PML) for a particular event (see Columns D and G, Figure 3.2), such as a one-in-250 year windstorm. While cedents and their brokers already provide underwriters with a modeled view of the deal using vendor models, underwriters run each deal again through these and potentially additional in-house models, as they adjust the available settings. Typically, underwriters have in-firm modelers who run the model on the deal, using particular scenarios and specific parameters. To select these parameters, an underwriter draws on knowledge about the cedent's exposure, which is also provided in the data pack, such as an overview of the number of insured residential homes according to specific building codes. As a simple example, underwriters may suggest setting the parameters to account for a higher concentration of residential or commercial buildings, or adjust the weightings of low- and high-rise family buildings, to ensure a close mapping to the specific details of the insured dwellings in a deal. Modeling quantifies the risk and results in specific figures from each model that is displayed in the spreadsheet (see the different shaded blocks for AIR and RMS in Figure 3.2).

Rating involves using a spreadsheet that includes aggregated financial information imported from the data pack such as the deal's total insured values and its structure (as exemplified in Section 3.2 by the layers in the FloTex excess-of-loss cover). Using the **rating sheet***, an underwriter will generate a technical rate for the deal, drawing on the modeled results generated during modeling (see tab at the bottom of the rating sheet, Figure 3.3). During this process, an underwriter adjusts the modeled results; for example, privileging a particular model because of perceptions that it is more accurate at calculating the details of a specific deal (Column F, Figure 3.3). The technical rate also includes a reinsurer's standard capital charges (which may be thought of as overheads and profit margins (see Kiln and Kiln, 2001: 215–218) that are applied to all deals. At this stage, all that has been calculated is the technical rate (see Column E, Figure 3.3), not the quoted price, which remains an empty column (Column G, Figure 3.3). We now return to John, the underwriter we observed at PCI in reinsurance-as-practice 3A, to show how he evaluates specific deals through technicalizing practices.

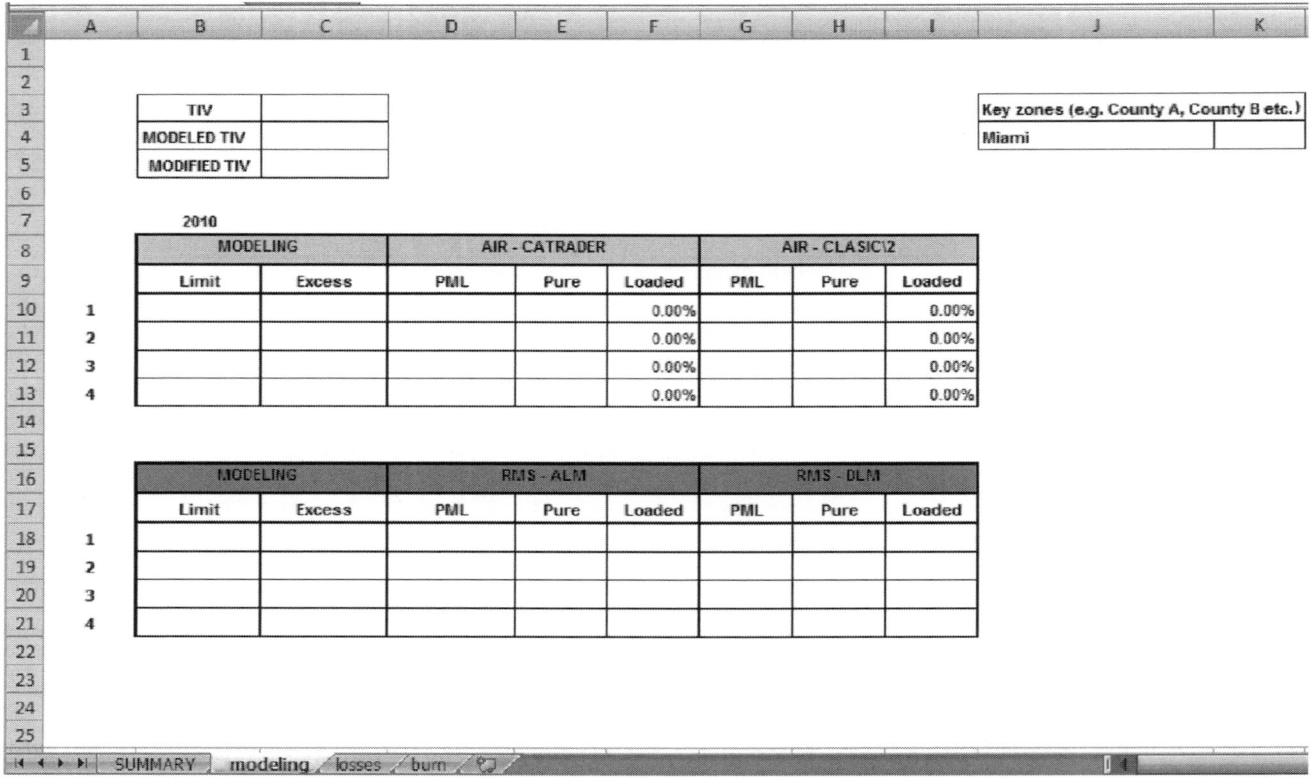

TIV	
MODELED TIV	
MODIFIED TIV	

Key zones (e.g. County A, County B etc.)	
Miami	

2010

	MODELING		AIR - CATRADER			AIR - CLASIC\2		
	Limit	Excess	PML	Pure	Loaded	PML	Pure	Loaded
1					0.00%			0.00%
2					0.00%			0.00%
3					0.00%			0.00%
4					0.00%			0.00%

	MODELING		RMS - ALM			RMS - DLM		
	Limit	Excess	PML	Pure	Loaded	PML	Pure	Loaded
1								
2								
3								
4								

Fig. 3.2. Simplified Sample Spreadsheet of Modeled Output on Deals

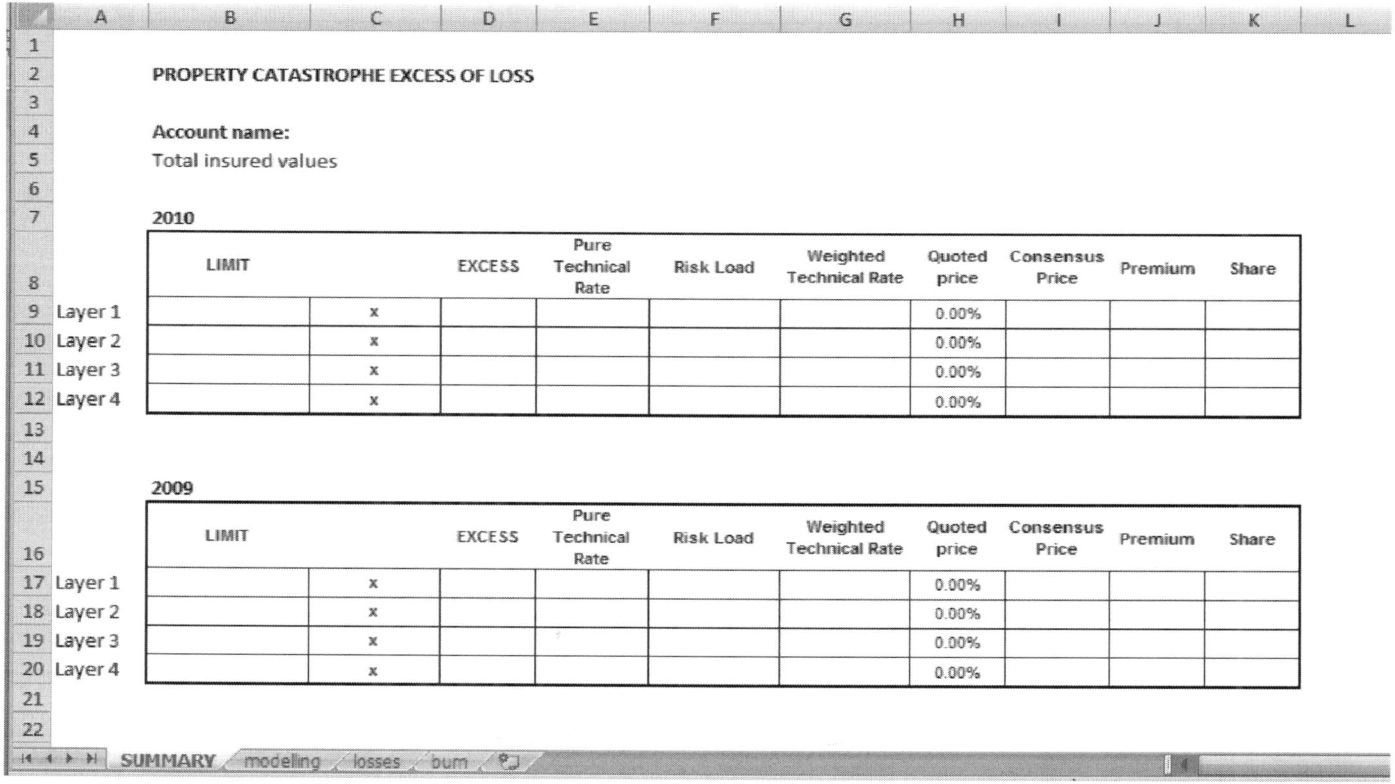

PROPERTY CATASTROPHE EXCESS OF LOSS

Account name:
Total insured values

2010

LIMIT		EXCESS	Pure Technical Rate	Risk Load	Weighted Technical Rate	Quoted price	Consensus Price	Premium	Share
Layer 1	x					0.00%			
Layer 2	x					0.00%			
Layer 3	x					0.00%			
Layer 4	x					0.00%			

2009

LIMIT		EXCESS	Pure Technical Rate	Risk Load	Weighted Technical Rate	Quoted price	Consensus Price	Premium	Share
Layer 1	x					0.00%			
Layer 2	x					0.00%			
Layer 3	x					0.00%			
Layer 4	x					0.00%			

SUMMARY / modelling / losses / burn

Fig. 3.3. Simplified Sample Rating Sheet for Deals

REINSURANCE-AS-PRACTICE 3B
Evaluating Deals Through Technicalizing Practices

On the morning of May 19, 2010 Paul arrives at Bermuda Re's office in a quiet side street in Hamilton, Bermuda, to shadow John. John is sitting in an open plan office, at his desk, which is piled with papers, his PC, and two computer screens. Around him are other underwriters at their similarly arrayed desks. John brings Paul up to speed with the current renewal cycle. To illustrate what has been happening in the past few weeks gearing up to June 1 renewal, which is dominated by Florida deals, John opens the folder of "submissions received" realizing that he is already behind where he should be for this current renewal cycle. During the past two weeks, John received raw data on most of his Florida deals, although he is still waiting for a few more. Bermuda Re dedicates a specified pool of capital to deals in Florida. As these deals are capital-intensive, John cannot participate on all deals submitted (capital availability and allocation are discussed more fully in Chapter 5). The deal evaluation process is therefore critical for identifying the "best" deals. Each one may cover residential or commercial properties, insured either in a single state or spanning several states, albeit with a concentration in Florida.

Modeling. At 8:52 a.m., John receives an email with the data on the excess-of-loss deal for FloTex, a cedent that Paula met while shadowing John during PCI. This data pack, which includes a server link to 2.5 gigabytes of data that John downloads, kicks off the deal evaluation process. It illustrates FloTex's exposure, meaning the total insured values of policies, differentiated and banded by type of property (e.g. residential, commercial, building structures, building codes, property values) by state (Florida or Texas) and zip code. It also contains information on FloTex's loss history, meaning the frequency and severity of losses that FloTex has had over the past eight years. All of John's peers in Lloyd's, Bermuda, and Continental Europe receive this same raw data.

In the PDF accompanying the raw data, John reads about changes in FloTex's exposure, which has gone down by 10 percent in Texas. FloTex seeks reinsurance cover against windstorm, which is the main risk in Florida and Texas. The deal's structure remains similar to last year, meaning that John can open a file on last year's pricing as a reminder of his previous approach. The threshold to trigger the reinsurance cover starts when damages caused to properties insured by FloTex exceed $20 million, and there are four layers at which a payout will be triggered. The first layer (Layer 1) is from $20 to $40 million. Accumulated damage exceeding $40 million falls within Layer 2, and includes payments for damages up to $60 million. Layer 3 consists of $60–$100 million. Layer 4 consists of $100–$160 million (see Figures 3.1 and 3.3).[10] As the greatest likelihood for payout is Layer 1, it also needs to generate the most premium for Bermuda Re. While the other layers have lower likelihood of losses, this will be reflected

[10] While there might be two deals with the same structure (for instance, split into layers comprised of 20m x 40m, and 40m x 60m as with FloTex), given the variation of insurers' insured premiums, location of the properties in relation to the risk, a direct comparison of deals on the basis of its structure is meaningless. A comparison of deals is therefore only available once modeling has been completed.

in lower premium figures. Therefore, evaluating a deal involves examining its general attractiveness, given the amount of exposure to the possible risk, as well as the attractiveness of each specific layer in order to achieve a return on equity for Bermuda Re.

Before John can work out a "price" for each layer, he needs to run FloTex's data through RMS and AIR, as he does with any other deal on U.S. Property Catastrophe that crosses his desk. While the broker who sent the data on FloTex also provided the RMS modeling output, John also runs the models in-house. "It's a black box how they get those numbers so we always run our own."

John sends the deal to his in-house modeler, suggesting in the cover email how they can adjust some of the parameters so that they reflect the FloTex deal.[11] While he recognizes that his competitors also run AIR and RMS on each deal, he explains to Paul that there are multiple parameters that can be applied when modeling a deal: "Even things like a standard model, we're running RMS, they're [our competitors] also running RMS. We may come up with different results from them, if they assume that the building stock conforms to a default RMS standard for a particular territory. Or if we say actually no, this portfolio is 90 percent glass and steel and 10 percent masonry. And then you come up with a different answer." He has asked the modeler to tweak some of the default assumptions in RMS, such as estimations of age of buildings, and buildings' structural components. John says, "We have always run FloTex's portfolio as 'average' in terms of these indicators of build-quality." Given FloTex's reduction in highly exposed properties in Texas, he anticipates that "it should look better than last year" particularly at the lower layers, but that the exposure reduction will be largely irrelevant at the higher layers. John has to wait until the modeler has run the data, so he turns to work on some other deals.

Later that day John receives an email with the modeled results, which have turned the deal into a specific set of numbers. Instead of looking at more than forty pages of tabled data on insured values by zip code, John now has specific numerical values that pertain to scenarios. He opens the outputs from AIR and RMS for FloTex on two separate screens (see below). These figures reflect losses for each layer according to the likelihood of an event, generated as a specific return period by the vendor models. According to AIR, Layer 1 corresponds to a one-in-twenty year event, indicating that payouts for losses covered by Layer 1 may occur every twenty years. As each vendor model is based on slightly different assumptions about the nature of the risk, modeling generates a variation in modeled output for a deal. While AIR assumes a one-in-twenty year event triggers losses in Layer 1, RMS for FloTex comes up with a one-in-thirty-six for the same layer. This variation between models is consistent throughout the layers, because these probabilities are not a very exact science, depending on how they attribute causality between an event and the resultant damage to property. Hence, AIR Layer 2 corresponds to a one-in-eighty event (RMS: one-in-105); Layer 3 to a one-in-165 year event (RMS: one-in-210); Layer 4 to a one-in-300 year event (RMS: one-in-420). For the next few minutes, John studies his two screens intently, comparing the results of AIR and RMS, which as usual are different.

---

[11] While underwriters make the decision regarding what deals to place capital on, they are assisted by modelers on Catastrophe deals, with whom they work closely.

	Screen1	Screen 2
Layer 1 ($20m to $40m):	AIR: 0.51;	RMS: 0.34
Layer 2 ($40m to $60m):	AIR: 0.29;	RMS: 0.21
Layer 3 ($60m to $100m):	AIR: 0.17;	RMS: 0.09
Layer 4 ($100m to $160m):	AIR: 0.11;	RMS: 0.03

Across the four layers, AIR assumes a higher likelihood for losses from windstorms than RMS. Generally, based on long experience using the models, John prefers AIR for deals covering windstorms in Florida: "I tend to think that AIR is very good on residential properties, homes and cars and things like that, where the law of large numbers makes it easier statistically to figure out losses. So, for example, if you have a big hurricane going across Florida which is mostly residential anyway, rather than commercial, and you've damaged X number of buildings, they all tend to be an average size. If you work out the average value of a home damage times the numbers, it's sort of quite easy to do it. On the commercial side it's much more difficult because buildings like hospitals or substantial buildings have different ways of being damaged and there are not a lot of them all around, they're dotted around the place." Based on his knowledge of the deal—FloTex is largely high-density residential property—and his modeling know-how, John is comfortable with a combined result that is weighted to the AIR output. To get a quick comparison on how the changes in FloTex exposure are reflected in the modeling, John opens last year's AIR and RMS results. He notes: "The models are favorable to the reduction in the Texas exposure," as the models reflect a 10 percent reduction in price from last year's results. These modeled results provide the basis for a technical rate (or price) for each layer (see Columns E and H, Figure 3.2) that indicates the amount of premium in percentage that John should charge for Bermuda Re's capital to provide FloTex with this cover against windstorm. To develop such a rate he turns to the rating sheet.

Rating. While the models ran on FloTex, John populated the rating sheet with the deal's structure and added FloTex's written premium: $85 million[12] in total across Florida and Texas. To generate a technical rate for each layer, John imports the modeled outputs from AIR and RMS into separate worksheets, which link to the rating sheet. Building on the information from these, the rating sheet populates the technical rate column (Column G, Figure 3.3), which incorporates Bermuda Re's capital charges and profit margin.

John then turns his attention to the modeled data inputs from AIR and RMS, clicking through the tabs in the Excel spreadsheet. Reflecting his preference for AIR, John stays with the worksheet of "AIR-modeling" manipulating the modeled output to reflect his privileging of the results over RMS Indeed, he adjusts some of the model's parameters, which are captured in the ratings sheet, thus varying the technical rate. Moreover, John looks at FloTex loss history (the losses that have hit the reinsurance layers in the past) and uses these to build in some

---

[12] As FloTex is a fictitious acronym, any figures on these reinsurance deals are also adjusted to ensure participating reinsurance firms' anonymity.

experience-based costs (known as a **burning cost***calculation), which he will then relate to the modeled results for Layer 1.

After manipulating the risk-loading within the rating sheet for thirty-five minutes—for example, in relation to the experience data on Layer 1 and to ensure AIR is weighted more heavily than RMS—John settles on the following technical rates for FloTex: Layer 1: 38 percent; Layer 2: 27 percent; Layer 3: 15 percent; Layer 4: 6 percent. These percentages are known as a **Rate on Line*** (RoL), which is a measure of the premium required for a deal relative to the potential of a loss measured by its probability. It shows how much premium a reinsurer would want as a percentage of the risk being carried. For example, a $10 million dollar catastrophe cover with a premium of $2 million would have a RoL of 20 percent, which provides a greater volume of premium for the reinsurer than a RoL of 10 percent, which would result in $1 million of premium. When a reinsurer quotes, they offer a RoL, as well as indicating what share of the deal they would like to take at that RoL. RoL is thus a reinsurance industry measure of price that incorporates a consideration of the return relative to the risk that the reinsurer is taking for this specific deal.

Through the calculative practices of modeling and rating, each deal is converted from the voluminous raw data into modeled results that represent its exposure to the risk, the underwriter's opinion on the accuracy of the modeled output in the form of the technical rate, and applied capital charges and profit margin. While the technical rate is derived from the calculative practices revolving around vendor models, it draws on John's knowledgeable practice in using the models, such as his preference for particular models depending on the particular region and the specific risk. As we have seen, the calculation enacted with multiple vendor models, and their manipulation in the rating sheet, detaches a deal from its physical characteristics and transforms these into a set of technical rates that comprise an initial basis for trading.

Yet, despite this extensive technical work, John says to Paul, "AIR and RMS are useful for comparison but the actual numbers are useless." While vendor models shape the technical rate, more work is required to determine the quoted price. The technical rate for deals generated through these models merely provides an industry benchmark.

....

3.5.2. Contextualizing

While models remain the central device used for evaluating U.S. Property Catastrophe deals, they are regarded with skepticism: as one [underwriter] remarked to us, "It's crazy that we've only [got data] for forty years and talk about one-in-500 year return periods. How the fuck am I supposed to know [whether this model is accurate]?" (Observation, Reinsurer, Underwriter, Bermuda). There is widespread recognition in the industry that models are at best approximations of risk. Thus calculation also involves contextualizing, which is the skilled practice of an underwriter bringing expert knowledge about contextual features into deal evaluation. It emphasizes the "qualitative" aspects or "judgment calls" involved in pricing deals. Contextualizing enables underwriters to deviate from the technical rate derived by the models. For instance, rating sheets usually have a means to adjust the "risk load" (Column F, Figure 3.3); that is, factoring the price up or down by some percentage points. For instance, an underwriter might want to add an "error" load if they are unsatisfied with the information quality they have received from cedents, inflating the price on such deals to compensate for the lack of information. Such deviation from the technical rate is not considered wrong; instead it is held to indicate an underwriter's calculative skill and know-how. It requires both an understanding of the limitations of the technical rate, and also an ability to relate that technical rate to the quoted price that a deal might command in a competitive market (McFall, 2011; Millo and MacKenzie, 2009). Contextualizing comprises three activities: i) evoking the physical characteristics of the deal; ii) incorporating the cedent relationship; and iii) incorporating the market dynamics (see Table 3.3).

Underwriters often know something about the physical characteristics of the insured properties, which they use to **evoke the deal's physical characteristics**. For example, in Reinsurance-as-Practice 3A, John knew from a site visit that FloTex had some relatively old warehouses in a particularly wind-exposed coastal area. During our observations, we witnessed underwriters using maps that illustrate lava flows, fault lines and hurricane paths, and looking at photos of buildings and damages. Looking at such materials, such as maps of coastal zones, taps into the underwriter's knowledge about the potential susceptibility of particular homes to the path of a windstorm in Florida for example, providing meaning to the RMS or AIR outputs. Evoking a deal's physical characteristics goes beyond the previous application of John's knowledge of the deal to tweak the modeling parameters during technicalizing. Here he delves into his knowledge of the underlying risk, the insured properties, and anything that might explain any losses incurred in the last twelve months.

Within the calculation of each deal, underwriters also try to **incorporate the relationship** with the cedent. This means that underwriters take into account the longevity of the relationship, both in terms of the expectations of reciprocity implied (see Chapter 2; Abolafia, 1996; Baker, 1984) and also how well they know the cedent's business, including how effectively they manage their operations. For example, in Reinsurance-as-Practice 3A John knew that BlingCo's staff checked the use of fire-resistant paint and monitored closely the contents of their high-value homes. Knowing the cedent so deeply arises from renewing business over many years (see Chapter 2, Section 2.4.1). Deep information is built up as underwriters tour local operations, catch up at industry conferences, welcome insurers to their own offices, and participate in social events such as corporate fishing trips and golf tournaments. We saw some of this information gathering during John's conference discussions (see Reinsurance-as-Practice 3A).

Knowing the cedent does more than simply give an underwriter confidence in the technical outputs of calculation. It can also frequently suggest modifications to the technical rate. For example, claims handling is a critical factor, as it determines the value of a reinsurer's payout following an event. Those insurers, such as BlingCo, that run good in-house claims handling are able to control losses, both by dismissing fraudulent claims, and by containing escalation of damage. Underwriters may thus be inclined to discount for insurers that are known to have good claims handling. Similarly, insurers who are known to check the quality of buildings, including the installation of window shutters and other features that contain loss, are more likely to be discounted. Another critical factor is the quality and accuracy of information provided by the cedent. This is not easily apparent simply from looking at the data packs, it also involves personal knowledge of what insurers have said they will do, such as reducing exposure in Texas, which can be compared with those figures presented in the data pack. As John has built up trust with FloTex over their eight-year relationship, he knows they will continue to follow through on this strategy, whereas he will treat the projections of a reinsurer he does not know with more skepticism. Underwriters will generally increase rates on deals from insurers whose information is shown to be unreliable or incoherent. Finally, underwriters take into consideration the relationship when renewing business. While this does not change the calculation as such, it changes the perception of it. As explained in Chapter 2, reinsurers are usually more likely to find a justification to underwrite a lower-priced deal they are renewing, than they are to take on a new deal at the same price.

Underwriters also **incorporate the market dynamics**, drawing on cues about what price a deal might achieve in the current market cycle. For example, as explained in Chapter 2 (Section 2.2.2), if the industry, or the particular region, is in a hard cycle of payback for significant losses from previous years, the reinsurer can adjust the quoted price up from the technical rate. Alternatively, if it is a soft cycle, the reinsurer may not even be able to achieve their technical rate, and must quote lower if they want to participate in the market. Information about the market dynamics is obtained from industry newsletters, conferences and gossip between colleagues. These market dynamics are factored into the deal evaluation and can provide a further element for slight adjustment to (although rarely a full reversal of) the technical rate. We now illustrate the practice of contextualizing by returning to John, as he evaluates deals for the June 1, 2010 renewals.

....

REINSURANCE-AS-PRACTICE 3C
Evaluating Deals Through Contextualizing Practices

Evoking the physical characteristics. John continues working on FloTex, saying, "I would like to send my quote out today." At the moment, he explains to Paul, he is refreshing his memory about any losses to the Florida portion of the FloTex deal. John brings up the in-firm database with notes he made on FloTex following PCI, and also reads this morning's email more closely on how FloTex's exposure has been developing from 2005 to 2010. When he met the Chief Underwriting Officer (Mick) at PCI, Mick indicated that FloTex planned to reduce exposure in high-risk areas by 15 percent in the forthcoming year. The submission email states an overall reduction of written premium of 5 percent. John identifies where this reduction has been achieved by referring to a table listing the aggregated data of 2009 to 2010. "Ah, there it is," John says as he spots a big decline in policies written in zip codes 32.xxx (Florida). To identify where these zip codes are located in relation to hurricane paths, John takes out a map, produced by RMS, which illustrates trajectories of past hurricanes that caused severe damage (e.g. Andrew, Katrina), mapped onto Florida's zip codes. Curious about the type of houses FloTex typically insures in an area he knows to be particularly hurricane-prone, he visits the website Google Earth, selecting "street view" to look at the houses in zip codes 32.xxx. The photo, which shows suburban houses with fancy swimming pools, neat lawns, two-car garages, and SUVs parked in the street, seems to have triggered a bad memory. John turns to Paul and says, "Do you see these pools . . . have I got a story for you!" John recounts why FloTex sustained such a large loss from hurricane Ivan in 2004. "FloTex had a lot of properties that had these things called pool screens that had these cages that go over pools to keep all the bugs out, insects. And they were very susceptible to wind blowing, and then the cages flying about caused more damage, hitting windows. As FloTex had a lot of those in their portfolio, they suffered much bigger losses than those [insurers] that didn't. For FloTex, it made up 30 percent of the loss." John adds, "These factors you can't put into the model," meaning characteristics of properties, such as pool fences.

John is also a bit concerned about FloTex's exposure in Texas, as "there's a lot of residential in here—but how many bloody trees?" Again he uses Google Earth's street view as a tool. He explains that, on a different deal with another cedent, he sustained a big loss because of the proximity of trees to residential properties, again a factor that has not been incorporated into any of the vendor models. John leans back in his chair to tell Paul his story: "Hurricane Rita comes along in Texas three years ago, and we ran the model before the loss and after the loss on the individual cedent . . . because he's claiming a lot of money against us. We were paying out a lot more than the model said. So the model was clearly wrong! Why? So we go and find out and do a lot of analysis and think ah, this part of East Texas has a lot of pine trees. I didn't know there were a lot of pine trees in East Texas until I went round there but there are a lot, and because the winds were very high, the pine trees were breaking off and because it's a nice sort of . . . very aesthetic to have trees very close to the house, they were falling on the houses. Plonk on the house and basically that's a whole new roof gone. Although the wind wasn't necessarily very high, they were snapping off and the individual average per claim was about $10–$12,000. Whereas the model suggested in a hurricane, a normal pitched-roof house, average claim was about $5,000 . . . The models don't discuss tree damage because how do we know whether this house has got a tree next to it? We're not told that, it's not in any application form or any of the data."

John goes back to identify how much of FloTex's exposure is located in Texas. Since it is still quite a significant proportion (20 percent of the $85 million written premium), John increases the risk factor in the rating sheet to "4" instead of

"3", which generates a weighted technical rate, that is adjusted upwards across the layers. Based on his deep knowledge of the physical properties of the deal, including the location of buildings and some of their structural characteristics, a new column has been generated, with a weighted technical rate that better reflects these features of the underlying risk. Evoking the underlying risk builds on an underwriter's knowledge of how a particular deal might respond in certain territories to certain types of events, as illustrated in the examples of pool fencing in Florida and trees in Texas. This knowledge can then be factored into the calculative practices, as part of ensuring the weighted technical rate reflects deal-specific knowledge.

Incorporating the cedent relationship. As he continues reading the submission email, John notes to Paul that Bermuda Re has been on this deal for eight years, "so we picked up losses from Ivan (2004) and Ike (2009) which means they are still in 'pay-back' mode". He thinks this also justifies the risk load of four he incorporated in the ratings. Still, John adds, "It is a cedent that we would like to keep as we think that is moving in the right direction." FloTex has started to scale back their exposure in Texas and the email says they intend to "reduce our exposure in high risk areas we had identified post-Ike and -Wilma by 20 percent." In particular, they are not renewing policies for older commercial properties, described as "very flimsy warehouses". John takes the exposure management for Texas as indicative that "FloTex have learned their lesson and done something about it", meaning attempting to contain losses by reducing their exposure in particular areas. Therefore he begins to wonder whether the risk factor of four is a little high.

While modeling is based on information about a deal's current exposure, it cannot account for a cedent's strategy for the forthcoming year, which is the period in which Bermuda Re will be covering the risk. As AIR and RMS build their analyses on the data points that reflect FloTex's exposure until the May 10 (the day data was extracted from the FloTex actuarial system), John has to factor in the planned reduction of their exposure in Texas. Turning to Paul, John murmurs, "This really depends on whether I trust the cedent." Looking at his notes from PCI, he comments, "This is in tune with what they were saying when I met them a few months ago." Taking into account these characteristics, John readjusts the risk factor from "4" to "3.5". The weighted technical rate now reflects the specific relationship with FloTex.

Incorporating market dynamics. Calculative practices that evoke the underlying risk and incorporate the cedent relationship have now been factored in through the generation of a weighted technical rate. Yet, as Chapter 2 has shown, John also has to situate the deal on FloTex in the current market cycle for deals renewing on June 1. In particular, he has to factor into the quoted price whether the market cycle for Florida and the Southern States is hard or soft.

John notes that regardless of what the vendor models might predict, rates have been declining and, given they had a "quiet hurricane season, reinsurers will just try and hold the rates as best as they can." While John senses that the rates will remain flat for the 2010 Florida renewals, he would like a small rate increase to factor in an additional risk of Floridian insurers' potential default—due to changes in their state regulation—which was the subject of gossip at PCI and has been further borne out in media reports. On the other hand, FloTex is a good cedent that is not likely to be caught up in the anticipated credit defaults. So there might be competition from other reinsurers who also want to write FloTex in preference to other Florida deals. John doesn't want to pitch too high and have his share squeezed by competitors. He says, "I don't want to look silly or unreasonable by providing a quote that is unrealistic within the current market context." He goes on: "Obviously there's a market, as well you know in your consideration of the quote. So if you say, 'Well taking all that into account, I want 15 percent— last year the market was charging 10 percent you know.' You might say, 'Well I think I can live with it and I know the market is flat this year. I quite like the cedent you know, his values are up a bit, I'm going to charge him 12 percent or something like that.'"

Based on his judgment of the market dynamics, and reflecting on this in relation to the weighted technical rate (see Column G, Figure 3.3), which already contains much of his contextual knowledge, John generates a quoted price for each layer in the rating sheet (see Column H, Figure 3.3). On Layers 1, these come out slightly lower than the weighted technical rate and the pure technical rate, as he feels he cannot get that price in the current market, but equal to the weighted technical rate for Layers 2 to 4. The quoted price, he explains, reflects both the current market dynamics and actual exposures FloTex has in Florida. However, before John sends the quote to the broker, he wants to compare it to the other deals he has so far evaluated.

3.5.3. Blending Technicalizing and Contextualizing: Generating a Comparable and Tradable Object

As we have seen, the deal as a tradable object is generated at the nexus of two practical understandings: technicalizing and contextualizing. Blending these two practical understandings during the evaluation process generates a quoted price for the deal that is abstracted from the raw data, yet reflects the underwriter's experience of such risks and deals. This blending takes place as technicalizing first generates a technical rate, and then contextualizing generates a weighted technical rate that is meaningful to the underwriter in relation to this specific deal and cedent, and a quoted price that reflects the market dynamics. Once this blending has occurred, a deal's quoted price may be compared with other deals for the purposes of deciding where to place capital. Essentially, **comparing** is a calculative practice that completes the deal evaluation process. It involves creating a graphical representation, typically in the form of a curve for each deal that has been evaluated in the run-up to the current renewal date. In John's case, it involves every deal that he has evaluated by May 19 for the June 1, 2010 renewal. As underwriters evaluate several deals, they are able to compare these on a chart displaying each deal's quoted price, so enabling the selection of those deals deemed most appropriate given the reinsurer's risk-appetite (see Chapter 5).

....

REINSURANCE-AS-PRACTICE 3D
Making Decisions on Deals

Comparing deals. John now wants to decide how best to place Bermuda Re's capital on deals in Florida, which means he needs to compare FloTex to other deals that he has already evaluated in the run-up to June 1. John clicks an icon on his rating sheet, which generates a graph with each of FloTex's four layers plotted on a curve according to the amount of premium for the amount of exposure at each layer. Over the past week, John has already evaluated twenty-five deals for Florida, using the same deal evaluation process as for FloTex. Each of these analyses has also been converted into a graph. He pulls up a screen that displays all of these graphs in a single sheet with different colored curves, each representing the pricing for a specific deal.

John imports the curve representing the FloTex deal. He looks at the screen for a few minutes, comparing the curves closest to the deal structure of FloTex; that is, having similar attachment points for the layers of cover. The graphical display of deals enables comparison of each specifically tailored deal on an ostensibly like-for-like basis, albeit that they all have different insured values, different properties, different exposures, and different deal structures. In comparing Bermuda Re's exposure to deals covering windstorms in Florida, John sees that FloTex is towards the top of the pricing curve, meaning that alongside his contextual understanding of FloTex's well-managed portfolio, price-wise they are a sensible deal upon which to place capital compared with many others he is considering. Given this, John decides to submit the quoted price he has generated for each layer of the FloTex deal, offering to take the same share as he took last year. To finalize the evaluation, he flicks back to his rating sheet, adding "10 percent" in Column K to indicate he is willing to take a 10 percent share again at his quoted price (see Figure 3.3).

As he writes the email, which builds on Bermuda Re's standard template for submitting quotes, John inserts his specific quoted prices for each layer and states, "I commit to renewing last year's 10 percent line [share] across Layers 1 to 4." As he clicks "send", John has committed his firm's capital. If his quote becomes the accepted consensus price, he is obligated to honor his commitment at that price for that share. He expects the consensus price, which will be set by FloTex in conjunction with the broker, to come within the next week (see Chapter 2, Figure 2.1).

The calculation John has enacted to reach a quoted price will impact how he reacts to the consensus price, a process that is outlined in greater depth in Chapter 5. As this chapter focuses on calculation we stop here. The deal evaluation is now complete; John has developed a view on the value of the deal and put that view into the market.

....

3.6. MAKING THE MARKET THROUGH
DEAL EVALUATION

Having explicated the specific practice of deal evaluation, we now zoom
out to explain the marketization of reinsurance risks within this everyday
practice of evaluating deals. John's practice is representative of the deal
evaluation process that we observed across many U.S. Property Catastrophe
underwriters throughout our three years in the field. John's quoted price is
one of many quoted prices on the FloTex deal, to use one example, that are
submitted by his peers. Each of these peers will have engaged in largely similar practice, although their particular view of the cedent, models, or market dynamics may have been somewhat different to John's, which accounts
for the range of quoted prices (see Chapter 2). Regardless of whether underwriters are located in Bermuda, Lloyd's or Continental Europe, the nexus
of technicalizing and contextualizing provides a common basis for their
individual decisions across vastly different U.S. Property Catastrophe
deals. This enables underwriters across a global market to take shares of
any particular deal based on consistent practice and consistent parameters
(incorporated in the model); they and their quotes are relationally connected through their common practical understandings of how to evaluate
a deal. At the same time, vastly different deals can be traded on a comparable basis, because all have been calculated within a similar evaluation
practice. We have thus explained how reinsurance risks are constructed as
tradable objects for the purposes of financial exchange, their marketization. This marketization of reinsurance deals underpins the relationality
through which individual underwriters are able to construct a consensus
price at which to collectively bear risk.

As we have seen in Chapter 2, each quoted price feeds into the consensus price and the market cycle. In this chapter we have further unpacked
our concepts of **relational presence*** and relationality by showing how that
quoted price arises through the blending of technicalizing and contextualizing. Through their use of a common suite of models within a largely similar evaluative practice, underwriters are relationally connected with each
other and with the deal that they are evaluating; it is the means through
which they connect with and understand risk as something that is tradable
(Çalışkan and Callon, 2009; 2010). In particular, in the case of U.S. Property
Catastrophe deals, the quoted price is built from a common basis in the
assumptions and mathematical calculations about risk occurrence and
potential losses that are incorporated within vendor models. Importantly,
calculation enables the generation of comparable valuations of different
deals, forming the relationality between different deals, as we saw with
John comparing FloTex as a deal on which to place capital, relative to other

Florida deals. Importantly, the use of consistent models for evaluation provides underwriters with some confidence in the basis of comparison for what are often vastly different deals.

Beyond this fundamental point, as U.S. Property Catastrophe deals arrive in the data pack with modeled data, other underwriters on these same deals also subscribe to these same models at least to begin their evaluation. Hence, the models provide a common reference point for underwriters distributed globally to arrive at technical rates on U.S. Property Catastrophe deals, even if they run the various parameters in different ways. In this way, models enable relationality between multiple dispersed market actors in generating the consensus price that emerges on any particular deal (see also Millo and MacKenzie, 2009; Beunza and Stark, 2012). The availability and acceptance of these models amongst underwriters, brokers and cedents thus shapes, although does not determine, the range of quoted prices across the global market for any particular deal. Indeed, as models have become the market standard for deal evaluation, they have shaped the ball-park within which deals are quoted, as this broker notes:

> The models without doubt have brought the pricing and quoting process within a narrower band than it had, so it's pretty rare. It happens but it's pretty rare we'll have a bunch of people quoting ten and a bunch of people quoting twenty. It'll usually be a narrower band than that. (Interview, Broker, London)

Vendor models reduce the variation in quoted prices on a deal because the way deals are presented and the technical rates produced by multiple competing underwriters are based on largely similar assumptions about the risk inherent in commonly used models. Variation in quoted prices still occurs in the transition from the technical rate to the quoted price which reflects, amongst other things, loadings based on an underwriter's professional knowledge of the underlying risk, relationship with the particular cedent and the current market dynamics. However, the models provide "boundaries" to this variation. The consensus price is based on multiple quotes, each shaped by different underwriters' knowledgeable practice in evaluating the deal. Yet, the source for each deal's evaluation, meaning the quantification of risk, has been provided by the same handful of models.

While the practical understandings of technicalizing and contextualizing complement each other, they provide an inherent relational tension that shapes the dynamics of the consensus market. On the one hand, the consensus market is established through standards in the technical analysis of reinsurance deals. In particular, vendor models constitute a common standard for transforming gigabytes of data into a calculable and tradable financial object. Vendor models thus shape the consensus market, as their output narrows the range of quoted prices across multiple underwriters.[13] On the other hand, variations in quoted price are generated through contextualizing the deal, based on an underwriter's specific expertise. As there are a myriad of ways to tweak and amend the outputs generated through vendor models, which may also be supplemented by additional in-house analysis and weightings, contextualizing creates variation in the quoted prices received from multiple underwriters. This relational tension between the standardizing effects of models and the variation arising from individual contextual knowledge is at the heart of the evaluation process from which the consensus price on every deal emerges.

In summary, calculation informed by vendor models is central to the relationality that forms between an underwriter and deal(s), and between various market actors all calculating the same deal as part of constructing a consensus price.

3.7. FURTHER THEORIZING

In addition to contributing to our particular concept of nested relationality, this chapter also presents a conceptual framework comprising technicalizing and contextualizing practices that speaks to other bodies of literature on evaluation, calculation, and the way that numbers are constructed and give legitimacy to decisions. We show how price is developed through the clustered expertise of underwriters, who are both technically skilled, and yet also attuned to the physical characteristics of a deal and the temporal dynamics of the market. We thus extend understanding of the "epistemization of economic transactions" (Knorr Cetina and Preda, 2001: 27) by developing a framework for analyzing the knowledgeable practice of calculation within evaluation. We now briefly outline how we engage with these literatures as the basis for future research.

Our framework of technicalizing and contextualizing sheds light on the **evaluation practice** and how a trader's expert knowledge is incorporated within the price that underpins financial exchange. The association between value as some apparently objectified outcome, category, or measure and evaluation practice is a growing area of sociological interest (Antal et al. 2015; Lamont, 2012) that is particularly pertinent to financial markets (Aspers, 2009; Helgesson and Muniesa, 2013; Zuckerman, 2012). We show that in the evaluation of a deal, technicalizing—importantly—provides an abstracted

---

[13] For example, Dupont-Courade (2013) shows that the type of deals most readily analyzed by vendor models (catastrophe business) are associated with the least variation (or standard deviation) among different underwriters quoted prices.

value of the risk, but that this abstraction involves knowledgeable calculation with vendor models including awareness of some of their limitations (Millo and MacKenzie, 2009). Contextualizing works around these limitations by situating this abstracted value within the underwriter's deep knowledge of the dynamics of the specific deal and of the market. That is, traders are both knowledgeable in the technologies of evaluation, even as they understand how to supplement them with other forms of knowledgeable practice (Knorr Cetina, 1999; Lamont, 2012). Thus, we show how evaluation practice blends different forms of expertise in order to generate a quoted price that remains meaningful in capturing the multiple types of evaluation applied by the underwriter even as abstraction is achieved (Aspers, 2009; Helgesson and Muniesa, 2013; Lamont, 2012). The practice by which meaning is attributed to an abstracted price is particularly critical in the context of financial markets, which are predominantly focused upon the derivation of price (Preda, 2007; Swedberg, 1994), often in the absence of an underlying physical good or asset to price (Aspers, 2009).

Our framework also speaks to recent studies on how financial models— or calculative devices more broadly—enact markets (e.g. Beunza and Stark, 2004; 2012; MacKenzie and Millo, 2003, Millo and MacKenzie, 2009; Muniesa et al., 2007; Preda, 2009a) and their role in the marketization of risk (Çalışkan and Callon, 2009; 2010; Callon and Muniesa, 2004). In particular, our study differs slightly from existing research into the role of models in calculation and the performativity of markets. This is because, unlike the price movements represented by the Black-Scholes-Merton model or the price ticker (e.g. MacKenzie and Millo, 2003; Millo and MacKenzie, 2009; Preda, 2006), vendor models do not represent the market. The model we focus on is not a pricing tool per se, but a probabilistic model that attributes degrees of causality between a possible peril, such as a hurricane, and the risk of damage to property (Cabantous, 2007; Cabantous et al., 2011; Grossi and Kunreuther, 2005). We show how these models generate ever-increasing legitimacy for calculative practice, yet at the same time underwriters arrive at prices that incorporate a complex understanding of the deal and the market that goes **beyond** the parameters provided in models. We thus provide more detailed insight into calculation that goes beyond consideration of the calculative devices to other, often quite normalized and widespread practices, such as evoking the client relationship in our case, that contribute to the number that is derived. Indeed, these contextualizing practices are explicitly understood to be central to knowledgeable practice and the appropriate use of the model to derive price. We have thus provided additional insight into the bundle of practices involved in calculation, and additional research might explore various other micro-practices that become entangled with models.

We also extend insight into the way these models develop connectivity among market actors (e.g. Beunza and Stark, 2012; Knorr Cetina and

Bruegger, 2000; Knorr Cetina and Bruegger, 2002a; 2002b; MacKenzie, 2004). Recent research into financial markets demonstrates how technologies connect market actors through making prices available instantly as flickers on a screen (Knorr Cetina and Preda, 2007; Preda, 2006; 2009a; Zaloom, 2003). In these financial markets, connectivity rests on the availability of information on a financial product's price movements. In contrast, the current price for a reinsurance deal is unavailable during the evaluation process. Thus, we show how connectivity among market actors is based on the standardized characteristics of a deal, which are disseminated to all actors on that deal and enable the same set of vendor models to be used as the starting point for technicalizing practice. These models' assumptions about the behavior of a risk strengthen the connectivity of actors, support the widespread consistency of evaluation practice, and shape the potential range for quotes (Dupont-Coutarde, 2013) and the eventual consensus price that emerges across a global market. We thus add to current understanding of both connectivity between traders in financial markets and the role of models in this connectivity (Beunza and Stark, 2012; Millo and MacKenzie, 2009).

3.8. CONCLUSION

In this chapter we have addressed the puzzle of how disasters that are as unpredictable, uncertain and diverse as hurricanes, earthquakes, and bushfires are constructed as tradable deals within a financial market. We have shown that the practice of making these perils tradable and comparable as deals is governed by a general understanding of marketization. Marketization involves the range of calculative devices and practices within which that trading is made possible (Çalışkan and Callon, 2009). In particular, the marketization of risk has spawned a set of statistical models that comprise the common standard for calculation within the reinsurance market for U.S. Property Catastrophe deals, coordinating the practices that enable a deal to be evaluated on a consistent technical basis by competing underwriters. We zoomed in on John's calculative practice to illustrate how technicalizing (through the use of vendor models) provides the reference point for contextualizing as individual underwriters bring their professional knowledge and judgment into deal evaluation.

As described in this chapter, an increasing demand for fine-grained data and continuous updates of vendor models reinforce the belief in the calculability and marketization of risk. Yet, as the calculative practices of contextualizing vividly demonstrate, technicalizing, which revolves largely around results generated from statistical models, is not enough to make meaningful evaluations. While these models extrapolate from past events to set the "knowable" parameters of risks, recent events have demonstrated that history can be rewritten any day. For instance, damages caused by storm surges from Hurricane Sandy (October 2012) had not previously occurred and were, therefore, not "known" or included in the parameters of the models. While excluded from the modeling, Sandy caused an estimated damage of $19 billion in reinsured loss ($65 billion economic loss) in the United States.[14] And these unmodeled losses happened in the United States, the most highly modeled territory in the world. How then, is it possible to write risks in other, less modeled territories, given that even highly modeled territories can be so prone to miscalculation of exposure? Chapter 4 will address this puzzle of the marketization of risk in the absence of standardized models.

Summary

In this chapter we have:

- Shown how **evaluating deals** is a fundamental site for market making activity.
- Shown how the **general understanding** of **marketization**—that vastly different deals can be evaluated, compared and traded at a price—is integral to making this market. We explained this general understanding through the daily practice of John as he gathers information about vastly different cedents (see Reinsurance-as-Practice 3A) and subsequently evaluates a U.S. Property Catastrophe deal (see Reinsurance-as-Practice 3B–3D).
- Shown how enacting **statistical models** coordinates globally dispersed actors who calculate deals according to similar assumptions (contained in the models) about risks.
- Shown the enactment of two **practical understandings**: technicalizing (such as modeling) and contextualizing (such as incorporating the cedent relationship) both of which are calculative practices that enable evaluation of reinsurance deals. Through the story of John we show that evaluation entails the blending of technicalizing and contextualizing practices (Reinsurance-as-Practice 3C).

---

[14] Aon Benfield, 2013. "Reinsurance Market Outlook: Reinsurance Capacity Growth Continues to Outpace Demand." January, Chicago: Aon Benfield.

4

Calculation at the Frontier

Evaluation in the Absence of Models

4.1. INTRODUCTION

> When we talk about modeling and our portfolio of deals, maybe half of it we
> think is modeled. The other half is partly or even not modeled. So 50 percent of
> the risk that's out there! How do you do it? How do you live with this, how do
> you price for it? (Interview, Reinsurer, Manager, Continental Europe)

Chapter 3 showed how the calculative practice around standardized **vendor models*** coordinates the **evaluation*** process within the reinsurance market. Yet, as our introductory statement shows, in many cases vendor models are not available to inform risk evaluation. Deals from many territories have insufficient data to be modeled (Gurenko, 2004) so that whole areas of the world are considered largely un-modeled from a catastrophe perspective.[1] Reinsurance also covers many other types of risks whose underlying causes are too complex to be standardized in models, including **Marine***, **Agriculture***, **Motor Liability***, and **Credit & Surety***, to name just a few (Alwis and Steinbach, 2003; Vergara et al., 2008). The asbestos case that cost reinsurers billions is an important example. There are no models that are able to predict or even assume the chain of events, such as changing environmental, medical, and legal frameworks through which a deal underwritten in the 1940s resulted in asbestos claims being made in the 1990s and 2000s. Yet, despite the lack of vendor models in many areas of reinsurance, the calculative purpose of the market remains the same: to turn these risks into tradable objects to which reinsurers can allocate capital (Callon and Muniesa, 2005; Çalışkan and Callon, 2010). Indeed, millions of dollars are traded on such un-modeled risks, as shown by the Thai floods where the reinsurance

---

[1] The RMS, EQE and AIR websites show the constrained scope of current modeling.

industry paid for over half of the estimated $16 billion in insured losses that were not modeled.[2]

In this chapter, we explore how marketization and calculation are practiced when vendor models, the central coordinating device discussed in Chapter 3, are not available. The chapter first introduces the many different **risk-types*** that characterize the reinsurance market as **sites*** (Schatzki, 2002; 2005) within which deal-evaluation occurs. Risk-types can be differentiated according to the modelability of deals, so adding further nuance to the notion of evaluating deals as **sites** of market-making activity that was the focus of Chapter 3.

Second, we return to the **general understanding*** of **marketization*** and the purpose of a market to transform risks into tradable and comparable financial deals (Çalışkan and Callon, 2010; Callon and Muniesa, 2005). The puzzle we address is how marketization is possible when information is sparse and/or the underlying peril is not standardizable, rendering the typical calculative practices of a market, such as financial models (MacKenzie and Millo, 2003; Millo and MacKenzie, 2009), less applicable.

Third, we explain how multiple **epistemic cultures**, each pertaining to a particular risk-type, enable the evaluation of different risk-types. Epistemic cultures, which are "how we know what we know" (Knorr Cetina, 1999, 1) are central in coordinating the marketization of these different risk-types. Expert professionals, such as John evaluating Property Catastrophe deals (Chapter 3) or another underwriter evaluating a different risk-type such as a Marine deal—wherever they are located in the world—each belong to a particular epistemic culture with its own calculative practice, such as the use of vendor models outlined in Chapter 3 that were specific to that culture. That is, the knowledge bases specific to each culture underpin the specific calculative practices germane to evaluating reinsurance deals within that risk-type. We show that underwriters specialize in different risk-types, which makes them part of specific global epistemic cultures (Amin and Roberts, 2008; Brown and Duguid, 2001), each of which has deep understanding of and shared practice in calculating deals within a particular type of risk, even in the absence of standardized financial models.

Fourth, we return to the **practical understandings*** of technicalizing and contextualizing outlined in Chapter 3, to show how members of different epistemic cultures enact the specific calculative practices that make deals within each risk-type tradable as financial objects. Different epistemic cultures each generate and apply those calculative practices appropriate to evaluating each of these less-modelable risk-types. We will explain how, despite their eclectic calculative practices, underwriters in these different cultures generate the

---

[2] Aon Benfield. 2011. "Thailand Floods: An Event Update." October, Singapore: Aon Benfield; "2011 Reinsured Cat-incurred Losses." 2012. *Reinsurance*, February 30.

same type of output, namely, a **quote***** expressed as a **Rate on Line (RoL)*****, which enables these vastly different deals to be compared and traded in a broadly consistent way. In this chapter we distinguish three types of epistemic cultures (based on the risk-types outlined above) and show their different calculative practices.

Finally, we outline how each epistemic culture helps to coordinate the wider market for reinsurance deals, comprising multiple different risk-types. Each risk-type constitutes a particular site of evaluative activity for market-making, for example, Marine underwriters interact to create the "Marine market" and Credit & Surety underwriters interact to create the "Credit & Surety market", each with its own specific deals, calculative practices, and consensus pricing. This means that an underwriter of a particular risk-type (such as U.S. Property Catastrophe) could not do the job of evaluating another risk-type (such as Credit & Surety) and vice versa. As many of these risk-types are characterized by a lack of vendor models or detailed statistical data, in this chapter we address the specific question of how deals from such risk-types are rendered calculable and tradable through the practices of their particular epistemic culture. We begin with the example of Ria, an underwriter for the Indian reinsurance market.

....

REINSURANCE-AS-PRACTICE 4A
Evaluating Deals in the Absence of Data and Models

Over three days during a humid Southeast Asian October, underwriters, brokers, and **cedents***** from all over the world arrive in Singapore to discuss Asia-Pacific deals at the "Singapore International Reinsurance Conference" (SIRC). Ria joins the mix of saris, turbans, hijabs, thobes, and suits. She has spent most of her career underwriting Indian-subcontinent risk; first from London, having moved from Delhi to study in London twenty years ago, and now from her company's Singapore hub. Her first meeting of the day is with Padma, a woman representing the cedent KolkataInc. Ria greets her warmly, and they agree it has been far too long since Ria has come to visit the company in Kolkata (the city previously named Calcutta). Padma then outlines the deal, highlighting its concentration in Kolkata and focus on newer commercial buildings, and the exposure to a number of perils including fire and flood. As they get into the conversation Ria outlines her concerns with the current pricing: "The more I look at the reports, the more I think Kolkata needs to accept some adjusted **loss-ratio***** figures for flood; especially given what has happened in Thailand and what it has told us about flood exposure." Padma hands Ria a single sheet of paper and explains, pointing to the paper, that the three-**layer***** structure of the deal is the same as last year. They have indeed made some changes to the assumptions; Padma explains, "The **return period***** for the top layer has been adjusted down slightly," meaning that they are assuming a higher frequency of large losses than before. She explains that this is due to recent industry losses, which suggest that the likelihood of severe flooding has been underestimated in the past. Padma then reiterates that the total sum insured (the number of properties they insure) has not changed, handing Ria another piece of paper to highlight her point. Ria reads the single page and says, "So your portfolio split has remained 70 percent commercial-Kolkata— same as last year, that's good."

Peter, Ria's junior colleague who is relocating to Singapore from London as part of their company's drive to grow in Asia, is listening with interest at his first SIRC conference as he joins Ria in her meetings. As the short meeting concludes, Ria stands up to leave—with her two pieces of paper—promising Padma that a visit to India is on her agenda early next year. Padma is off to meet one of Ria's competitors who will also underwrite her deal. As Ria also moves quickly to the next meeting, Peter races to keep up. "So will the broker be sending you the information later?" he asks as they move through the crowds. "Well yes," she says, waving the sheets of paper at him; "I'll get electronic copies of this deal structure and this total sum insured by region." Guessing that Peter expected much more data, she explains, "It's not like we have the models to run any detailed information anyway." She smiles at his obvious disquiet. "Don't worry, I've known the cedent company as well as Padma for years, they mainly insure new properties and only deal with a few trusted building contractors. And their whole book is pretty sound." Peter silently wonders how, given the lack of information on the types of property, or even about their actual location relative to the Hooghly River, Ria and the cedent come up with the deal structure they had discussed. Comparing those sheets of paper with the megabytes or gigabytes of data he demanded to even consider a deal as a U.S. Property Catastrophe Underwriter in London, he truly does not know how Ria is going to put a price on that deal. Perhaps this move to Singapore is going to be harder than he had thought.

....

4.2. EVALUATING WITHIN RISK-TYPES AS A SITE OF MARKET-MAKING

We now turn the kaleidoscope to focus on the varied calculative practice involved in evaluating different risk-types, which we conceptualize as particular sites of market- making activity (Schatzki, 2002; 2005). These risk-types are differentiated by two dimensions that inform the modelability of deals: **information quality and standardization** (see Figure 4.1).

4.2.1. Information Quality

Information is a key differentiating dimension of risk-types, as its quality and availability is the basis of a deal's modelability (Figure 4.1, *x*-axis). For example, a U.S. Property Catastrophe deal is generally information-rich; it

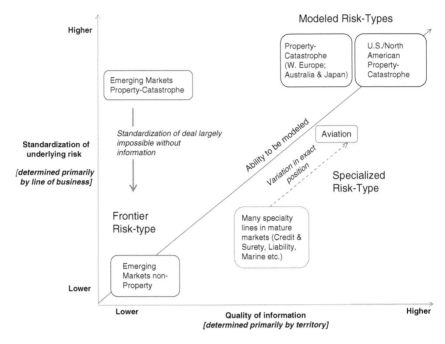

Fig. 4.1. Variation in Risk-Types

comes with gigabytes of detailed data about location, constructions standards, weather patterns, and so forth (Chapter 3), which can be fed into models. By contrast, deals within other risk-types may have very sparse data, as shown in the Indian deal where Ria received two pages of information (Reinsurance-as-Practice 4A).

Typically, information quality is connected to the geographic territory of a deal. Deals originating in mature, developed territories have regulatory structures that provide impetus to collect information, a history of collecting relevant insurance data, technological infrastructure to support information collection, and largely stable profiles in which information can be updated on a regular basis. Hence, North American, Western European, and Australian deals tend to have high information quality, with the most detailed being North American data, which can be parsed by zip codes and structural building codes. By contrast, cedents in less-developed countries often struggle to collect and provide robust statistical data for a variety of reasons, including lack of infrastructure to collect information, and weak historical experience, due to changes in their portfolios arising from rapid growth in such markets. For example, the Thai floods in Chapter 2 occurred in a recently industrialized area that had formerly been small agricultural holdings, and so had no prior loss-experience data.

4.2.2. Standardization

A second dimension for distinguishing risk-types is the extent to which they may be **standardized** around common parameters for modeling (Figure 4.1, *y*-axis). For example, U.S. Property Catastrophe deals may be standardized around common parameters regarding the underlying peril, such as the likelihood of a particular level of hurricane or magnitude of earthquake in a particular geography. Such defined probabilities can then be applied as "standard" to any deals in that region involving that particular peril, which facilitates modeling. This ability to standardize is largely differentiated by **line of business***, a term which denotes different types of reinsurance risk such as Motor Liability, Credit & Surety, Marine and the Property-Catastrophe we examined in Chapter 3. Certain inherent features, or specifically the underlying causes, of many of these risk-types mean that they are difficult to standardize against widely applicable benchmarks. For example, in **long-tail risks***, such as Casualty, the payout on a deal may be made years after the premium is paid, as illustrated by the fifty-plus years of asbestos claims. Unlike a **short-tail risk*** such as hurricane damage to properties, where costs can be assessed relatively quickly, long-tail losses might take years to develop, and can be determined by factors which are not static, such as the legal or economic environment at a future point in time. In these risk-types, the many evolving and unknown future social factors impede the standardized application of set scenarios to a large number of deals. Such risks are thus very difficult to model through standardized and definable parameters (Raim and Langford, 2008). Other factors affecting standardization include understandings of causality, and the extent to which the factors that may trigger a loss can be captured within consistent modeling parameters. For example, the causes of insolvency are relatively poorly understood in Credit & Surety reinsurance, but reinsurers understand the causes of fire much better, and are thus able to standardize them as consistent parameters for multiple deals (Alwis and Steinbach, 2003).

4.2.3. Three Categories of Risk-Type

While each risk is distinct, for analytic convenience we can delineate risk-types into three categories distinguished by these two dimensions of standardization and information quality (see Figure 4.1).[3] First, **Modeled**

---

[3] Within each of these categories there is enormous variation in the underlying perils, territory, and cover sought. However, for the purposes of simplifying the narrative they can be clustered into three groups that share certain characteristics that enable us to contain our argument within the scope of this book (see Figure 4.1).

risk-types pertain to deals that are data-rich, with very granular information, such as zip-code-level detail of properties, their building codes and values, and these data can be standardized for the purposes of modeling. Such granular information is captured in shared, industry-level databases that support standardization within industry-wide modeling parameters. For example, the PERILS Industry Exposure and Loss Database, or the Catastrophe Risk Evaluating and Standardizing Target Accumulations (CRESTA) database, are widely available and regularly updated with new information on catastrophes, losses, and exposures: "For Catastrophe business we've got some loss-data at industry level that everyone can use to understand storms; for example, there's a couple of storms that cost $10 billion, another that's $15 billion. We've got that industry level data and it's getting better and better" (Interview, Reinsurer, Underwriter, London). As shown in Figure 4.1, Modeled risk-types are usually Property Catastrophe deals from mature markets, such as the U.S. Property Catastrophe deals discussed in Chapter 3.

Second, **Specialized** risk-types consist of deals that are moderately data-rich but less capable of being standardized. The Specialized risk-type encompasses a wide range of what the industry calls "specialty lines" such as Credit & Surety, Marine, and Agriculture, as well as long-tail business such as Liability. These risk-types are data-rich at the level of the deal, and are therefore amenable to various actuarial calculations. However Specialized risk-types do not have widely shared industry databases, even where there is good data quality at the level of the specific deal (Alwis and Steinbach, 2003). This in turn inhibits the standardization of data, the specification of industry-wide modeling parameters, and the development of vendor models. Indeed, the inherent features of many of these risk-types mean that they cannot be standardized against industry-wide benchmarks. For example, Marine or Agriculture risks have too many contingencies to be amenable to standardized modeling parameters:

> There were approximately 1,000 brand new Lexus cars, they were very expensive and were on the Kobe wharf the night before the [2011 Tohoku] earthquake. The ship then came along and took them all away. Had the earthquake happened the day before, it would have been a massive loss . . . So you're trying to hit a moving target. (Interview, Reinsurer, Underwriter, Continental Europe)

> Agriculture business is difficult to model, because it's dynamic.[4] Every year it's a different crop in a different place and a different combination of the weather conditions. So there are too many variables, you cannot model this. (Interview, Reinsurer, Underwriter, Continental Europe)

In short, it is hard to standardize parameters for how Specialized risk-types might behave, due to the number of economic, social and behavioral

---

[4] For example, weather conditions, world shortages or over-supply all impact (and change) the price between years.

contingencies, regardless of the information available. This means that standardized models for these risks are not generally available, in contrast to the Property Catastrophe risks discussed in Chapter 3.

Third, **Frontier** risks are low on technical information. For example, there is little information on potential for flood in newly industrialized zones in emerging markets such as parts of Asia, and weak data on the value of properties exposed to any potential flood. As there is little data to "crunch", there is also a paucity of statistical models available for analysis: "I haven't got a decent model for Indonesia, so what do I do? Particularly in Asia, many of the models are pretty poor or nonexistent" (Interview, Broker, London). As this suggests, even when models are starting to be developed for such territories, they are generally dismissed due to their evident inaccuracy or embryonic nature in such regions.

Frontier deals usually originate in emerging and fast-growing territories where the information is either not available, due to lack of technological systems for capturing data, or changing so rapidly that it cannot be collated. Data packs for such deals may be only a few pages of information rather than the fifty-plus pages that accompany Modeled risk-types. They are also usually hard to standardize—and are therefore situated low on both axes of Figure 4.1—because the information they do have is changing too rapidly to enable standardizable parameters to be built:

> The Russian market is an emerging market. Structures are relatively young and in flux, so everything is changing . . . we cannot rely on what has been there last year. We have to be very careful when using historical data because the information looks usable, but actually the business behind that has totally changed. That is if we have historical data at all. (Interview, Reinsurer, Underwriter, Continental Europe)

We term these Frontier risk-types because the details of the deals and their parameters are in constant flux and development. From year to year, they are at a continuously shifting frontier.

Buyer's Perspective 4: How the Cedent Manages Different Types of Deals

In pursuit of further international expansion the cedent GlobalInc purchased a small Puerto Rican firm, which now trades as a local operating entity under the GlobalInc umbrella. Jane's colleague Ian is in Puerto Rico buying reinsurance for their small Puerto Rican Motor deal. The level of detailed information Ian has, and can provide his reinsurers, is very different from the gigabytes of data Jane has included when structuring GlobalInc's main U.S. Property Catastrophe deal (see Buyer's Perspective 1 and 3). For example, for Ian's Motor deal, GlobalInc only has loss figures going back four years; before that the company had not offered Motor insurance. In general, Ian's data is approximate and unreliable and not backed up with any market statistics or vendor modeling.

The lack of "experience" or claims data for Ian's Motor deal is critical; these statistics on losses allow reinsurers to see and understand the development of any losses over time and to price on that basis (**experience pricing***). The data on historical losses are as critical to how reinsurers evaluate Motor deals as vendor models are to how they evaluate U.S. Property Catastrophe deals. For GlobalInc's Puerto Rican Motor deal, not only will reinsurers not have industry-wide models, they will not have detailed loss data to inform their actuarial pricing techniques. Given the paucity of the data, Ian is justifiably very anxious about how he will be able to attract enough reinsurers to get the cover he needs. In the information pack that he provides to reinsurers, Ian therefore includes some general information about trends in Motor Liability insurance in Puerto Rico and goes into detail about GlobalInc, such as the strict internal quality controls they have implemented in the Puerto Rico local operating entity in the last year. This deal will still not be understandable to many reinsurers on GlobalInc's main "Catastrophe" deals. To assess this risk, they will need expert underwriters who specialize in Latin America, know how Motor Liability works in Puerto Rico, and who can make their own judgment in the absence of detailed models and statistics.

4.3. GENERAL UNDERSTANDING: MARKETIZATION OF VARIED RISK-TYPES

Marketization—the rendering of diverse Acts of God tradable (Çalışkan and Callon, 2010)—is a pervasive **general understanding** regardless of risk-type. Typically, marketization is associated with robust calculative devices, as shown in the explanation of vendor models in Chapter 3 through which deals are transformed into prices that can be compared for the purposes of capital allocation. However, for many risk-types, as outlined above, such devices are not widely available. Indeed, it is perhaps surprising that many deals with these underlying risks may be traded at all within a global finance industry, given their paucity of information and the great variation in factors that might affect loss. Nonetheless, such deals comprise much of the global market.[5]

As marketization involves making deals calculable for the purposes of trading, some form of technical valuation that results in a price is necessary (Callon and Muniesa, 2005; Preda, 2007). It is unthinkable to trade risks within a financial market without engaging in calculative practice. As one underwriter of a non-modeled risk-type noted: "Where there's no [model] . . . you try and

---

[5] Global Property Catastrophe (some of it itself un-modeled) makes up 38.5 percent ($89.9 billion) of the total premium in reinsurance, with long-tail Liability business, as one example, comprising of an additional (and important) 26.3 percent ($55 billion) (see "Global Reinsurance." 2013. *Marketline Industry Profile*, October).

find a technical way of doing it, you try and find something technical to hang your hat on" (Interview, Reinsurer, Underwriter, London). Indeed, the pervasiveness of marketization is evidenced in the ubiquity of the **rating sheet*** that we introduced in Chapter 3. Wherever we were in the world, and whatever type of deal we were observing, a rating sheet was used to express the RoL or price of a deal numerically in a spreadsheet. A rating sheet is a basic calculative device; it must be filled in with numbers, regardless of the information at hand, so rendering all deals, regardless of the underlying peril(s), calculable or "modelable" at some level. Thus the practice of underwriting different risk-types involves calculation regardless of variation in information quality and standardization.

This general understanding means all deals are allocated a somewhat comparable output, in terms of a price that represents some form of evaluation, according to the specific indicators of the **rate of return*** used by any particular reinsurer as the basis for capital allocation.[6] Hence, in the absence of vendor models such as RMS and AIR, there must be some other way to coordinate multiple actors within a global market to generate such prices. We now turn to this issue.

4.4. COORDINATING MARKET PRACTICE— EPISTEMIC CULTURES

In this section we explain how **epistemic cultures** (Knorr Cetina, 1999) coordinate the practice of globally dispersed underwriters in transforming vastly different and often un-modeled risks into tradable financial deals. Epistemic cultures are "how we know what we know"— meaning how a particular group of experts (Knorr Cetina, 1999: 101) such as finance professionals (Kalthoff, 2005; Knorr Cetina and Preda, 2001)— generate expertise. For example, the professional training, relationships and associations that comprise **how** they know, and the profession-specific tools, technologies and concepts through which they practice **what** they know. In reinsurance this knowledge is concentrated around calculative practices for evaluating risk, as introduced in Chapter 3. For example, being part of a U.S. Property Catastrophe epistemic culture, and therefore knowing how to access and use the appropriate tools, enabled John in Chapter 3 to engage in calculation of Modeled deals. Indeed, as part of this culture, he and other U.S. Property Catastrophe underwriters in

---

[6] Specific "profitability" measures vary between firms and can include focusing on combined ratio, return on equity, and return on risk adjusted capital. These measures will also not be strictly comparable, since some types of more volatile risk command higher RoE than others because they are likely to have a higher severity loss if they are triggered.

offices all over the world enact common calculative practices. Underwriters, therefore, participate in distinct epistemic cultures that provide the particular bases of knowledge for the specific calculative practices through which their respective risk-types are turned into tradable deals.

4.4.1. Epistemic Cultures and Evaluating Varied Risk-Types

The diversity between cultures and their knowledge bases is central to the concept of epistemic cultures (Knorr Cetina, 1999; Robertson et al., 2003). This diversity is important in the reinsurance market because different risk-types cannot be evaluated in the same way—due to variation in both their information quality, and the extent to which they may be standardized for modeling. Underwriters therefore develop specific practices for evaluating and calculating a particular risk-type within a particular epistemic culture. In short, U.S. Property Catastrophe underwriter John (Reinsurance-as-Practice 3A) could not calculate the Asian risks evaluated by Ria in Singapore (Reinsurance-as-Practice 4A) and vice-versa; they have unique bases of knowledge stemming from their different epistemic cultures. The practices specific to an epistemic culture enable its members to knowingly evaluate and calculate these deals:

> Previously if there was Motor business from Italy, they'd probably say we don't understand it, why should we do it? We now have somebody who understands Italian Motor insurance law. Previously the deal had to have such a big profit margin to pay for the insecurity over the evaluation, but now we have people who understand it so the margin won't be that big. (Interview, CEO, Continental Europe)

While a particular risk might not necessarily be "modelable" using vendor models, underwriters from a particular culture generate and enact the specific calculative practices of their culture, which enable them to turn that particular **perils*** into a tradable financial deal. Epistemic cultures are thus critical in making a market for less-modeled risks. Knorr Cetina (1999) describes the bases of knowledge that underpin the calculative practices of distinct epistemic cultures as **technical**, **empirical**, and **social**. We will briefly address each in turn, illustrating our concepts through the experiences of Brent, a Marine underwriter, in Reinsurance-as-Practice 4B.

....

REINSURANCE-AS-PRACTICE 4B
Underwriting Within a Marine Epistemic Culture

We shadowed Brent a couple of times a week over some months in Bermuda. As the only Marine underwriter in the Bermuda office he was a bit of a mystery to his peers. When Paula mentioned that she was about to interview Brent, senior Property Catastrophe underwriter Tony remarked that he didn't really know what Brent, who sat across the office from him, did: "Marine . . . well it's a whole new world—I don't know about it really!" (laughs) I get the impression (lowers his voice slightly in shock) . . . they don't really have models as such!" While Tony could not understand Marine, Brent's lens on the reinsurance sector was steeped in it: "I was at sea . . . I know what a boat looks like. I went into primary Marine insurance, and I was involved in the claims and primary underwriting, then reinsurance buying as a cedent before I moved into Marine reinsurance, so I understand . . . nobody could say to me the cedent wants this or this is what happens, because having done it with my own hands, face to face, getting my hands dirty, I know exactly how it's done." As Brent explained, the complexity of Marine demanded this level of lived experience: "It (the risk) is a moving target and that's why it is so specialized and why to make any money in it, you have to have specialists. You have to have people like me who know and live and breathe this stuff."

Brent was also embedded in Marine underwriting social networks. He had just returned from a global Marine conference: "Everybody knows everyone. At the most recent International Union of Marine Insurance Conference there were about 500 people . . . and you're probably talking about 90 percent of the people that practice this business worldwide. I do London business and I'm now reinsuring all my former peers: we all grew up together, if that makes sense." Indeed, when he was not in London, much of his day was spent on the phone connecting to those in the Marine reinsurance community in London. This included the Marine underwriters within his company in the London office, but also those from other firms—"I know them all!"—as well as Marine brokers. Sometimes this contact was transactional or deal-specific; however, more often than not it was just to have a good gossip about the latest goings-on in the Marine market.

As we got to know Brent we also saw that he had his own methods of evaluating Marine deals that did not involve the same vendor models being used by his U.S. Property Catastrophe colleagues. This was often the source of ribbing and teasing: "I've got a deal with no real data here—but then again, it's probably more analyzable than what Brent's working on!" and, due to different profitability expectations about Marine versus Property, "Gosh this RoE (**return on equity***) is so low, even Brent might decline it!" In terms of his daily practices—how he calculated deals and what he considered an adequate basis to place capital—Brent was more connected to others underwriting Marine risk in the global market than he was to his immediate organizational peers underwriting Property Catastrophe.

In the reinsurance industry, the **technical** practices that form the basis of knowledge are the generation and use of calculative devices that are specific to each risk-type. For instance, while Brent's colleagues underwriting U.S. Property Catastrophe knew how to use vendor models, Brent had other specific ways of calculating Marine risk. As an actuary explained to us, there was considerable variation in the calculative devices used for analyzing all the different risk-types in his company:

> We have nearly ten specialty lines of business [e.g. Agriculture, Credit & Surety, Marine etc.] . . . and the tools and models are specific to each line with not much of a possibility for one line to use the other model for the other lines . . . you cannot use the same tools at all. (Interview, Reinsurer, Actuary, Continental Europe)

Furthermore, underwriters are "shaped and transformed" with regards to the kinds of technologies and techniques they use (Knorr Cetina, 1999: 32). That is, underwriters such as Brent become more embedded in and so also reproduce the technical practices of their particular culture as they use them to evaluate risk.

There are also different **empirical** practices that form bases of knowledge; in reinsurance, connection to the different underlying characteristics of the risks being assessed enables their evaluation. For example, a Marine underwriter such as Brent has a deep knowledge of ships, derived from having been at sea, and having worked in the Marine primary insurance industry. In short, underwriters often have lived experience within their specific risk-type that enables them to calculate those risks. They tend to enter reinsurance either focused on a particular risk-type or to train in one main risk-type. For example, an underwriter for Agricultural deals described his deep immersion within its epistemic culture: "I was basically raised on a farm and studied agricultural economics. And then I gained a Ph.D. on agriculture policy. And I worked in food development aid, mainly in Asia, before becoming an Agriculture underwriter" (Interview, Reinsurer, Underwriter, Continental Europe). Such specific experience in Agriculture or Marine or Catastrophe modeling, both within and outside the reinsurance industry, constructs underwriters as members of an epistemic culture who perpetuate that culture through their practice and whose expertise enables them to construct the calculative practices within that culture.

Finally, in reinsurance **social** practices form bases of knowledge that are specific to each risk-type and underpin the knowledgeable enactment of calculation for underwriters within a particular epistemic culture. For example, Brent was continuously interacting with other Marine underwriters, brokers, and cedents who traded Marine deals, at conferences, on the phone, and in informal social meetings, and this was a critical source of knowledge in evaluating risks. To support such social interactions, there are specific conferences for, amongst others, Agriculture, U.S. Property Catastrophe, and Credit & Surety lines of business.

> No, I didn't go to Monte Carlo. That is not an Agriculture event . . . For us, there is an international conference on insurance of agriculture production. And there we have clients worldwide and also competitors; some 100 people. For the U.S. and Canadian business, it's normally the national crop insurance conference in the United States [he brings out a leaflet of conference attendees and goes through, showing how he knows almost all of them]. (Interview, Reinsurer, Underwriter, Continental Europe)

Within firms, underwriters working on the same risk-type are clustered together based on their collective expertise, sitting in the same space, often underwriting in teams and providing training for newcomers. For instance, an underwriting assistant working with a Marine underwriter is learning the "art of the trade", not only in underwriting generally, but specifically in becoming a Marine underwriter, including learning the specific tools for analyzing Marine deals. Indeed, lacking colleagues in the Bermuda office, Brent was often on the phone to his Marine underwriting colleagues in the London subsidiary of his firm. Thus, underwriters of particular risk-types interact with each other, contributing to and sourcing knowledge that comprises their specific culture, rather than dealing with members from other epistemic cultures.

4.4.2. Epistemic Cultures and Connectivity

The specificity of calculative practices to the particular epistemic cultures associated with each risk-type is a source of connectivity between underwriters. That is, specific bases of knowledge that enable risk evaluation are common to dispersed underwriters within a particular epistemic culture even as they act individually.[7] These underwriters, regardless of whether they are co-located, enact a collective practice that extends beyond the organization (Brown and Duguid, 2001). For example, Brent in Reinsurance-as-Practice 4B has deep experiential understanding of the calculative practices appropriate to underwrite Marine risk. He shares this deep understanding of Marine risk with other underwriters within his epistemic culture, whether located in Bermuda or elsewhere in the world. He is thus more connected in his calculative practice to those in his epistemic culture, even if they are located in other firms, than he is to his U.S. Property Catastrophe colleagues in the same firm, who cannot understand how he can analyze his deals. Epistemic cultures are thus critical to making the market for particular risk-types because they enable collective, supra-organizational practices (Brown and Duguid, 2001), such as reaching a consensus price on a particular type of risk. For example, the market for a Marine deal exists within its particular epistemic culture where Marine underwriters engage in and comprise the market for Marine deals, turning them into tradable objects. Indeed, the relational connections to competitors that are so central to the quoting process (Chapter 2) and the ability to contextualize a deal (Chapter 3) are enacted within the practices of a

---

[7] Importantly, while shared epistemic machineries denote connections, they do not denote unity or uniformity. They are similar to Schatzki's (2006) general and practical understandings, which indicate something shared or common to practices, but do not signify a unified way of doing something. Rather, there is still large variation in opinion and localized translation across the culture. The very idea of epistemic cultures which embrace different, often competing organizations suggests that within these epistemic cultures, there may be ongoing competition and "non-community" aspects. Nonetheless, just as violin players may all play the violin differently (and indeed accomplished players may have robust arguments regarding elements of technique) we can still talk about violin players sharing a collective and knowledgeable practice that is distinct from, although related to that of cello players (for example, when playing in an orchestra).

particular epistemic culture. The capacity to participate in a particular market resides in underwriters' membership of that epistemic culture. In this chapter, we thus foreground how connections between dispersed actors in the reinsurance sector are coordinated by epistemic cultures and their associated, common epistemic practices in evaluating deals within their particular risk-type.

4.5. PRACTICAL UNDERSTANDINGS: VARIATIONS IN BLENDING TECHNICALIZING AND CONTEXTUALIZING AMONG EPISTEMIC CULTURES

In Chapter 3 we introduced the two practical understandings, technicalizing and contextualizing, that constitute the basis for evaluating deals, establishing consensus price, and placing capital. These practical understandings are central in enacting the marketization of deals, transforming them into tradable financial objects that may be compared for their relative rates of return (Çalışkan and Callon, 2009; Callon and Muniesa, 2005). These practical understandings are equally important in the marketization of all risk-types, each of which is rendered calculable through the knowledgeable blending of technicalizing and contextualizing that is specific to its epistemic culture (Knorr Cetina, 1999). Blending is thus shaped by the interplay of technical, social, and empirical bases of knowledge within an epistemic culture as underwriters enact the practical understandings of technicalizing and contextualizing for their particular risk-type. That is, the particularities of blending vary according to risk-type. Namely, Brent (a Marine underwriter evaluating a Specialized risk-type) would blend technicalizing and contextualizing in a different way to John (a U.S. Property Catastrophe underwriter evaluating a Modeled risk-type).

As we saw in Chapter 3, technicalizing starts the evaluation process for U.S. Property Catastrophe deals (Modeled risk-type, see Figure 4.1) because the calculative practice of that epistemic culture revolves around models. Contextualizing then supplements technicalizing with deal-specific knowledge. This chapter focuses on other epistemic cultures, which have different calculative practices that are not driven by vendor models and hence have a different approach to both technicalizing, and how and when to blend that with contextualizing. With deals that lack the detailed statistical information or standardization necessary for vendor models, technicalizing practices still occur; yet their composition and interaction with contextualizing during the deal evaluation process varies according to particular characteristics of the risk-type (see Table 4.1). In evaluating deals of a Specialized risk-type, technicalizing and contextualizing practices co-constitute each other, meaning that contextual knowledge about the deal is integrated into the decisions about which analytic and rating tools to use, while with Frontier deals evaluation begins with contextualizing, evoking the physical characteristics of the risk and the cedent relationship in order to ascertain what technical tools might be applicable and to construct a price out of whatever information might be at hand (see Table 4.1). Hence, blending technicalizing and contextualizing involves a different knowledgeable practice for deals within Modeled, Specialized, and Frontier risk-types, that is underpinned by the varied social, technical, and empirical base of each epistemic culture (see Section 4.3). Having already illustrated the calculation of Modeled deals (Chapter 3) we will discuss Specialized and Frontier risks in turn.

4.5.1. Blending Technicalizing and Contextualizing for Specialized Risk-Types

As there are no vendor models available, evaluation of Specialized risk-types begins with a combination of technicalizing and contextualizing; that is, they **co-constitute** each other. Technicalizing practices, such as modeling and rating (see Table 4.1, 2B/C) and contextualizing practices such as incorporating cedent relationship (see Table 4.1, 2E) do not take place separately but are used together to construct knowledge about the deal. Specifically, unlike Modeled risk-types, there are no modeled outputs available to begin the process, so that with Specialized risk-types contextual features of the deal (such as evoking the physical characteristics of the risk) guide the selection, application and sometimes construction of actuarial pricing tools that will be used for modeling.

In this way, calculative practices of technicalizing go hand in hand with, and are co-constituted by, the calculative practices of contextualizing. For instance, knowing how one type of ship behaves relative to another is often critical to identifying which tools are appropriate to use with the available information on the movement of a vessel and its cargo. As we shadowed underwriters evaluating Specialized risk-types it became clear that a plethora of different in-house technical tools (as opposed to vendor models) are selected and used (Table 4.1, 2B-C), according to the underwriters' contextual knowledge of this risk-type and deal (Table 4.1, 2E-F). Blending thus occurs throughout the deal evaluation process and involves constant iteration between technicalizing and contextualizing practices (see Table 4.1, 2A). This process is illustrated in Reinsurance-as-Practice 4C where we illustrate deal evaluation in the specific epistemic culture of Credit & Surety; an example of a Specialized risk-type where technicalizing and contextualizing co-constitute each other.

Table 4.1. Variation in Blending Technicalizing and Contextualizing

Calculative Practices		Variation 1. Modeled [see Chapter 3]	Variation 2. Specialized [Reinsurance-as-Practice 4C]	Variation 3. Frontier [Reinsurance-as-Practice 4D]
A. Different ways of Blending		*Technicalizing then Contextualizing* *Technicalizing is central and supplemented through contextualizing*	*Technicalizing and contextualizing are co-constituted* *Continuous iteration; contextualizing and technicalizing co-constitute each other*	*Contextualizing then technicalizing* *Using contextualizing to construct numbers and tools to technicalize*
	B. Modeling	**Start of calculative practice.** Skilled use of specific vendor models, setting standards for modeling.	**Start of calculative practice.** Multiple actuarial tools and calculations selected, modified, and used in the rating sheet in a way that is specific to each deal. Rating not strictly separate from modeling.	Making do with actuarial tools that can be borrowed or modified to support rudimentary modeling of deal and satisfy rating expectations.
	C. Rating	Blending modeled results as foundation to determine price.		**Start of calculative practice.** Enables the construction of deal-specific technicalizing [usually based on the geographical characteristics of a territory].
	D. Evoking the physical characteristics of the risk	Contextualizing tailors assumptions in models, imbuing technical rates with underwriter's contextualized understanding and experience.	**Start of calculative practice.** Knowledge of particular risk characteristics (e.g. specific type of credit bond deal) central to calculation.	
	E. Incorporating cedent relationship	Used to avoid "the models taking over" and to imbue the price with meaning.	Incorporated to tailor ratings and use of tool if it provides insight into quality of particular "risk" and future performance.	**Start of calculative practice.** Underwriters overcome the lack of data by seeking in-depth knowledge about the 'best' cedent in a particular territory.
	F. Incorporating market dynamics	Incorporated as part of final consideration of quoted price.	Incorporated as part of final consideration of quoted price.	Becomes a central part of calculation when there is little else to go on.
	G. Comparing	Comparing quoted prices of deals that have been evaluated to finalize capital allocation. Based on graphical representations of the deal evaluation in form of curves.	Comparison to other similar deals used to build assumptions that can be incorporated within evaluation. Comparison feeds into calculation, e.g. to check 'fair' evaluation for other deals.	Comparison to other similar deals helps construct numbers to feed into pricing. Comparison feeds into the calculation, e.g. an E.Q. cover in Pakistan is compared with an E.Q. deal in India.

....

REINSURANCE-AS-PRACTICE 4C
Evaluating a Specialized Risk-Type

Task 1: Contextual understanding enabling the use and selection of technical tools. Stan, a Credit & Surety underwriter being shadowed by Rebecca, starts a typical busy pre-renewal day at Global Re with "Average deal" for ModerateInc, a company with credit exposure in Italy. The deal is average in that it is moderate in size (about $400,000 in **premium*** at his firm's current level of participation) and in its predicted return. Global Re has a plethora of specific in-house actuarial tools to model these risks from which Stan can choose. While they are developed in-house, not as industry-wide models, most of Stan's peers in the Credit & Surety world use similar tools, and develop in-house databases (based on credit ratings) that enable them to run specific analyses for this type of risk. Stan opens the ratings sheet (Figure 4.1, 2B), into which he has already entered the data, invoking his knowledge of the deal and client as he does so (Figure 4.1 2D, 2C), by commenting that this cedent "has shown me all their assessments of the companies they insure; ModerateInc has a number of larger specific credit risks in their portfolio we have to pay detailed attention to." He therefore selects one specific tool that is helpful for developing a more fine-grained sense of the exposure within a cedent's portfolio (Figure 4.1, 2A).

The deal has plenty of well structured information, with the insured companies it covers represented as ratings of "A", "B", or "C" according to their financial **security*** and risk of default. Stan states dismissively, "Of course you can't believe the cedent 100 percent; you have to make your own assessment. I've got a pretty sound idea of their specific exposures [in this case the financial risks] as all I do is look at Credit & Surety deals like this and we might see a particular exposure across many of our deals over many years!" Consequently, to get this "sound idea" Stan draws from his team's contextual knowledge of the specific risks (Figure 4.1, 2E), which involves, among other things, going through ModerateInc's ratings of their key exposures, as well as those of rating agencies (e.g. Standard and Poor's), and adjusting them based on his own knowledge of the cedent's financial security. Stan's assistant has already worked with the actuary to enter these internal exposure rankings into the ratings sheet. This is what **exposure pricing*** entails for Credit and Surety.[8] Stan flicks over to that tab and makes calculations that adjust the base premium exposure figure based on this risk assessment of the cedent's portfolio. He scans the technical result, in which the main exposure has been adjusted based on his team's ranking of ModerateInc's security. Thus, the tools being used—and the resultant technical rates—are constructed from deep contextual knowledge of this cedent, and of the Credit & Surety deal. Here, technicalizing and contextualizing are not enacted in isolation but are closely entwined to generate a technical rate (Figure 5.1, 2A).

---

[8] Just as underwriters such as John (in Chapter 3) of U.S. Property Catastrophe and other Modeled risks have in-house modelers who can run the data on deals through the vendor models, so underwriters working on Specialized and Frontier risks have access to in-house actuaries who can run the data on these deals through the actuarial tools that are developed in house.

As Stan quickly flicks through the rating sheet tabs it is evident that this tool is only one part of his analysis; he continues to make other calculations, using these to weight the technical rate. In particular, devising a sense of the "expected losses" based on an assessment of historical losses is an important way to project the deal's performance into the future. Stan incorporates cedent knowledge (Figure 4.1, 2F) to reach a figure for this year's expected losses (a loss ratio), by studying various statistics on the cedent's losses, stating, "As we have a lot of history with this cedent we can at least base the attritional loss ratio [how much they might expect to lose in any given year] on prior experience (an experience rating or **burning cost***). However, as the company has done a little bit of restructuring I will give them a discount for the shock loss [larger losses that only occur infrequently] as they got rid of some of the nasty risks in their portfolio." As he states: "The idea is to come up with a loss ratio for the coming year—you are thinking into the future and therefore the rating we base on prior experience only takes us so far before my knowledge of the cedent and the types of financial risks they have in their portfolio comes into play." He adjusts the loss ratio figures, changing the standard deviation setting in the rating sheet to reflect his assumption about decreased volatility in the deal, in order to generate a price he can quote (Table 4.1, 2BC; 2F). Finally, he is ready to send out his quote, invoking his knowledge of the market by commenting that his competitors will also be aware of the cedent's changes and likely to treat the prior-experience data in a similar way (Table 4.1, 2G).

Task 2: Comparing deals: Comparing deals and simultaneous technicalizing and contextualizing. After lunch Stan heads to a meeting with the rest of the Credit & Surety team (underwriters and the actuaries who help them with technical analysis) to finalize the pricing on deals from the two largest cedents in Global Re's portfolio—SuperSurety and MegaCredit. In the meeting they discuss the construction of the cedent-specific loss ratio "picks". The pick is a number projecting losses for the coming year; a higher number reflects their in-house assessment that there will be more losses. They relate each cedent to a market average (or market loss-ratio pick) they have calculated as a means to finalize the number for each specific cedent. This process of devising a market loss-ratio blends contextual understanding of market dynamics and the physical characteristics of risks in that market with the technical generation of the market loss-ratio pick (including financial and economic data), which is a type of benchmark for assessing price (Table 4.1; 2B-2E, G). They then compare the two main cedents, invoking cedent knowledge to determine their loss-ratio picks in relation to the market average they have constructed (Table 4.1; 2D). In particular, they have assumed that SuperSurety will have more losses in the year ahead due to their aggressive growth strategy, which might mean they are accumulating lower-quality risk, and thus need to be allocated a higher loss ratio. However, David, Stan's colleague, argues: "I am not confident that we should allocate a higher loss-ratio pick for SuperSurety than MegaCredit." Stan pushes back: "On what basis? I was just in a meeting with [renowned Credit & Surety broker] where we talked about SuperSurety getting more aggressive and pursuing growth not quality." He invokes cedent-specific knowledge, pointing out that certain Spanish defaults hit SuperSurety more than MegaCredit and that this could mean a few loss-ratio points (Table 4.1 2D, 2F). In this way, comparing the deals is very much a contextualized practice (in contrast to Modeled Risk-Types). However, while they compare the relative profitability of the different deals in this way, the team does not question the use of the loss-ratio figures that they have generated as an appropriate basis upon which to place capital. Rather, they all recognize the two deals as "valuable" and ones they wanted to underwrite, based on blending their deep knowledge of these companies, and their relative performance within the current market (contextualizing), with the specific actuarial calculations they have selected (technicalizing).

An hour later, Stan opens the rating sheets for both deals, which now contain the actuarial adjustments discussed at the meeting. The output is now incorporated in the rating sheets as a loss-ratio of 57 percent (SuperSurety) and 53 percent (MegaCredit) respectively based on their assessment of each cedent's future performance. They will use these ratings to generate quotes and, comparatively, place capital on these two deals. Thus, just as modeled outputs provided the initial basis for comparative decisions in Modeled risks (see Chapter 3); in Specialized risks there is also a technical basis for comparative capital allocation. Here, however, it has been informed from the start by contextual understandings of the market and cedent rather than being a simple comparison of technical outputs after they have been generated (Table 4.1 2D–G).

Task 3: Finalizing pricing through deep knowledge of Credit &Surety. Towards the end of the afternoon, as Stan completes the last few jobs for the day, his connection to the epistemic culture outside his firm becomes clear. He smiles as he looks through a contract he needs to authorize to finalize his share of a deal: "This is the old [well known competitor's] legal contract; I've known this for years." He explains that he knows the competitor would have checked it very thoroughly. He was at the Credit & Surety conference in Rome last week and met with the underwriter, Gerald, who was responsible for developing this very wording. Gerald's company spent a lot of time tightening up this deal, including the terms and conditions and thus what types of risks were included. Based on this knowledge of his competitor (market dynamics, Table 4.1, 2G), and of this particular contract, he already knows that the wording has strict parameters about what is included in the deal. He looks through the contract and admits he actually loves dissecting the wording and after years of experience knows what to look out for, to ensure no ambiguities sneak in (Table 4.1, 2E). After having a close read of the document he confirms that he can take a share in confidence as the contract parameters established by his competitor are up to scratch. "Gerald and I agree on that!" "And the RoE is perfect," he adds, kissing his fingertips in satisfaction as he sends off his acceptance of his share of the deal. Indeed, his original quote was not far from the consensus price, and his final assessment is aligned with those of other underwriters in his epistemic culture, allowing him to quickly accept (Figure 4.1, 2G). By contrast, just before we were about to pack up for the evening he looks at another deal and mutters "Yuck"—as a particular type of credit risk had been included. He explains that this cedent has got to be dreaming: "No matter how profitable these might look I won't touch them." He pauses. "No real Credit & Surety underwriter will anymore, so good luck to the cedent finding reinsurers!" (Table 4.1, 2E). In this way, the knowledge of market dynamics and characteristics of the risk that are central to being a "Credit & Surety" underwriter enable Stan to make decisions regarding these particular deals.

Stan's story demonstrates that knowledge of the actual risk, in this case the underlying type of financial product, is particularly central in blending technicalizing and contextualizing to calculate Specialized deals (Figure 5.2, 2E). Knowing the risk, the deal and the cedent are all central: tools are developed, selected, used, and their technical ratings made sense of, in relation to the in-depth contextual knowledge of the underwriter. Technicalizing and contextualizing are closely entwined to enact each task as part of evaluating Specialized risk-types; the two practical understandings are blended in an iterative process of co-constituting each other. Finally, it is clear that calculation is conducted within an epistemic culture: Stan referred to and engaged with his Credit & Surety competitors in other firms, Credit & Surety brokers, and his own colleagues, with whom he constructs knowledge about the risks and common calculative practices.

4.5.2. Blending Technicalizing and Contextualizing for Frontier Deals

In Frontier risk-types, not only are there no vendor models but individual deals also come with very little statistical information. Hence, contextual knowledge of the specific risk, territory, and market is critical to the practice of calculation. In contrast to Modeled and Specialized risk-types, the evaluation process commences with contextualizing (see Table 4.1, 3D and 3E) which provides the basis for constructing relevant measures to evaluate deals of a Frontier risk-type. For example, the construction of numerical benchmarks to compare deals and to generate market averages for a particular territory is based on an underwriter knowing the pool of deals comprising the market, and knowing the particular characteristics of the territory and underlying risk. In evaluating Frontier deals, blending thus involves contextualizing the deal in order to construct the numbers upon which technicalizing is then based and from which a quoted price is constructed. This is illustrated in Reinsurance-as-Practice 4D, where we rejoin Ria, the underwriter we met at the SIRC conference in Singapore, as she evaluates Indian and Pakistani deals.

....

REINSURANCE-AS-PRACTICE 4D
Evaluating a Frontier Risk-Type

Task 1: Constructing numbers through contextualizing. Ria is focused this Monday morning on a Pakistan deal. She explains to Paula that this deal, which reinsures commercial properties in Karachi and other cities in the Sindh province for fire, has very little relevant loss history information. However, she knows the cedent and the market for Pakistan; she believes that this is one of the best deals in Pakistan (Table 4.1, 3E and 3F). Ria frowns at how little there is to work on; however, she goes through her files, saying that she has "some knowledge regarding the checks this cedent makes regarding whether the building code was followed." She explains that she's been to Karachi a few times and since the 2005 earthquake and regulations that followed, "you do see modern commercial buildings now being engineered and maintained to modern fire standards and these are the ones this cedent reinsures." She points to her notes: "Look, see; the cedent brought up the fact that they conduct checks on the fire extinguishers." She already has an empty rating sheet open, waiting to be populated with numbers, and after a few moments thought, she opens another Excel spreadsheet. She explains that she will benchmark the potential loss using some data from a deal focused on commercial property in India, where they have more information and thus slightly more accurate statistics on fire. It is not perfect but she invokes the physical characteristics of the risk. She knows how the two regions behave "after all these years" so she can adjust the assumptions for Pakistan to reflect the differences—namely, Pakistan is more exposed to earthquake (one potential cause of widespread fires) and has less responsive systems for fires. From this information, she is then able to use this tool, which relies on a few simple parameters to estimate exposure based on the number of properties, and to load for peak catastrophe losses, in this case earthquake. She copies over the figures from the Indian deal and then reduces them by a certain percentage point. As she generates a quoted price for the deal, Ria makes a note in the rating sheet so that peers and her **Chief Risk Officer***** can trace where she "dreamed up" the pricing and estimated RoE.

Ria's ability to generate numbers with which to practise technicalizing and construct a price for the deal is based on her knowledge of the cedent and territory, as well as how to generate comparative benchmarks from her knowledge of Indian deals. Her contextual knowledge enables her to construct numbers to satisfy the expectations of the ratings sheet and, most importantly, reach a price that aligns with her knowledge of this cedent and market. She knows that this is the "best deal in Pakistan" to allocate capital on, despite the limited amount of quantitative information available (Table 4.1).

Task 2. Territory and cedent-specific knowledge enables technicalizing. This example extends on Task 1 above to show more directly how cedent and market knowledge are central to rendering Frontier deals calculable, despite the paucity of modeling tools.

Later that morning Ria has a **bouquet deal***** on her desk. Bouquets are a type of deal rarely seen in developed markets, except from very small cedents. It is called a bouquet because it bundles all the risks that usually comprise separate deals together in a single deal, often because each of these is too small to be placed on its own. In this case, Ria's deal incorporates both Indian Motor Liability and property. As she opens the information pack on the Motor portfolio, looking for claims that have hit the reinsurance layer in the past, she says, "There's simply not enough claims information to run an analysis of the losses." However, she has some market rates for Motor in India that she and the actuaries estimated last year, based on her understanding of the market and any data they had been able to collect from all the deals she has seen over the years (Table 4.1, 3B, 3C, 3E).

"Most reinsurers develop their own market averages like these from their experience of these particular types of risk," she explains. "Not completely accurate but it's a number that can be applied." She brings up a folder with the market benchmark and invokes her cedent knowledge as she applies it: "This particular cedent's portfolio is actually relatively low risk, compared to most Indian Motor Liability, which has terrible losses." She pauses, looking through the sparse demographic estimates of the portfolio: "I think it deserves a discount of about 11.5 percent from the market average we have." She then inputs the discounted modeled industry average into her rating sheet as a loss ratio and uses that to build the rest of her pricing. As she does so she picks up the phone and calls the broker in India, whom she knows well, quickly clarifying how up to date the cedent's demographic summary is, and having a general chat about how the broker is finding the renewal this year. As she puts down the phone, she shakes her head and laughs, invoking knowledge of the market dynamics to explain that the exact price doesn't really matter. India has been below the technical rate for Motor for years; she and others dealing Indian Motor have always been participating on deals below the technical rate! She explains that she had been at the India Rendezvous in January and she had managed to talk to a few of the other international reinsurers on the deal—"Bill from Mega Re and Raj from Eastern Re." All had moaned about the price; but none believed the local context would change this year for Motor. If she put in what she thought she should get, then she would be vastly out of line with her competitors (Table 4.1, 3G). She will wait to get the Property pricing back from the actuary, in order to combine it with her view on the motor.

Later, over coffee, Paula asks Ria how she knew that a discount of 11.5 percent was appropriate. Ria explains that she had visited this cedent recently and knows that they are not growing the Motor portion so she didn't have to account for growth in exposure. The company will also continue to focus on affluent demographics with expensive cars that tend to be a little newer and safer, as well as better looked after. She also knows that they keep a close eye on fraudulent claims rather than simply passing them on to their reinsurers, an issue you have to control for in Motor insurance. The importance of such deep contextual knowledge is again evident when, back at her desk, Ria opens an email from an assistant she is training. It contains his assessment of the Property portion of the deal, which Ria will bring together as one price with the Motor she has analyzed. The RoE is negative. "That boy sure knows how to price!" she mutters, referring to the fact that he was comprehensive. She explains she'd talked him through what to do as she tweaks a few things in his pricing, although the RoE remains negative. Without missing a beat she puts the information together in one sheet with the rates already generated on the Motor and emails the cedent: "I am pleased to advise participation of 20 percent share." She has placed her firm's capital. As she does so, she explains: "I don't give a shit about the RoE, and it's a small treaty so I can write it just like"—she snaps her fingers—"without asking my boss." Ria laughs, explaining: "Some people you can just trust with your eyes closed and this is what these people"—she gestures in the general direction of the analysts (actuary)—"these number crunchers—don't understand . . . they're only looking at numbers. But the issue on this business is trust. You place your trust in the cedent and that they will execute the plan they have explained to you. In this particular company this is what is happening." This company is one of her best cedents in India and, displaying her knowledge of the market dynamics, she points out that if she quoted as high as she might like, she would be laughed out of the market! She also explains that despite the RoE, it is important to remember that there will still be cash flow on this deal if there is no loss. As far as her company is concerned it is a small diversifying piece of business that is part of their overall portfolio strategy to balance out their concentration of U.S. Catastrophe Property deals (see Chapter 5).

Again, Ria's contextual knowledge of the cedent, and the Indian market territory has enabled her to write a risk that, by technical standards alone, appears unprofitable. However, she understands that these technical assumptions need to be overridden in order to generate a price that the deal can command in this market context. Otherwise, they would be unable to write any business in India, and yet, as she notes, the deals she has been writing for many years have not been making losses for her firm.

....

As shown in Reinsurance-as-Practice 4D, the lack of available data on Frontier deals means that evaluation cannot begin with technicalizing; there are neither vendor models (Modeled risk-type) nor actuarial tools (Specialized risk-type) available. Contextualizing practices are thus essential to construct the deal in a numerical form. The data for these numbers is created through knowing the risk, the cedent, and the particular territory, and positioning that within the market dynamics of that territory. Contextualizing provides the means to **construct** numbers and enact technicalizing in the absence of detailed statistical information.

4.5.3. Constructing the Market Through Variations in Blending

In order to underwrite any reinsurance deal, it is necessary to come up with a number; specifically, a price expressed as a RoL. Despite the fact that many deals around the world lack the data to be calculated using standardized models, they are all evaluated using a combination of technicalizing and contextualizing practices to reach this number. Yet the way these practices are blended varies according to the information and standardization characteristics of the risk-type. In the case of **Modeled** risk-types, which are both information-rich and highly standardizable, technicalizing practices commence the deal evaluation process (see Table 4.1 and Chapter 3). Yet, as these models are widely acknowledged to be flawed, contextualizing is used to supplement the modeling and make the evaluation process meaningful in accordance with the underwriter's lived experience of the risk (see Chapter 3). In **Specialized** risk-types, which are information-rich but unstandardized, technicalizing and contextualizing are blended simultaneously, or co-constituted, with contextualizing enabling the construction, selection, and use of actuarial tools. In contrast to the Modeled risk-type, contextual knowledge of the risk informs technicalizing from the start of the evaluation process, as illustrated by Stan (Reinsurance-as-Practice 4C). By further contrast, information on **Frontier** deals is often scarce, may be inaccurate, and cannot be standardized. Models are thus unavailable or deemed unreliable. Contextualizing forms the dominant calculative practice in the deal evaluation process, as it provides the basis to construct adequate information to practice technicalizing and generate a price for the deal. A price is compiled through the bringing together of whatever information and tools might be at hand from a variety of sources. Thus, blending centers largely around contextualizing which enables technicalizing.

While blending varies across risk-types, its role in enacting the marketization of reinsurance risk is very consistent. Each evaluation renders a deal, regardless of its apparent "modelability" (see Section 4.2), calculable and tradable as a financial object; it has a price attributed to it, which provides the basis for a decision. That is, despite such wide variation in deals and risk-types, an RoE is generated to inform the decision of whether to place capital on any deal, which we explore further in Chapter 5. Blending of technicalizing and contextualizing is thus at the heart of making a market for reinsurance risk, despite the incredible diversity in risk-types, the incommensurability of the underlying risks, and the vast difference in calculative devices and practices available for such risks.

4.6. EPISTEMIC CULTURES IN THE RELATIONALITY AMONG ACTORS, DEAL, AND MARKET

We have examined how the evaluation of deals pertaining to particular risk-types is coordinated within epistemic cultures (Knorr Cetina, 1999). The specific calculative practices that are common to members of each epistemic culture (whether John in Chapter 3, or Stan or Ria) enable the transformation of risks into tradable financial objects, regardless of the availability of standardized models. We have zoomed in on the variation in the calculative practices and blending of technicalizing and contextualizing, illustrating them in the Reinsurance-as-Practice sections. We now zoom out to explain the relationality through which epistemic cultures coordinate the market practice for specific risk-types. We discuss five relationalities through which the market is coordinated, as summarized in Table 5.2.

First, epistemic cultures coordinate the market as they construct the practical understandings of how to evaluate a particular deal within a particular risk-type. They are fundamental to the relationality between market actor, and deal, in terms of deal evaluation and calculability. The different ways in which deals are evaluated for different risk-types demonstrate that each has a distinct epistemic culture governing its calculative practices. Each epistemic culture is built upon specific technical, social, and empirical bases, which enable the market for that risk-type to be made. Underwriters tend to belong to one particular epistemic culture: because of differences in the way a Specialized deal is evaluated compared to a Frontier deal, Ria would struggle to evaluate Stan's deals and vice versa. Indeed, an underwriter will only see a deal if they are a member of that epistemic culture; no cedent or broker would send Ria a Credit & Surety deal, or Stan an Indian Motor deal. Hence, the relationality between an actor and that actor's ability to evaluate and quote on a deal is specifically informed by the epistemic culture to which the actor belongs.

Second, epistemic cultures construct relational connectivity between actors within a particular culture. The calculative practices to evaluate deals of a specific risk-type are collectively constructed by the globally dispersed underwriters within that culture; yet diverge from the ones outside of that epistemic culture (Amin and Roberts, 2008; Brown and Duguid, 2001). For example, Stan has more in common with his peers who evaluate Credit & Surety deals on the other side of the world, than with his colleagues in the same organization who might evaluate U.S. Property Catastrophe deals. Epistemic cultures ensure specific calculative practices transcend organizational or geographic boundaries and build relationality between globally dispersed underwriters evaluating particular risk-types. This connectivity is established in different ways within different cultures. Vendor models are central to connecting underwriters evaluating deals within the Modeled risk-type; these models belong to the technical practices of the culture (Knorr Cetina, 1999). Contextual knowledge about the underlying risk provides the source of connectivity within the epistemic cultures formed around Specialized and Frontier risk-types; this contextual knowledge stems from the empirical and social practices of the culture (Knorr Cetina, 1999). We thus move beyond the existing focus on models (Millo and MacKenzie, 2009), face-to-face interaction, (Baker, 1984), or technological platforms (Knorr Cetina and Bruegger, 2002a; MacKenzie, 2004) to show the multiple ways that common practices enable the **relational presence** between market actors within an epistemic culture.

This relational connectivity is important because it enables a consensus price for a particular deal to be formed by those actors who are part of the same specific epistemic culture. The way the quoted price becomes meaningful, and indeed, the "appropriate" price or rate of return for a particular deal, both rest on the shared calculative practices within that epistemic culture. That is, what constitutes an acceptable price is not an absolute measure through which deals across risk-types are deemed profitable, or below which all deals are not profitable. Rather, what constitutes an appropriate price for any deal and risk is understood relationally **within** an epistemic culture. Consensus pricing and collective risk-bearing thus emerges from the relationality between actors within an epistemic culture as they evaluate deals using common calculative practices. This connectivity within globally dispersed epistemic cultures is central to the professional "oversight" that enables the promulgation and monitoring of the norms of behavior that are central to this market (see Chapter 2).

Third, epistemic cultures enable relational comparisons between deals within a risk-type, so that their price and relative rate of return may be calculated on a like-for-like basis (Çalışkan and Callon, 2010). That is, an Indian Motor deal is neither compared to a British Motor Liability deal, nor to an Australian Property Catastrophe deal. Instead, comparisons are confined to deals that are evaluated within a specific epistemic culture, so reducing the scope of commensuration within the evaluation process (Espeland and Stevens, 1998; Huault and Rainelli-Weiss, 2011). In this way, epistemic cultures enable the comparison of risks as financial deals, which is a critical element of making them tradable within a market. Namely, actors can compare the relative profitability of one deal over another for the purposes of placing capital (see also Chapter 3).

Fourth, the notion of epistemic cultures provides an additional important nuance to the dynamic of **temporal coordination** over market cycles. As we saw in Chapter 2, at any particular renewal date, actors pitch their quotes on each deal in relation to the market cycle that they are constructing. Yet, as the "ripple effect" showed, not all deals are equally affected by events, so all deals do not rise or fall consistently in response to an event. Rather, the actors on those particular deals that have been affected by any event are at the center of constructing increases in price for those deals. Typically, these actors will be members of a particular epistemic culture, relationally constructing price rises on deals within a particular risk-type that have experienced losses from a specific event, such as floods in Thailand, or medical malpractice claims in France. The possibility of shifting the pricing of India Motor deals by a few points might not feature as a general industry cycle, or be reflected as general industry news. However, people within that specific epistemic culture are attuned to such shifts. Because of that awareness, they construct the many small "cycles-within-a-cycle" on particular deals and risk-types, which shape and are shaped by larger market shifts in pricing (Chapter 2). Thus, through the concept of epistemic cultures, we provide a way of understanding not only large pricing shifts (or cycles) but also subtle localized ones that might either support a "rising tide" in global pricing, or that do not mirror the general global cycle but nonetheless enable a ripple of increased pricing within the specific risk-type.

Finally, this chapter also implies an underlying relationality **between** epistemic cultures and their associated risk-types. Despite the variation in

Table 4.2. Summary of Relationalities Among Risk-Types

Relationality A	The relationality formed through epistemic cultures between deal and underwriter that enables calculation of particular risk-types.
Relationality B	The relationality formed by globally dispersed underwriters within an epistemic culture calculating the same risk-type, which enables the formation of consensus price.
Relationality C	The relationality formed between deals of a similar risk-type as they are compared within an epistemic culture.
Relationality D	Building the relationality between market actors within an epistemic culture and pricing cycles of a particular risk-type over time.
Relationality E	Relationality is formed across risk-types, despite variation in practice, through an ostensibly similar and comparable output (a price expressed as RoL) that enables all of these different risks to be traded within the reinsurance market.

calculative practices we have outlined between epistemic cultures, there is still a recognizable process whereby both technicalizing and contextualizing are brought together, albeit blended in different ways, in a rating sheet to come up with a similarly expressed assessment of value (i.e. a price and a rate of return). The commonality of a ratings sheet and the common requirement to derive a rate from the evaluation process supports the relationality across risk-types. Namely, there is the construction of a numerically expressed price and assessment of return for every deal, regardless of risk-type. This common evaluative output enables all of these risk-types to be traded within the reinsurance market, regardless of the vast variation in the underling perils and risks, so supporting relationality between risk-types within a global market.

4.7. FURTHER THEORIZING

In addition to its contributions to our theorizing of relationality, this chapter speaks to a number of specific concepts: marketization, evaluation, connectivity between dispersed market actors, and the epistemic foundations of financial markets.

First, this chapter describes the calculation of financial deals where no widely accepted models exist and where there is little numerical data. Our framework, which shows the considerable variation in technicalizing practices and the way that they are blended with contextualizing practices, addresses the recognized tendency for existing research to "treat practices of economic calculation in a somewhat undifferentiated manner" (Miller, 2008: 52–53). In doing so, it extends the concepts of marketization and calculation (Çalışkan and Callon, 2010) within financial markets into less ostensibly model-driven or "numerical" domains. Our detailed illustration of marketization in less modelable settings contrasts with the dominant focus in Social Studies of Finance on how models and technologies—albeit imperfect or inaccurate ones—enact the market (Beunza and Stark, 2004; MacKenzie, 2011; 2012; MacKenzie, 2006; Millo and MacKenzie, 2009; Pinch and Swedberg, 2008). Generally, studies have focused on settings where there is abundant numerical information, usually available in real time (Beunza et al., 2006; Carruthers and Stinchcombe, 1999; Knorr Cetina and Bruegger, 2002a; Knorr Cetina and Preda, 2001; MacKenzie, 2012; Preda, 2006; 2009), and where widely used calculative devices exist (Beunza and Stark, 2004; 2012; MacKenzie, 2011; Millo and MacKenzie, 2009). Our framework extends these former studies by explaining how calculation can occur in financial markets where risks remain largely un-modeled and/or where numerical data is sparse.

We show that calculation in such un-modeled domains is different from those where there are widely accepted sophisticated models, such as that described in Chapter 3. Nonetheless, the conceptual framework of the evaluation process developed in Chapter 3, based on blending **technicalizing** and **contextualizing** practices remains valid, enabling marketization in a wide variety of calculative settings (Callon and Muniesa, 2005). We have also shown that this is possible due to the specific bases of knowledge held by market actors who belong to distinct epistemic cultures (Brown and Duguid, 2001; Knorr Cetina, 1999; Knorr Cetina and Preda, 2001). Valuation does not start with the "device" (Beunza and Stark, 2004; 2012; Callon and Muniesa, 2005; Millo and Mackenzie, 2009), but more fundamentally, with calculative knowledge (Knorr Cetina and Preda, 2001). In doing so, we elaborate upon the pervasiveness of marketization (Çalışkan and Callon, 2010) as a general understanding that transcends the lack of statistical information and widely used models. Specifically, we show that vastly unpredictable and uncertain risks are assumed to be tradable in a financial market to the extent that actors construct calculative practices and generate financial measures (Callon and Muniesa, 2005). This takes place **even** in the absence of information that might enable the more standardized calculative techniques that are normally associated with calculation in financial markets (e.g. Beunza and Stark, 2004; Millo and MacKenzie, 2009).

This chapter has extended our framework of the evaluative process through which price is established, by providing deeper insight into the role of contextualizing. Providing additional insight into judgment within calculative cultures (Mikes, 2009; Mikes, 2011), the "social" elements of pricing (e.g. Beunza et al., 2006; Beunza and Stark, 2004; Beunza and Stark, 2012), and the way that specialist knowledge of the "material and legal realities" of risk (Mackenzie, 2011: 1,808) supplement models. Our finding about variations in blending explains how such contextualizing practices enable the selection and use of calculative devices (in Specialized Risk) and even more dramatically construct the numbers upon which technicalizing in based (in Frontier Risk). Such contextualizing practices therefore fulfil a role that is far more than supplementary, providing empirical substance to Callon and Muniesa's (2005: 1,231) point that calculation does "not necessarily mean performing mathematical or even numerical operations." By moving beyond a dominant focus on highly modelable settings, we better theorize the role of contextualizing practices in constructing the numerical basis for the marketization of risk. Contextualizing practices are therefore at the heart of our theorization of the construction of price in financial markets, not only as important supplements (e.g. Beunza, et al., 2006; Beunza and Stark, 2004; Mackenzie, 2011), but also as drivers of calculation. In doing so, we elaborate upon the role of knowledge and expertise in financial markets (Knorr Cetina and Preda, 2001) by exposing the technical, social, and empirical foundations of trading practice.

Third, this chapter also adds insight into connectivity between globally dispersed market actors, an issue that has preoccupied social studies of finance (Beunza and Stark, 2012; Knorr Cetina and Bruegger, 2002a; Mackenzie, 2004). We show how epistemic cultures enable connectivity in the calculative practice of globally dispersed actors (Amin and Roberts, 2008; Brown and Duguid, 2001). Importantly, we show that this connectivity develops in different ways within different epistemic cultures (Knorr Cetina, 1999). While the vendor models in Chapter 3 are one manifestation of common calculative practices that enable connectivity (e.g. Millo and Mackenzie, 2009), the underlying epistemic culture, rather than the models, is the engine of this connectivity. We move from focusing on the models, to the **knowledgeable** use of the models and also show how other knowledgeable practices of calculation build connectivity in the absence of models. By contrast, the social studies of finance literature have been largely focused on the technological infrastructure that build this connectivity and enable actors to be "plugged in" to each other and the market in real time (Knorr Cetina and Bruegger, 2000; Knorr Cetina and Bruegger, 2002a; 2002b; Preda, 2009a; Zaloom, 2003). This, in turn, was a direct step away from foundational work based on a more traditional sociological approach, which drew from network theory (Granovetter, 1985) to show how relationships and real-time face-to-face interactions (Abolafia, 1996; Baker, 1984) built connectivity in financial markets.

Fourth, we foreground the epistemic foundations of markets more generally (Knorr Cetina, 1999; Knorr Cetina and Preda, 2001), building upon understandings about the role of knowledge in enacting markets (e.g. Mackenzie, 2011; 2012). We have further developed the implications of Knorr Cetina and Preda's (2001) work which links epistemic cultures to the practices of actors in financial services firms, providing a detailed study of the technical, social, and empirical bases of calculation as epistemic work. Market-making in this sense depends on people's knowledgeable practice both with and without models. While many have talked about the importance of knowledge in financial markets (Aspers, 2009; Carruthers and Stinchcombe, 1999; MacKenzie, 2006; 2012), we have provided a detailed exploration of what that means: specifically, that the epistemic practice of a market is enacted through belonging to an epistemic culture, as part of which actors construct knowledge and perpetuate that culture. In so doing, we have married the notion of epistemic culture (Knorr Cetina, 1999) with that of marketization (Çalışkan and Callon, 2010).

4.8. CONCLUSION

We have now traversed the expanse of the global reinsurance industry and its many, varied risk-types. The various deals discussed in Chapters 3 and 4 are representative of the variety of risks that make up the reinsurance market.[9] Despite the vast differences in risk-types, the evaluation of deals forms a coherent and recognizable process, which draws from common calculative practices such as "rating" or "evoking the physical characteristics of the risk." We have also turned the kaleidoscope once more to show the way epistemic cultures coordinate the market. Epistemic cultures are founded on common knowledge that enables variation in blending technicalizing and contextualizing within any particular epistemic culture. Even in the absence of any commonly practiced vendor models, we have shown that market actors are relationally connected through the epistemic cultures within which they construct and share calculative practices. The market is thus created through the calculative practices enacted within epistemic cultures.

Yet a puzzle remains. We have observed multiple risk-types in this chapter, each associated with distinct epistemic cultures. Yet definitions of what constitutes an appropriate price for a deal are constructed within a particular epistemic culture and can differ wildly between cultures. Such variation raises questions regarding how and why what appears to be business with a lower rate of return is underwritten. Why do reinsurers bother to underwrite deals on ostensibly lower return risk-types? Allocating capital is not only the preserve of decisions **within** a particular epistemic culture, but is also a consideration made within firms about what constitutes a desirable portfolio of risk-types. Consequently, while we have described deal evaluation and

---

[9] Our study is confined to non-**life*** reinsurance meaning all types of reinsurance apart from life.

pricing within an epistemic culture we still need to explore what happens when the pricings generated by these different cultures are compared within a firm, in order to decide where it should put its money. In Chapter 5, we will address this additional puzzle by exploring the firm as the site for capital allocation.

Summary

In this chapter we have:

- Shown how the different evaluative practices enacted within **risk-types** are fundamental sites for market making activity.
- Shown how the general understanding **that risk can be marketized** is still maintained in the **absence of models**. That is, when information is sparse and/or not standardizable, so that the typical calculative practices of a market (such as financial modeling) are less applicable. We illustrated this **general understanding** through the story of Ria in Singapore, evaluating deals that had little informational or statistical basis (Reinsurance-as-Practice 4A).
- Shown how **epistemic cultures** coordinate the market in the context of multiple risk-types; explaining how these cultures enable knowledgeable calculative practice and connectivity between underwriters within a specific risk-type. We illustrated this coordination through the Marine underwriter Brent and his close connection with the practice of other Marine underwriters globally (Reinsurance-as-Practice 4B).
- Shown the **practical understandings** of contextualizing and technicalizing being blended in different ways within different epistemic cultures. We highlighted this **variation in blending** through Stan the Credit & Surety underwriter (Reinsurance-as-Practice 4C) and Ria, underwriting deals from India and Pakistan (Reinsurance-as Practice 4D).

5

One Firm's Trash is Another's Treasure

Competing in a Consensus Market

5.1. INTRODUCTION

The **consensus price*** developed on individual **deals*** is central to the functioning of the reinsurance market. Consequently, competing on price—by undercutting the market, for instance—is considered dysfunctional by both supplier (reinsurer) and buyer (**cedent***) (Chapter 2). However, the consensus terminology should not obscure the intense competition between reinsurers; they are for-profit corporations that are expected to maximize profit by their shareholders. Yet, given that reinsurers sell their capital at the same consensus price for any particular deal, how do they compete and over what do they compete?

While it seems intuitive that reinsurers will compete for the deals with the highest designation of value, such as the highest **rate of return***, this chapter shows that not all firms compete for the same deal and **risk-type***. For example, some competitors may jump at one deal at a particular price, while others may consider that very same deal severely underpriced and unattractive for their capital. Just as beauty lies in the eye of the beholder, so the attractiveness of a deal, or the extent to which firms will compete for it, has no clear, universal definition. Rather, competition is relative, depending on different firms' varying appetites for particular deals and risk-types.

This chapter, therefore, examines the firm as the **site*** for allocating capital to deals and risk-types (Section 5.2). We explain the **general understanding*** of competition in this market: firms compete to shape the consensus price, and to maximize their share of those deals for which they have an appetite (Section 5.3). We then show how variation in reinsurers' risk-appetite **coordinates** which particular firms compete for, and so construct, the market for particular deals and risk-types (Section 5.4).

We demonstrate how competition occurs throughout the renewal process, as underwriters enact their firm's particular **practical understandings*** of risk-appetite, which includes their optimum diversity in **risk-types***; the value they attribute to the longevity of business relationships; and fluctuations in their capital availability (Section 5.5). This competition through enactment of **risk-appetite*** is brought to life in a Reinsurance-as-Practice example of the competitive actions of four firms as they **quote*** and take shares in a deal (Section 5.6). Finally, we zoom out to demonstrate how our focus on the firm-as-site builds **relationalities*** among risk-types (see Chapter 4), and how risk-appetite coordinates the relationality among firm, deal, and risk-type (Section 5.7). These relationalities enact competition and consensus while shaping the market for reinsurance within and across risk-types.

5.2. FIRM AS SITE

The variation in risk-types noted in Chapter 4, with their different levels of risk and rates of return, creates a challenge for reinsurance firms in deciding which risk-types will make the best use of their capital. The following illustration describes an internal meeting within a reinsurer, which introduces the notion of firm risk-portfolios and highlights why a reinsurer might compete on risk-types and deals that vary dramatically in their profitability.

....

REINSURANCE-AS-PRACTICE 5A
Expanding the Portfolio* of Risk-Types on which to Compete

The Zurich-based subsidiary of Growth Re is having its quarterly meeting between the head underwriters of different **risk-types***. Among them is Harry who is managing the company's European Property Catastrophe array of deals, having previously been running their U.S. Property Catastrophe team in Bermuda. A large portion of the meeting is taken up with providing overviews of the performance of each risk-type. Harry presents the Property Catastrophe portfolio first, showing that they are well above the profitability target.[1] Relatively robust figures from the **Credit & Surety*** team and the "reasonable" rate of return from the small Engineering portfolio are then discussed.

Michel then outlines the European **Casualty*** business. Growth Re has historically avoided Casualty deals. Through this Zurich subsidiary Growth Re is, however, testing the water in this new risk-type and has hired Michel from a competing firm to lead this expansion. The **combined loss-ratio*** (the profitability

---

[1] Reinsurers will use different measures of profitability such as return on equity (RoE), **return on risk adjusted capital (RoRAC)***, or **combined ratios***.

measure used at Growth Re) flashes up on the PowerPoint and Michel outlines what he has achieved during the renewal. Harry is frowning as Michel talks and before long jumps in: "If the business is **this** bad, I mean it's below adequacy by that figure, why should we even bother competing in this space?" And indeed the next slide suggests that the profitability of their Casualty business is negative. Harry again interrupts, "I mean this proves my point, it seems to be really counter-intuitive to place capital at these profitability levels!" Michel begins to get frustrated. "What the combined ratio is not showing," he explains, "is that these cedents **never** actually lose money. There's less severity—it balances out your big multi-million-dollar hurricanes—and therefore we can afford lower prices." The CEO steps in to move the conversation on, outlining that it is a new area for the company and they are not looking to compete "hard" in this space yet. Instead, they are taking a "softly, softly" approach on just a few deals to test the water.

As this example shows, the enactment of **firm-specific appetite** for different risk and deals is the site of practice and is where different risk-types come together. Our focus on deals and risk-types in previous chapters has, temporarily, pushed firms into the background. While underwriters evaluate and make decisions to place capital on deals, it is their firms that bear the risk and hold the capital reserves to pay out on losses. As we move from a focus on underwriters appraising deals within particular risk-types to a focus on **capital allocation**, so the firm becomes a critical site for the activity of market- making. As illustrated in the example of Growth Re wrestling with different assumptions about profitability on different risk-types (Reinsurance-as-Practice 5A), these firms span multiple risk-types, which broadens our focus to explaining how trading practices are enacted within firms.

Underwriters evaluate deals as attractive and compete to allocate capital to them in relation to their firm's risk-appetite. By doing so, underwriters enact the reinsurer's portfolio of risk-types and deals. They might compete strongly for one deal or particular risk-type (such as Catastrophe in the example of Growth Re) based on that appetite or even not at all. Focusing on the reinsurance firm as site provides insight into how competition shapes evaluation practice and the allocation of capital to particular deals. Underwriters situated in **different** firms make these decisions as part of enacting their firms' varying appetites for different risk-types and deals. These firm-specific risk-appetites are another reason why underwriters might evaluate and quote very differently for any particular deal.

Why does this diversity exist and persist between firms? Such variation may be partly explained by the distinct cultural-historical foundations of reinsurers (Borscheid, et al., 2013). For example, many Bermudian firms originated in the wake of U.S. Property Catastrophe **events*** to provide capital to that market (Cummins, 2007), and some of them continue to focus primarily on U.S. Property Catastrophe deals. They are not interested in competing on deals such as the European Casualty business described in Reinsurance-as-Practice 5A. Lloyd's firms, with a historical foundation in Marine; and Continental European firms, with a historical foundation in underwriting their cedents' entire portfolio of risk-types, also similarly grew out of their own particular cultural-historical settings. However, geographic location and history does not totally determine variation in risk-appetite, which is specific to each reinsurer and can evolve over time as firms position themselves in the market. For example, many Bermudian firms have deliberately expanded beyond U.S. Property Catastrophe, increasing their exposure to a range of risk-types. The point is that individual reinsurers are attracted to different risk-types and thus actors from different firms compete in different ways for any particular deal. These issues will be explored further in the discussion of competition, firm risk-appetite, and their varied enactment by underwriters.

5.3. GENERAL UNDERSTANDINGS: BASIS OF COMPETITION

Reinsurance firms do not compete by trying to get a higher price than their competitors or by trying to win a deal through offering the lowest price (see Chapter 2). Rather, the general understanding is that reinsurers compete through a very specific renewal process, first to shape the eventual consensus reached on price, and then to take greater shares of those deals that—for various reasons—they consider most valuable.[2] We will describe this general understanding of competition through the various stages of the renewal process below.

5.3.1. Competition to Establish and Influence the Price

At quoting, competition is limited to a reinsurance **panel***** that is selected on a deal-by-deal basis by the cedent, usually in conjunction with the **broker***. Quoting a deal is a competitive move for reinsurers because it establishes the ballpark from which the cedent sets the consensus price they are willing to pay reinsurers for holding capital to cover a deal. As we saw in The Buyer's Perspective in Chapter 2, when faced with the quotes from a panel of reinsurers, the cedent wants to select the lowest price they can—in order to pay the least possible for reinsurance—yet they must select a price high enough

---

[2] As explained in Chapter 2, we saw no evidence of collusion or reinsurers operating as a cartel to set the consensus price. Indeed, a 2013 European Commission report conducted by Ernst & Young into the London market, which has the most potential for such collusion, found no evidence of improper alignment of premiums and noted that the intensely competitive nature of the reinsurance market ensures that reinsurance is traded on competitive terms (Ernst & Young. 2013. "Study on Co(re)insurance Pools and on Ad-hoc Co(re)insurance Agreements on the Subscription Market." Luxembourg: European Commission).

to ensure that enough reinsurers want to take shares to ensure **full cover-age*** of the deal. During quoting, reinsurers seek to both shape the consensus price and assert their power and significance as **market-makers*** in the quoting process (Abolafia, 1996; Baker, 1984). For example, an underwriter in a small firm with a limited number of employees explained the importance of quoting: "We don't have a lot of resource but want to quote as much as we can. We want to be a voice in the price" (Observation, Reinsurer, Underwriter, Continental Europe).

Because this is a competitive process, underwriters do not know what others are quoting, but must pitch their own evaluation "blind". As noted in Chapter 2, there is a rule of thumb that firms want to be on the high side in their quote, in order to shape the consensus price upwards. Indeed, many underwriters explained to us that they aimed to be in the top 25 percent of all quotes. As one underwriter reflected, his strategy was often to explicitly say: "I'm going to quote up here [i.e. be expensive] . . . because if I quote high there's a chance that'll help drag up that [eventual consensus] price a little bit" (Reinsurer, Interview, Underwriter, London). However, at the same time underwriters never want to be too high, in case they are not considered for a share by the cedent (the other basis upon which they compete). As those in the industry explained: "If our quote is far too high the chance for getting any share is just gone" (Interview, Reinsurer, **Account Executive***, Continental Europe); "If I'm too far out [of the benchmark] they'll ignore it, if it's within a reasonable range they take it into account [in devising the consensus price]" (Interview, Reinsurer, Underwriter, London).

Reinsurers may not always want to quote on the high side, however. Sometimes, based on a firm's risk-appetite, a deal may appear particularly attractive to an underwriter during the evaluation process, perhaps because they want to grow in this type of risk, so resulting in a less expensive quote. A less expensive quote is a strong signal to the cedent that a reinsurer is interested in a deal, and it may secure that reinsurer the desired share. However, the reinsurer will never want to provide a quote that is **too** low that it becomes a market outlier; if so, the cedent will disregard it as a naïve price that other reinsurers will not follow.

Signaling a reinsurer's significance as a partner to the cedent during quoting is also a critical competitive move in terms of setting the price. As one manager explained about a deal where his firm's quote was selected as the consensus price: "We were able to get the price we wanted, because the customer values our relationship, our technical expertise, and that we understand what they are doing" (Interview, Reinsurer, Executive, Continental Europe). That is, the cedent had confidence in this reinsurer's expertise in evaluating their deal, because of their long-term relationship. The reinsurer's reputation with peers can also be important to the cedent. For instance, ReinsurerA might have a recognized reputation for technical expertise that means other firms will follow their price if it is set as the consensus price—that is, other reinsurers will recognize ReinsurerA's price as a well-researched one, and will be encouraged to take shares at that price. Further, because cedents wish to be certain that reinsurers will pay out in the event of any loss, they therefore consider quotes in the light of the reinsurer's **security rating***, as an indication that they are strong enough financially to pay the claims if "the big one" hits; and their claims handling, for instance whether firms pay claims quickly or slowly. Reinsurers know that all these desirable qualities can be used competitively, to encourage the cedent to take their quoted view of the price.

Finally, through their quote reinsurers indicate the share they want at the price they are quoting, and this is a formal obligation to provide that share if that quote is accepted as the price. Hence, at quoting, underwriters commit their firm's capital. As those firms offering a bigger share are typically more important to cedents (Dupont-Courtade's, 2013), this allows firms willing to offer a large share to stand out from a reinsurer offering a small share. Through these various means, some reinsurers become market-makers, whose voice is privileged on particular deals (Abolafia, 1996; Baker, 1984).

5.3.2. Competing for Share During Quoting and at the Point of Capital Allocation

Even during quoting, reinsurers are already competing for their eventual share of a deal. In particular, quoting is perceived by cedents and brokers as an important service in evaluating a deal (Chapter 2). Those who quote are typically seen as serious competitors and rewarded with larger shares. The main shares on a cedent's deal will go to reinsurers who have provided quotes within the ballpark of the eventual consensus price:

> If you quote and even if the final price is not your quote but it's still within the range, and then you wish to have a share, then usually you get a share. If you quote, usually you will get a share if you are still within the market and not too far off. (Interview, Reinsurer, Executive, Continental Europe)

During quoting, underwriters already indicate the share of a deal they are willing to take at a particular price. This then becomes the basis of competition for a share of a deal once the consensus price is set. Nonetheless, the competition for share is most apparent once the consensus price is set: "We're all going to get the same [price] at the end of the day. The difference is how much we get out of that deal" (Interview, Reinsurer, Executive, Bermuda).

If a reinsurer's quote is the consensus price chosen, they are obliged to provide the share given at quoting, if the cedent offers that to them. Otherwise, after the cedent issues the consensus price, competition is enacted through underwriters identifying whether to continue to participate, and then whether to reduce, retain or increase share on the deal relative to the quote, or to last year's share. Even when the panel of reinsurers providing capital on a deal is consistent from year to year, the actual share each takes fluctuates at each renewal according to the competitive dynamics. In particular, as reinsurers compete to retain or increase their desired share on the deals that are most attractive to them, this can often mean taking a share from others on the deal. Our field observations help to illustrate this point. One evening as the renewal deadline approached, an underwriter, Felix, received an email regarding the share he had been allocated by CedentA on an attractive deal. Leaping to his feet, he punched the air with exhilaration, exclaiming, "Yes! I screwed Capital Re [competitor]. I got an extra US$200,000 share off CedentA and Capital Re lost out!" (Observation, Reinsurer, Underwriters, London). Felix and his colleagues all considered increasing their share, at the expense of Capital Re, to be a competitive win.

After the consensus price is established, competition is also opened up to additional reinsurers that are approached to take a share of the deal at that consensus price. Namely, reinsurers who not quote often still compete for a share once the consensus price is set, if the deal's consensus price meets their internal model for profitability. This increases the number of competitors at this stage compared to the more limited panel of reinsurers during quoting. The newcomers at this stage are sometimes termed **capacity*** providers, or following markets, helping to fill out coverage of a deal by following a price that has been made without their input.

5.4. COORDINATING COMPETITION: REINSURER RISK-APPETITE

As we have seen in Chapter 4, deals fall into many different risk-types from Aviation, to Property Catastrophe, to Casualty, each of which is more or less attractive to a reinsurer according to its risk-appetite. Risk-appetite is defined as "the amount and type of risk an organization is willing to pursue or retain"[3] and in financial sectors it is considered part of risk management systems, quantitative tools, and measures (Grossi and Kunreuther, 2005; Mikes, 2011; Power, 2009); usually set and monitored at the "executive" level; primarily by **Chief Risk Officers (CRO)*** and **Chief Underwriting Officers (CUO)***. In reinsurance, risk-appetite is fundamentally a reinsurer's appetite for different risk-types (see Chapter 4) and, specifically, particular deals within those

---

[3] British Standards. 2008. "BS 31100: Risk Management. Code of Practice," ISO 2002. "ISO/IEC Guide 73: Risk Management: Vocabulary, Guidelines for Use in Standards."

risk-types. As risk-appetite is firm specific, it coordinates which reinsurers compete, and how hard, upon particular deals.

The fundamental concept underlying risk-appetite is diversification. As early as 935 BC the book of Ecclesiastes advised its readers: "Divide your investments among many places, for you do not know what risks might lie ahead," and diversification has long since been a cornerstone of modern portfolio theory (Markowitz, 1952). Reinsurers diversify their portfolios in order to withstand the potential for severe and unpredictable losses (Cummins and Trainar, 2009). Specifically, they assemble a portfolio of risk-types and deals described as non-correlating, which involves spreading the portfolio between different territories, such as Japan and the United States, and risk-types, such as Aviation, Casualty, and Property Catastrophe (Elango et al., 2008). For example, a bushfire on the U.S. West Coast and a flood in Thailand are not apparently correlated: occurrence of one is not likely to exacerbate the occurrence of the other. Consequently, diversification suggests that in cases of a major loss that affects a particular region or risk-type (for example, a hurricane in Florida affecting Property Catastrophe deals), there is still **premium*** income from other non-affected deals to cover the loss. Hence, the risk-appetite of reinsurers—their tolerance for exposure to particular risk-types—is expressed through their portfolio diversification, which varies from firm to firm. For example, some firms will maximize their diversification to cover all risk-types illustrated in Chapter 4 (see Figure 4.1), while others will tend towards primarily Property Catastrophe risks, diversifying only into highly modelable regions.[4]

Risk-appetite is enacted in the way a reinsurer allocates "pots of capital" between risk-types in their portfolio. As reinsurers must hold capital in reserve for all the deals across risk-types that they write, they plan their capital allocation annually according to their desired exposures to particular types of risk: Gulf of Mexico windstorm, Californian earthquake, Japanese earthquake, U.S. Casualty, and so forth. These separate pots of capital form the boundaries within which underwriters make decisions on specific deals during the renewal. For example, once they have committed their allocated pot of capital for Japanese earthquake during the renewal process, they cannot safely commit any further capital to such deals, even if they are attractively priced. If they do, they will over-expose the firm to that risk.

Underwriters therefore enact the firm's risk-appetite in the way they place capital on deals during the renewal, within the risk-appetite framework set by the likes of their firm's CRO and CUO. As underwriters are usually involved in the business planning of their own sections of the portfolio, they

---

[4] As shown in Dupont-Courtade's (2013) study which outlined that while the majority of reinsurers placed capital on the Catastrophe line of business (81 percent) only 39 percent of reinsurers in her sample had placed capital on Liability.

are usually very aware of the firm's capital allocation plan, and this shapes their judgments on how much to allocate to renewing or new deals. Most obviously, within the pots of capital that form the boundaries of their risk-appetite, underwriters will pre-allocate capital to renewal deals, specifically setting aside capital for their most important deals, as a way of enacting the general understanding of renewal business (Chapter 2).

These capital allocation plans are an expression of a reinsurer's risk-appetite; their view of what constitutes adequate diversification to maximize capital efficiency and minimize loss, given the variation in volatility of different risk-types. Highly volatile risk-types, such as Florida wind-storm where losses could run into the billions following a severe hurricane, are capital-intensive; they can be supplemented with deals that require less underpinning capital due to lower volatility, such as a German Motor Liability where losses are stable and infrequent. As one Chief Underwriting Officer explained, a lower-priced and less apparently profitable risk-type, such as Agriculture, can be an important part of the portfolio because it provides capital efficiency in hedging for more volatile, albeit higher-priced risk-types:

> The maximum exposure out of one event that we write in Agricultural is $20 million . . . So you need much more capital to support the catastrophe exposures than in Agriculture. The same applies for the cost of capital. The Agricultural **quota share*** business has a probable maximum loss of something like a 170 percent **loss-ratio***. A catastrophe treaty in the year where a loss occurs, you have a total loss that is 10,000 percent loss-ratio. So the cost of capital to cover an Agricultural deal is very different from Property Catastrophe. If you don't consider that, you're not getting to a reasonable portfolio. (Interview, Reinsurer, Executive, Continental Europe)

Thus, allocating some pots of capital to less volatile deals and risk-types can be seen as an efficient use of capital to supplement the capital-intensive deals a firm might have, even where these less volatile deals might have an ostensibly lower price (Diers, 2011).

Diversification helps to explain how different firms can view the same deal so differently and therefore why they might compete for that deal very differently. We frequently saw underwriters reject deals that paid well, because they had used their pot of capital and further placement would make them over-exposed to the particular risk-type. By contrast, a competitor who was not over-exposed in this profitable territory would have a stronger appetite and be competing strongly for these deals during the same renewal. In general, the relative attractiveness of a deal depends on its level of correlation with other pieces of business already in a reinsurer's portfolio, which is unique to each firm. In the next section we explore the enactment of the firm's risk-appetite.

5.5. PRACTICAL UNDERSTANDINGS: ENACTING RISK-APPETITE

Each reinsurer's unique risk-appetite is defined at the nexus of three intersecting practical understandings (Schatzki, 2002):

- **Diversification**: does the particular deal fall within the range of risk-types (see Chapter 4) for this firm's portfolio? This indicates the extent to which the firm will value the diversifying benefit of that deal.

- **Relationship longevity**: is there a long-term relationship with this particular deal and cedent (see Chapters 2)?

- **Capital availability**: how much capital has the firm allocated to deals of this type and how much remains unplaced at this point in the renewal (see Section 5.4)?

We will show that these practical understandings enact both a reinsurer's risk-appetite, and firm-specific conceptualization of profitability. Reinsurance-as-Practice 5B will introduce two of these practical understandings, diversification and relationship longevity, before each is discussed in turn. As it shows, in practice these understandings are enacted simultaneously rather than separately.

....

REINSURANCE-AS-PRACTICE 5B

Shaping Competition: Diversification and Relationship Longevity

Shaping the consensus (Reinsurer A): Quoting and competing for share. James is an underwriter specializing in Eastern Europe. He works for Diversified Re, a large Continental European reinsurer that underwrites most risk-types and has a presence in many emerging markets. Diversified Re is still expanding into Eastern Europe and is a market-maker there, being one of the main players shaping the price through their strong presence and quotes. As James explained: "The good thing is that most of what I underwrite just tends to diversify the book of business of the firm. So even if a deal does not have a very high price, you still want to write some of them because they are just bringing the diversification." One afternoon a Property Catastrophe deal from a Polish cedent arrives in his inbox requesting that he quote. James immediately sits up in his chair, opening and quickly looking through the material. He has a strong relationship with this particular cedent, having renewed their business for five years. "I've visited them every year since 2005," he explains. "They are one of the best cedents in Poland and I am pleased with their current strategy." He explains that last year they had had a little discussion about price, as he had not been thrilled that it had decreased slightly. However, he goes on: "If I make a fuss over a couple of **RoE (return on equity)*** points then I could lose a long-term cedent I know very well." He opens the **rating sheet*** in Excel explaining: "I will analyze it now but won't confirm my quote until I see their Engineering and Property per-risk deals; I want to drive home that the three are a single package as far as I'm concerned."

Not within their risk-appetite (Reinsurer B): do not quote. A few weeks later, the consensus price has been established for this Polish deal, and a broker offers the deal—at the consensus price—to Mark who evaluates International Property deals at Analytic Re, a London firm mainly focused on Property Catastrophe risk. He has never seen this deal or met the cedent and, as he looks through the submission documents, he laughs at what he considers to be very little data. "They expect me to write it based on this? They are dreaming," he says. He comments that as things are "boringly quiet" this afternoon, he'll look at the numbers. He makes some quick calculations to get a sense of the deal's parameters, and snorts, "With the price as low as this what's the point of looking more closely?" He doesn't want the broker to take the trouble to come back to him and just sends a quick email to say "Thanks but no thanks." As he explains to us: "It's hard as we do want some international diversifying exposure so don't want to cut the communication with Eastern Europe completely. But you also want to get the message to the brokers not to send us the crappy, low-priced stuff." He admits that he doesn't tend to get shown too many deals like this as Analytic Re is known for being quite technical and placing capital on the most analyzable deals. Later that evening, going down in the lift, Mark recalls the "trials" of poorly priced deals at the international desk to his colleague who evaluates U.S. Property: "I do wonder who writes this stuff."

....

5.5.1. Enacting Risk-Appetite Through Diversification Across Risk-Types

There is no magical mathematical formula that determines what level of diversification is required or optimal. While any reinsurer diversifies, each has a vastly different perception of the degree (and type) of diversification that is desirable. Acts of God do not follow a strict law of averages; even uncorrelated events can strike with atypical concentration. For instance, in 2011 earthquakes hit Japan and New Zealand, severe floods affected Thailand and Australia, and five severe windstorms blew through the United States; all of them non-correlating events occurring during the same year. Consequently, diversification is a social practice that manifests differently in different firms. Many firms **do** believe in maximum diversification, competing across many different risk-types and considering each attractive for its diversifying benefits (even if they fluctuate in their price). Other reinsurers will still diversify but within a smaller array of risk-types. Indeed, some firms might describe diversification into lower-return risk-types as "worsification", believing that maximum diversification erodes profitability because it encourages them to evaluate those lower-priced or harder-to-calculate risks explained in Chapter 4. Risk-appetite thus involves the values attributed to particular metrics (e.g. Aspers, 2009; Helgesson and Muniesa, 2013; Lamont, 2012),

Table 5.1. Examples of How Diversification Shapes Appetite for Risk-Types

	U.S. Property	Western Europe Property	Marine	Credit & Surety	Indian Motor
Reinsurer A (low span, largely diversifying on modeled risk-types)	✓	✓	X	X	X
Reinsurer B (moderate span)	✓	✓	✓	X	X
Reinsurer C (maximum span to enable maximum diversification)	✓	✓	✓	✓	✓

which are socially constructed in interaction (Mikes, 2011; Power, 2009) and enacted in different ways by different firms.

Variation in the degree of diversification across reinsurers, as illustrated in Table 5.1, leads to differences in the deals and risk-types for which each reinsurer competes. As noted in Chapter 4, the practice of evaluating any particular risk-type is germane to underwriters within a particular epistemic culture (Knorr Cetina, 1999). A firm will not allocate capital on deals without the appropriate expertise to evaluate that risk-type. Hence, reinsurers enact their varying beliefs in diversification through their epistemic span. Firms with a risk-appetite for maximum diversification will have a high epistemic span, meaning they will have different types of underwriters, such as Marine, Property Catastrophe, Credit & Surety, Aviation and so forth, each able to evaluate a specific risk-type. An example is Diversified Re above, which has different teams of underwriters, each dedicated to the evaluation of different risk-types through which the firm's diversification is enacted (Reinsurance-as-Practice 5B). By contrast, a reinsurer with a risk-appetite based on moderate diversification will have a narrower epistemic span. Such reinsurers are often focused on a few risk-types, often dominated by Property Catastrophe, and typically tend to expect higher returns on a narrower range of deals. For example, Mark was one of only a few underwriters in Analytic Re not trading in U.S. Property Catastrophe. In evaluating the Polish deal as unattractive, he was enacting his firm's moderately diversified portfolio of primarily Property Catastrophe risk in more analyzable territories such as the United States, Western Europe, Japan, and Australia.

A reinsurer's practice of diversification shapes the way profitability is calculated. Maximum diversification results in a view of profitability on the basis of the stream of premium income accumulated from a cedent's multiple deals. For example, as James places capital on the Polish deal, which is ostensibly unprofitable to Mark in another firm, he is enacting his firm's risk-appetite, which is based on the view that portfolio diversification is the best use of Diversified Re's capital to mitigate losses and use capital efficiently. Such firms might allocate capital on deals with lower returns in pursuit of their diversified portfolios, as one reinsurance executive explained: "We need to be mindful of the margin on any particular deal as well, but when you have an across-the-board approach, at least you have a more robust portfolio. If you have a loss you have more diversity so it doesn't impact as much of your portfolio" (Interview, Reinsurer, Executive, Continental Europe).

Furthermore, Diversified Re receives multiple deals from the same cedent, such as the Property Catastrophe deal in the United States, the Casualty deal in France, and the Motor Liability deal in the United Kingdom. Instead of treating each deal as a unit to measure profitability, the overall profitability of the sum of deals, referred to as **whole account***, is taken into consideration. Within a whole account, less profitable deals are balanced out by preferential access to a cedent's most profitable deals. A broker explains: "Things are looked at as a whole ball of wax. You underwrite deals which, in isolation, nobody in their right mind would ever do" (Interview, Broker, London). Reinsurers that are highly diversified across risk-types may thus allocate capital on deals with a relatively low profitability measure from a particular cedent, because they gain both a diversification benefit from the deal, and also access bigger shares of those deals that are more profitable. As diversified reinsurers have an appetite for a cedent's entire portfolio (whole account) of deals, their significance to, and competitive position with, that cedent is enhanced.

By contrast, reinsurers with a low diversification across risk-types typically evaluate profitability differently. Underwriters in these firms, like Mark in Reinsurance-as-Practice 5B, focus more on deal-specific return, rather than the overall diversification effect of a deal or the cedent's whole account profitability. An executive explained: "We are obsessed with finding deals that we think are good on a stand alone basis" (Interview, Reinsurance Executive, Bermuda).

5.5.2. Enacting Risk-Appetite Through Relationship Longevity

As explained in Chapter 2 (Section 2.4.1) renewing business across hard (high-priced) and soft (low-priced) **market cycles*** is an industry norm that underpins security and stability of cover. It provides competitive advantages to the reinsurer, because long-term relationships provide important information to support deal evaluation (see Chapters 2 and 3), and also enhance a reinsurer's chances of being allocated bigger shares of deals during **hard market*** cycles. Relationship longevity is therefore a critical consideration for risk-appetite. Committing to long-term relationships with the same cedents requires the continuous allocation of capital to support their deals. The allocation of capital thus does not start with a blank slate. Typically, reinsurers privilege repeat business and have a higher appetite for deals where they have a historical relationship with the cedents.

Indeed, the consideration of relationship longevity also influences a reinsurer's portfolio planning, which in turn shapes the quoting of deals and the allocation of capital to them. On any particular deal, competing underwriters enact relationship longevity to different degrees, according to whether they have an existing long-term relationship with the cedent. For example in Reinsurance-as-Practice 5B, James, who placed capital on the Polish deal, had a long-term relationship with the cedent whom he visits every year. By contrast, Mark had never seen this deal before, and this shaped his view on the deal's attractiveness. This example highlights the fact that on any one deal some underwriters might be privileging, and enacting, their firm's relationship longevity with a particular cedent; while others, who might have strong relationships with other cedents, are not. A cedent will give those in the second group less attention during quoting, and may also give them a lower share on their deal.

Furthermore, the emphasis given to the relationship with a cedent shapes the view of a deal's profitability. Some reinsurers are inclined to consider any deal's profitability on an annual basis, rather than renew a deal in a lower-priced year because of their long-term relationship with the cedent. One executive explained that this was his firm's stance:

> We don't write business we don't think is profitable. We just say: "Look, this is what we do for a living. You can show us your deals and we'll write them or not. Here's the price, here's the capacity"; and it's more or less "take it or leave it."
> (Interview, Reinsurer, Executive, Bermuda)

Such reinsurers will have stricter cut-off points regarding a deal's profitability. At the other end of the spectrum, some reinsurers privilege long-term relationships as a means to compete and will almost always renew business. As one reinsurance executive explained: "It's multi-year, it's a partnership with the cedent without any end . . . the cycle for us is not something that will drive us in a decision to participate or not in a deal" (Interview, Reinsurer, Executive, Continental Europe). Underwriters in such firms are able to take a long-term, relationship-based view of a deal's profitability. Even if the deal is less well-priced one year, the reinsurer retains their appetite for a deal, with the expectation that profitability is generated over the duration of the relationship, as prices on that deal fluctuate across the market cycle. As another reinsurance manager noted, in assessing a deal: "We first consider the cedent, the relationship, and not the relationship of today but the relationship of the past and the prospect of the future" (Interview, Reinsurer, Executive, Continental Europe).

In enacting relationship longevity, all reinsurers will have slightly different thresholds for any particular deal regarding when the particular consensus price is no longer acceptable. For example, while James considered the lower price of the Polish deal adequate (in the light of his long-term relationship with the cedent), Mark did not. Hence, reinsurers' appetite for a deal will vary according to the degree to which they privilege relationship longevity.

5.5.3. Enacting Risk-Appetite Through Capital Availability

A reinsurer's risk-appetite involves another practical understanding, capital availability, which we described in Section 5.4 in terms of the "pots of capital" a reinsurer allocates to different risk-types within the portfolio. The amount of capital a reinsurer makes available for each risk-type may change on an annual basis. In addition, the amount that is available to underwriters to allocate to a specific deal also shifts as the renewal process unfolds, according to how much has already been placed, as Reinsurance-as-Practice 5C shows.

....

REINSURANCE-AS-PRACTICE 5C
Enacting Capital Availability

Leading up to the January 1, 2010 renewal we met Noah, a Property Catastrophe underwriter in Lloyd's who was carefully managing his European windstorm pot of capital. As his firm was reducing their exposure in Europe, Noah had a reduced amount of capital available compared to the previous year, and so was being even more selective on which deals he quoted: "There is little point in sending out multiple quotes I do not then have the capacity to follow up; that would just be embarrassing." Similarly, he accompanied quotes with an explanation of the low share he offered; for example, "I have a limited amount of capacity to allocate this year." By contrast, a firm we were observing in Bermuda had a capital plan to grow in Europe and was therefore quoting on numerous deals that Noah had to bypass.

Capital availability also shaped Noah's activities once the consensus price was released. Noah was generally not competing for large shares on deals; some of his competitors were offering 25 percent shares on the same deals where he was offering 2.5 percent. Yet he also had to be careful to fully allocate his pot of capital so that he would not be left with spare capital after the renewal deadline. For instance, on December 15, Noah accepted the consensus price of some deals with the proviso that his acceptance was dependent on his allocated share being confirmed before a particular date. He explained that this was to protect him from having spare wind-storm capacity on the January 1 that he did not have time to redeploy: it was precious and he needed time to place it on another deal if he did not get the signing he wanted on this deal. The broker got back to Noah that afternoon, explaining that this cedent would not be confirming the share for reinsurers until December 28. Noah explained his rationale to the broker: "I have to have time to allocate this capacity elsewhere if I do not get the share I want." Noah asked the broker to just give an indication of "what you expect us to be signed." When the broker shrugged, Noah said, "So you can't tell me if I will get a share of Layer 3? I would still need to reserve an extra $5 million for Layer 3. Things then become difficult for me if I don't get the share I am requesting and don't have the time to redeploy the capacity!" There was nothing the broker could do that day, but he promised to be back early next week as he might have a clearer picture by then. Noah reiterated that he could not back down on his deadline to confirm the allocation of his share. That evening in the office, Noah looked through his other deals to see which he might be able to allocate the capital to, if the share offered to this deal fell through.

The story of Noah shows that the capital available for one-deal **changes** throughout the renewal due to the capital committed on other deals as the months go by. The available amount of capital changes right up to the **renewal date***, so that all deals on which a reinsurer is quoting and offering shares are considered in relation to one another as part of the competitive process. While capital availability is pre-planned to a certain degree (as outlined in Section 5.4), there is always ambiguity, as reinsurers do not know how much share of any deal they will actually get until very late in the quoting process. Consequently, we often observed underwriters like Noah explode with frustration as they suddenly lost share on deals late in the renewal process, and did not know if they could reallocate that capital on other deals before the end of the renewal.

Capital availability influences a firm's appetite for deals. At one extreme, a lack of capital availability means a reinsurer does not compete at all:

> It depends on capacity. Reinsurers typically say, "I've got this much money I'm willing to devote to Japanese wind storm." If they've got a couple of big contracts they may find they've used up all their Japanese wind storm . . . and then they say to us, "Sorry, we can't do any more, we're closed." (Interview, Broker, London)

Alternatively, if reinsurers have additional or spare capital—perhaps because they have lost shares in some other deals—they will compete more strongly to use that capital on other deals within the designated risk-type. As a result, reinsurers scale up and down the size of shares depending on the available capital for a particular risk-type.

Firms will often alter their capital availability for different risk-types between renewals. This is most dramatically apparent as firms respond differently to large events that cause huge payouts. For example, in the case of the Japanese earthquake and tsunami, which we outlined in Chapter 2, some reinsurers scaled down their exposure to Japanese Catastrophe risk. By contrast, we observed other firms increasing their capital allocation to Japan, seeking to take bigger shares of deals in that territory, to make the most of rate rises. As reinsurers shift the capital made available to particular risk-types or territories, the overall capacity in the market may change, triggering a turning point from a **soft** to a **hard** market cycle, as explained in Chapter 2.

5.5.4. Enacting Variations in Evaluations of Profitability Based on Risk-Appetite

In summary, a reinsurer's risk-appetite comes to bear at the nexus of these three practical understandings. Every reinsurer's risk-appetite is thus unique as its underwriters enact each practical understanding as a nexus during quoting and capital allocation. Table 5.2 offers a brief glimpse of the variation in enacting risk-appetite depending on the emphasis given to diversification, relationship longevity, and capital availability, crudely differentiated between "low" and "high".

The emphasis given to each aspect of risk-appetite is enacted through variations in a reinsurer's conceptualization of profitability. For instance, a reinsurer with low diversification across risk-types considers a deal on a stand alone basis, in contrast to a more diversified reinsurer who may take a holistic view of a cedent's multiple deals spanning differing risk-types (see Table 5.2). As illustrated, the measure of profitability is not only determined by differences in the price metric, e.g. the output of Return on Equity (RoE), Return on Investment (RoI) or Return on Risk-Adjusted Capital (RORAC), but is shaped by a reinsurer's view of the benefits of diversification, or their attribution of value to long-term relationships with particular cedents.

This overview of how a reinsurer's risk-appetite shapes the assessment of a deal's profitability, for instance as "attractive" or "acceptable" (or "appalling!"), adds a final layer of detail to the picture of the deal evaluation process sketched out in Chapters 3 and 4. The practices described in Sections 5.5.1–3 show how evaluation is an enactment of a reinsurer's risk-appetite, in which

Table 5.2. Risk-Appetite Shaping a Reinsurer's Conceptualization of Profitability

	Low	High
Diversification	Profitability calculated on a **deal-by-deal basis**; diversification concerns less central to considerations of a deal's profitability.	Profitability can be calculated on a **whole account basis** to enact a highly diversified "book" of business as part of risk-appetite.
Relationship Longevity	Profitability calculated on an **annual basis**; makes it more difficult to privilege relationship longevity as part of risk-appetite.	Profitability can be calculated on a **multi-year basis**; makes it easier to privilege relationship longevity as part of risk-appetite.
Capital availability	Sets the (fluctuating) parameters within which the calculations take place.	

there is variation in the conceptualization of profitability and the notion of what constitutes a "good value" deal.

5.6. ENACTING RISK-APPETITE AS A COMPETITIVE PROCESS

Enacting a firm's risk-appetite through these three practical understandings unfolds dynamically throughout the renewal process. Such enactment is critical to competition, as it shapes which firms quote upon any particular deal and which are able to access shares once the cedent releases the deal's consensus price. We first outline this process (Section 5.6.1) before highlighting the unfolding competitive dynamics through an illustration of three different firms competing for the same deal (Section 5.6.2).

5.6.1. The Process of Enacting Risk-Appetite

The process through which these practice understandings enact competition is depicted in Figure 5.1, which we now explain.

Which reinsurers quote? The degree of diversification determines whether a reinsurer has the epistemic span that would enable them to quote on a deal. Only a select number of reinsurance firms with the requisite know-how are selected (Figure 5.1, B) to quote for the deal, while many firms do not quote (Figure 5.1, C), of which some would not have the epistemic span to underwrite such a risk-type anyway. Reinsurers are also more likely to quote on a deal if there is high relationship longevity (for instance, if the deal is a renewal) and if they have pre-allocated capital to this deal within the risk-type (capital availability is high).

Quoting on deals. As shown by the shaded section (the ballpark), the quotes from these firms shape the ballpark from which the cedent decides the consensus price (Figure 5.1, B–C). As indicated by the various circles depicting quotes, reinsurers position their quotes in terms of both price and share (see Section 5.3) according to its fit with their risk-appetite. For example, if a deal fits within a firm's approach to diversification, is a renewal deal on which they value the relationship with the cedent; and if they have ample capital available for this risk-type, their quote might be priced competitively within the ballpark (not so high that it prices the reinsurer out of the market) and a large share might be offered. By contrast, if a deal is less aligned with a firm's risk-appetite they might indicate that they want a small share, or price more highly because the reinsurer is willing to walk away if the consensus price is too low (this process will be further illuminated in Reinsurance-as-Practice 5D). Within this process there may also be outliers, indicated by the circles outside the shaded ballpark area in Figure 5.1, which are

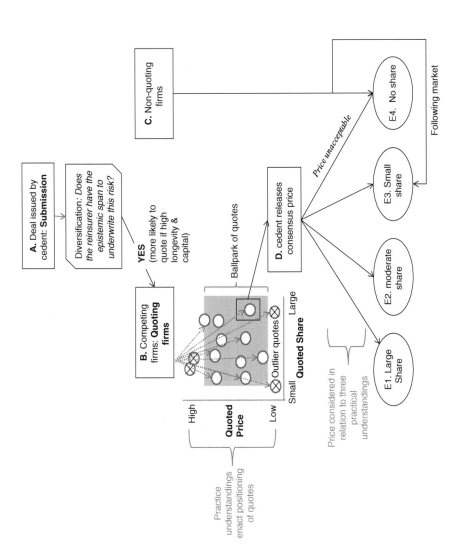

Fig. 5.1. Enacting the Three Practical Understandings During the Renewal Process

reinsurers who have misinterpreted the market by quoting too high or low, so that their quotes are discarded by the cedent in deciding consensus price.

Enacting risk-appetite at consensus price. Once the consensus price is released, underwriters consider its adequacy in relation to their firm's risk-appetite. That is, whether the deal has diversifying benefits in their portfolio; whether they have a long-term relationship with that cedent; and the amount of capital they still have available for deals of that type. These practical understandings inform whether a reinsurer seeks a large or small share, or even no share, at that consensus price. For some firms the consensus price might be attractive, largely reflecting their quoted price and aligning with one or more aspects of their risk-appetite. In such instances a firm will seek a large share (Figure 5.1, E1). By contrast, firms might take a smaller share for a number of reasons. The price might be lower than their quoted price; yet a firm that still has capital available and a long-term relationship with the cedent might decide to take a moderate share (Figure 5.1, E2). Another firm that values maximum diversification might take a small share of less attractively priced business because of its diversifying benefits (Figure 5.1, E3). Finally, for any firm there is a point at which the price is simply "not right" and they decide not to take a share of the deal (Figure 5.1, E4).

An additional subset of reinsurers (Figure 5.1, C) also enters the renewal process at this point. While these reinsurers are excluded from shaping the price, they may evaluate the deal at its consensus price, calculating its profitability according to their risk-appetite. If it is deemed attractive, they may then compete by offering to take a share of the deal. By taking a small share on a deal, they become a "following-market" (see arrow from Figure 5.1, C to E3); that is, a reinsurer who competed for a share without shaping the consensus price (see Section 5.3). This group of reinsurers can be essential to cedents to provide capacity—that is, the capital necessary to ensure full coverage of the deal, when it is not fully shared by the quoting reinsurers.

5.6.2. Enacting Competition Through Practical Understandings: An Empirical Illustration

We now illustrate the process depicted in Figure 5.1 through an empirical illustration that shows how the enactment of several reinsurers' risk-appetites forms competition for deals. We do this in three parts. We will first illuminate how competition is enacted through variation in reinsurers' risk-appetite at the stage of quoting and consensus price (Part A). The decision-making processes of the cedent in establishing both the consensus price and the shares to allocate to firms are then explained, to show how and why reinsurers gain traction through these competitive actions (Part B). We conclude by showing competition for a share after the consensus price has been set (Part C).

Part A. Competing during quoting. We observe the dynamics of three players with varying risk-appetite for BigCat, a large Property Catastrophe **excess-of-loss*** deal (the most common form of deal) from a major global insurance firm, GlobalInc. GlobalInc has multiple deals in the market aside from BigCat as it insures several risk-types in many regions of the world. Two of the three reinsurers, Mega Re and Property Re, have a strong risk-appetite for the BigCat deal, while Price Re's appetite is less strong, and this affects how they each compete—both to shape the consensus price, and for a share of this deal.

....

REINSURANCE-AS-PRACTICE 5D

Quoting: Competing to Shape Price and for Share

Company 1. Mega Re—submission (December 2). Christina is a senior underwriter for Mega Re, based in one of Europe's main reinsurance trading hubs. She has been preparing for the arrival of BigCat from GlobalInc for a few weeks. With her assistant and **modelers***, she has done a preliminary analysis and is waiting for the finalized figures to complete the detailed analysis. As Mega Re is a major reinsurer on most of GlobalInc's deals, she has also had a couple of meetings with the Account Executive and her colleagues to coordinate their thinking about the approach to GlobalInc's multiple deals. She currently has a 25 percent share of the large BigCat deal, and Mega Re has provisionally set aside the capital to do so again. Last year her quote was accepted as the consensus price for the lower two layers of BigCat and she plans to follow the same "thorough" pricing strategy this year.

Mega Re—quoting (December 9). After numerous meetings and comprehensive rounds of analysis, Christina sends off her quote. She and the Account Executive had a telephone meeting with the broker the previous day. While the broker warned they had to be price-competitive if they wanted to keep their lead position on the deal, Christina has not reduced her pricing. She is confident that because of their long history and the large amount of capital they can provide, she will be able her to retain her share. She remarks: "They'd be crazy to try and play games with us; they rely on us for capacity on so many other deals as well!" She admits, however, that the reliance goes both ways, as Mega Re accesses various good deals through GlobalInc; she further admits that Mega Re would struggle to reallocate that capacity if GlobalInc were to consider its quote uncompetitive. She feels that her price on BigCat reflects this mutual relationship across all of GlobalInc's other deals, which span territories (such as South America) and risk-types (such as Casualty and Engineering). Indeed, the range of deals they write for GlobalInc is central to their own approach to diversification, making GlobalInc a valuable cedent for them. Hence, they have always offered GlobalInc an attractive price on this deal as they are able to consider the profitability of the client's multiple deals over time as a single package: "We think about it as a sort of package; we know exactly what we are getting from them overall to make it worthwhile." She explains that that means they don't have to be overly aggressive on their pricing on any one deal.

Company 2. Property Re—submission (December 2). Jim at Property Re, a large Bermudian reinsurer, yells out, "GlobalInc's arrived," to the rest of the Property Catastrophe team. He had been waiting for this deal and opens the attached information straight away. After a quick scan he emails it off to the modelers: "Please give this the full works and quickly. Thanks, Jim." As he continues to pore over the data, reacquainting himself with the details, he explains that it is one of Property Re's largest deals; they have been placing a lot of capacity on BigCat over many years. As such, he needs to be careful in his quoting to provide a view that is "tough but also fair" in order to maintain their share whilst trying to push up the price from last year. Later that day he rings the broker to let him know analysis is in full swing, reaffirming that he enjoyed the visit he had with GlobalInc's U.S. team a month ago. He then pushes on with the business of talking the price up: "The windstorm . . . [interruption and listening] yes, yes, I know the tornado didn't actually hit this deal but we did suffer losses on other deals and the recalibration of the models has bearing; particularly for Layers 1 and 2. GlobalInc doesn't live in a vacuum here!" He assures the broker that Property Re has put aside the capital for this deal, but leaves the threat hanging: "The capacity is there if the price is right." As he puts down the phone he laughs, explaining that he is playing a dual game. He wants to maintain his share as he knows the cedent well and he will not find a better quality deal to reallocate his capital; but at the same time he wants a price increase.

Property Re—quoting (December 9). Negotiations have broken down on another of Jim's renewing deals and he has offered a much smaller share. This means he suddenly has a little more capacity to play with in the territory covered by GlobalInc's deal and he is keen to use this capital to cement this critical relationship. Jim therefore provides a quote for GlobalInc that seeks to push the price up a little, while also being a clear statement of the significant amount of capacity he can provide. He knows he is a large enough player to impact the price. However, it is a critical relationship and he wants to be sure to place his pre-allocated capacity. As he explains: "I will not be too aggressive as that might mean I price myself out of the market and get a decreased share." Given that he now has spare capacity he had increased his offered share on all layers to 17.5 percent, ringing the broker to confirm, "At the price I've quoted the capacity is there. If GlobalInc needs it they'll have to work with me on the price." He has sent a clear message: he is committed to the deal and if GlobalInc is prepared to increase the price, then he is prepared to increase his share.

Company 3. Price Re—submission (December 3). Sean at Price Re (a larger Lloyd's firm) opens the deal from GlobalInc that the broker gave him yesterday. They are not a core cedent for him any more, as for the last few years GlobalInc has been reducing the price. Hence Sean has also been reducing his share on BigCat, even though GlobalInc has great data, and this deal fits with Price Re's Property Catastrophe portfolio. He has maintained a small share on the deal as it "ticks a lot of boxes." As he sends it off to the modeler he explains that while it is a reasonable deal and the type of risk with good data that Price Re likes, in recent years he has built more important relationships with some other major cedents that take up a lot of the "precious" catastrophe capacity he has available. Plus, this year the whole company is really under pressure to reduce its exposure to the perils covered by BigCat, so he's not really in a position to increase his share even if the price is good. He laughs that, in his assessment, the price for the past few years was only "washing its own face" rather than making money. He expects he will offer a small "renewal line" at 4 percent for the bottom layers and 2 percent for the top.

Price Re—quoting (December 13). Sean is a couple of days later than he would like in providing the quote for GlobalInc; other things have been keeping him busy. He tells the broker, as he signs his quote, "We have very little capacity for a deal with this type of exposure unless it's priced very well and look—it just hasn't been priced well; I told you last year enough was enough." As he explains to us afterwards, he had decided to quote a little aggressively to send a strong message that an increase in the price is vital. He wants to do his bit to try and get higher rates; "I'm sick of the bullshit cedents think they can get away with in a soft market."

As this case illustrates, each reinsurer pitched their quote differently, based on variation in the way they enact the three practical understandings of risk-appetite. Two firms have a strong appetite for the deal based on their capital availability for this deal and their relationship longevity with this cedent. Both Mega Re and Property Re are consequently **competing strongly** to shape the price and to get a large share of the deal. They are, however, competing slightly differently. The diversification of Mega Re means that they evaluate multiple deals from GlobalInc and are considering every deal's quote in light of those other deals. This is not the case for Property Re, who are focused on this single Property Catastrophe deal and their key role on it.

By contrast Price Re's appetite is very different. They do not have a lot of capital available for GlobalInc and are therefore not too concerned about renewing a large share. Furthermore, they privilege relationship longevity less on this deal compared with other cedents with whom they now have more significant relationships. They are therefore **not competing strongly** for a share of the deal.

Finally, while only two of the three firms are competing for significant shares, all are competing to shape the price. For example, Price Re is still competing to shape the price, with their higher quote explicitly being a competitive move designed to push the price upwards. While the cedent will only select one consensus price for each layer of the deal, all quotes from these and other competitors on this deal, form the ballpark from which that consensus price is selected.

Part B. The cedent sets the consensus price. Following the dynamics outlined in Reinsurance-as-Practice 5D, the cedent GlobalInc receives all of the quotes from reinsurers, including from the three players described above (see Table 5.3). A spread of views on the attractiveness of BigCat is evident, which is grounded in reinsurers' various risk-appetites for such a deal. Based on these quotes GlobalInc must now decide on the consensus price for each layer of their deal and issue the consensus price. For an indication of this step in the process please refer to Buyer's Perspective 5.

Buyer's Perspective 5: The Cedent Considers the Quotes

Out of the fifteen quotes to which the cedent pays attention, the three from Mega Re, Property Re, and Price Re all represent good quality security, long-term relationships and pay their claims. Furthermore, Mega Re and Property Re provide GlobalInc a huge amount of capacity, with GlobalInc considering them, along with a couple of other reinsurers, to be their key partners on this deal. Jane, the senior reinsurance buyer at GlobalInc, knows that Mega Re and Property Re pay their claims on time and are highly secure, meaning that she doesn't need to worry about them not being able to pay if they have a big claim.

Discussing the quotes with the broker, Jane thinks GlobalInc probably aren't going to be able to push the consensus price down this year, which she had hoped to do. However, she is pleased to note that Mega Re—their most valuable reinsurer given their share on this deal and many others—is not pushing for a rate rise. Nonetheless, she can see that Property Re is set on a price increase, which is aligned with the conversations she had with their underwriter Jim during a recent visit. After some discussion, she accepts that she cannot push the price down, given that they cannot afford to lose that large amount of good quality capacity provided by Property Re. Furthermore, Price Re's high quote, along with a couple of others, is indicative that the broader market is expecting rate rises. She worries, with the broker, that if GlobalInc pushes too hard they might end up with a shortfall where they cannot attract enough capital for the deal. Eventually, Jane decides to make the consensus price more aligned with the Property Re quotes (see Table 5.2) on Layer 1 this year to keep that important reinsurer happy. However, on the other layers she feels she can afford to stay with the same price as last year. This is mainly because with Mega Re's lower quote and their large share, she feels confident that a slight concession on Layer 1 is enough to "appease" the market and get the capacity she needs. Nonetheless, it is a little bit of a gamble. As she sends the consensus back to the reinsurers, Jane hopes that the slight increase on Layer 1 guarantees a large share from Property Re and appeases smaller players such as Price Re to maintain their share on the deal.

Table 5.3. Competing on BigCat: Different Positioning According to Risk-Appetite[5]

	Quoted price	Quoted % share
Mega Re	L1: 55% RoL*	L1: 25% share
Competing "hard" to shape	L2: 16.5%	L2: 25%
price and for share	L3: 5.2%	L3: 25%
Property Re	L1: 57.9%	L1: 17.5%
Competing "hard" to shape	L2: 20%	L2: 17.5%
price and for share	L3: 7.5%	L3: 17.5%
Price Re	L1: 63%	L1: 4%
Competing to shape price	L2: 22%	L2: 4%
	L3: 9.2%	L3: 2%

[5] GlobalInc received more than the quotes described here. However, for illustration purposes we focus on the variation between these three.

Part C. Competing for share based on consensus price. Once GlobalInc has established and released the consensus price, competition ensues as each reinsurer decides how much capital to place on BigCat. Here we introduce a fourth player, Peripheral Re, who did not quote but who takes a share of the deal at this stage.

....

REINSURANCE-AS-PRACTICE 5E
Consensus Price: Competing for Share

Company 1. Mega Re finalizing the deal. When she receives the consensus price, Christina is pleased she has got the shares she wanted. She has been pretty confident that she would get what she wanted as Mega Re's capital would be hard for GlobalInc to replace, especially given that Mega Re also writes a lot of their other deals. Indeed, just a few days ago Christina was copied into some correspondence from the Account Executive to GlobalInc's broker enquiring about their signing, and subtly letting GlobalInc know that Mega Re considered participation on their deals as a package, including the less attractive ones that GlobalInc might be having difficulty placing. The inference was that if GlobalInc "mucked them about" on BigCat, Mega Re could reduce their capacity on a whole range of deals.

As the renewal process comes to a close, she hears from her colleagues that, in addition to her large share on this deal, they have increased their share on some other deals with GlobalInc in ways that also help them to meet Mega Re's capital diversification plan. It appeared that the relationship with GlobalInc was solid for another year.

Company 2. Property Re finalizing the deal. Jim is disappointed that there has not been movement on the second and third layer of BigCat. However, he is pleased that the price has increased on the first layer, in line with his quote. He is able to tell his boss that he has pushed through a price increase. Even so, he decides to reduce his share (from 17.5 percent to 10 percent) on the third layer, which is the furthest away from his quote, as a statement that its price is not good enough. However, he maintains his offered share of 17.5 percent on the bottom layers. About an hour after he emails his offer to the broker, he receives a call. While GlobalInc has considered his increased share favorably on the bottom layers, they are disappointed about the reduction on the top layer. They ask if he would also consider taking a small share of an additional "umbrella" deal they have in the market (which is one that Jim has generally ignored). The broker implies that it is only through taking a small share on this additional deal that Property Re could guarantee getting the shares Jim wants on BigCat. While annoyed at the request, Jim weighs the odds and decides the small share on the other deal is acceptable to keep a long-term cedent happy and secure his share on BigCat. On reflection he is pleased. It is actually one of his success stories of the 2011 renewal; he has helped to push the price up, increased his share and reallocated spare capacity.

Company 3. Price Re finalizing the deal. Over in London, Sean swears a bit when he sees the rates. "No one has any brains in this business anymore," he mutters about his competitors, who have obviously not pushed with him to significantly increase the rates. For him it is an easy "price not right" decision, especially as he has so little capacity left because Price Re is reducing their exposure to the territory for this deal. He tells the broker his new offer, staying on the bottom two layers with a reduced share (2 percent) but coming off the top layer completely. The broker is not happy and a lengthy conversation ensues, with the broker threatening to kick Price Re off the deal completely if they don't maintain their share across all the layers. Sean just keeps reiterating, regarding the price: "I warned you last year and the year before." In the end he agrees to maintain a 4 percent share on the bottom two layers, but refuses to budge on walking away from the top layer. It is a strong message; his capacity is there if the price is right but he is willing to walk away, including on the bottom two layers if they do not improve price by next year.

Company 4. Peripheral Re finalizing the deal. The broker scrambles to find the capacity they have lost from Price Re and some other reinsurers who are also playing "hard-ball" on price. Luke, an underwriter at Peripheral Re, a smaller Lloyd's firm who were not approached to quote on BigCat, is approached just before lunch on Christmas Eve with the option to take a share on the deal. As it happens, this year he has spare capacity. Therefore, after sending it to the modelers for a quick, although not complete, analysis; late that afternoon he commits to 2.5 percent on the top two layers. As he explains: "We prefer to be a market follower, we don't quote especially in the areas we don't know so well, we like to follow." It's fine to do that if you are just after a small share, he explains, especially in areas where cedents always need capacity such as Catastrophe deals. The lower layer is too close to the risk (the most likely to be hit by losses) for his liking, given that he does not know the deal well, so he focuses on the two top layers which are less likely to suffer losses. In the end the 2.5 percent he puts on the deal helps use up that spare capacity he had. However, he knows he will never be a major competitor on this deal, or if he will place capital on it again.

Again, competition over the consensus price is shaped by variation in the way reinsurers enact their risk-appetite, as reflected in their different shares on the BigCat deal (see Table 5.4). As we saw:

- Mega Re competed strongly, referencing the package of deals it under-wrote with GlobalInc, based on their **diversification,** to secure their share. It did so due to its high **relationship longevity** and high **capital availability** for this deal (and other of GlobalInc's deals). Writing this deal enabled them to further cement their relationship with GlobalInc's other deals, which was central to their strategy of seeking maximum diversification.

- Property Re also continued to compete strongly for a share of BigCat, both because its **capital availability** was high, and because Property Re valued the **relationship longevity** on the deal. As this particular deal was central to their portfolio, which was concentrated around Property Catastrophe, they were ultimately willing to take a small share on another deal to secure their share on BigCat.

- Price Re was less concerned about competing for share, having failed to shape the price to the degree they wished. In particular, their **capital availability** was lower than Property Re's for this deal, as they

Table **5.4.** Share of Capital Placed on the BigCat Deal Based on the Consensus Price

	Quoting (Fig. 5.1; A–D)		Consensus price	Share taken by reinsurer	Other deals
	Quoted price	% share			
Mega Re Competing "hard"	L1: 55% L2: 16.5% L3: 5.2%	L1–3: 25%		L1: 25% L2: 25% L3: 25%	Multiple deals
Property Re Competing "hard"	L1: 57.9% L2: 20% L3: 7.5%	L1–3: 17.5%	L1: 57.9% L2: 16.5%	L1: 17.5% L2: 17.5% L3: 10%	Umbrella deal
Price Re Competing	L1: 63% L2: 22% L 3: 9.2%	L1–3: 7.5%	L3: 5.2%	L1: 4% L2: 4% L3: 0%	n/a
Peripheral Re Competing minimally	n/a	n/a		L1: 0% L2: 2.5% L3: 2.5%	n/a

were scaling down their portfolio's exposure in a key territory the deal covered. They were consequently willing to decline a share on one layer.

- While BigCat was not central to their portfolio and they did not quote it, Peripheral Re came on to the deal with a small share at the consensus price because, due to losing out on another deal at a late stage in the renewal, they had capital available.

While the case of BigCat is an example of a single deal, firms play out their competitive position on each and every deal through a dynamic enactment of their various risk-appetites, which remains fluid and changeable until the very moment that any particular deal has full cover. As we have shown, there is considerable variation in the risk-appetite of reinsurers and thus in how they compete. We will now explore the wider picture of how these competitive actions construct the reinsurance market.

5.7. RELATIONALITIES OF COORDINATING COMPETITION IN A CONSENSUS MARKET

We have investigated competition in a consensus market by zooming in on the enactment of risk-appetite by underwriters, which informs variations in firms' competitive responses to deals. We will now zoom out (Nicolini, 2009) to discuss the relationalities through which risk-appetite coordinates competition within a market based on consensus pricing.

5.7.1. Relationality Among Deal and Portfolio of Risk-Types

The market for any reinsurance deal is made through the relationality between deals and the specific portfolio of risk-types incorporated within a firm's risk-appetite. No deal is considered in isolation; instead, it is traded in relation to its particular value within each reinsurer's specific portfolio. This central dynamic is particularly illuminated through the fluidity of the capital allocation process. Enacting the relationality between any particular deal and a reinsurer's portfolio evolves during the renewal process as underwriters respond to unexpected disappointments and opportunities that shape their ability to fulfill the portfolio. In particular, changes in other deals in their portfolio impact how they attribute relative value to, and hence how hard they compete for, any particular deal. This continuously unfolding relationality among deal, risk-types and firm portfolio plays out in underwriters' competitive actions of quoting and attaining shares, as they make multiple micro-adjustments throughout the renewal process to enact their firm's risk-appetite.

5.7.2. Relationality Among Firm and Multiple Risk-Types

This chapter has also illuminated the relationality among firms and the vast variation in largely incommensurable risk-types, from Motor Liability, to Terrorism to Medical Malpractice (see Chapter 4), that comprise the reinsurance market. A firm's risk-appetite spans one or more of these multiple risk-types according to the way it conceptualizes diversification as a hedge against the volatility of reinsurance risk, in which over-exposure to a single disaster can blow a firm's balance sheet. Hence, while Chapter 4 explained how the market for each risk-type is made among underwriters across firms, in this chapter, we show that the market is also made within firms, through the relationality between a firm and its particular appetite for these various risk-types. The firm as the site of market-making activity (Schatzki, 2001) thus brings together the relationalities involved in calculating particular deals (Chapter 3) within each specific risk-type (Chapter 4) to understand how relationalities **across** risk-types are formed within the competitive actions of firms. The reinsurance market, with its multiple, varied and yet interconnected risk-types and deals, is also made within firms as their underwriters construct and enact their portfolio of deals.

5.7.3. Relationality Among Firm and Deal

This chapter has also depicted additional dynamics inherent in the relationality among reinsurers in constructing the consensus price for deals that is so critical to the functioning of this market (see Chapter 2). This relationality can be understood in two ways: the firms' risk-appetites coordinate both **which** firms compete for particular deals and **how** these firms compete.

First, risk-appetite coordinates which firms comprise the relevant sub-set of competitors on any particular deal. Only those with a clearly signaled appetite for a particular risk-type, such as Credit & Surety, will be shown deals within that risk-type. Risk-appetite thus narrows the scope of who is competing on, and making, the market for any particular risk-type and deal. Importantly, the wide variety in risk-appetite is critical to match the wide variety of risk-types (Chapter 4), ensuring that they can be brought together within the reinsurance market.

Risk-appetite also coordinates the relationality among different firms' competitive moves, in constructing the consensus price for a deal, as shown in Section 5.6 where we observed three reinsurers all pitching for the same deal on a different competitive basis. While this competitive variety makes pricing more complex, it has a stabilizing effect on the overall availability of capital to cover reinsurance deals. The variation means that even when one competitor considers a deal less attractive, and perhaps reduces its capital, there will likely be other firms with alternative risk-appetite that continue to compete strongly for that deal, as in our case of the BigCat deal. Variation in how firms compete on deals consequently means that both price wars and vastly inflated prices are less likely. A reinsurer cannot radically undercut competitors based on price, as the other competing firms will have varied views of the deal's value that will shape the ballpark from which consensus price is established (see Figure 5.1). As cedents want to gain complete cover for a deal from a panel of reinsurers (see Chapter 2, Section 2.4.1), they tend to establish consensus price not from outliers but from a quote that can be met by a wide number of competitors, stabilizing both the flow of capital and maintaining the underlying principle of collective risk bearing across multiple reinsurers. Variation in risk-appetite therefore constrains (Abolafia, 1996) the extremes of opportunistic competitive behavior in pricing by any individual player.

How firms compete on any particular deal also shapes their influence on the market for that deal. Some firms are market-makers (Abolafia, 1996; Baker, 1984; Zaloom, 2006) in the competition for any particular deal. For example, in Reinsurance-as-Practice 5D, Mega Re and Property Re were particularly influential in shaping the consensus price on BigCat. While Price Re was still important as part of the overall shaping of price, it was not a market-maker. That is, some reinsurers dominate the shaping of consensus price for a deal. Yet this dominance is not absolute, but always relational to the actions of competitors. If Mega Re, for instance, misread the actions of its competitors, the stage of the market cycle, or the price tolerance of the cedent, the collective actions of others in the market would mean that Mega Re could lose the position of market-maker on that deal to another competitor. The practice of individual market-makers is, therefore, still related to the collective practice of the market (Schatzki, 2001). Even extreme moves from one market-maker will be smoothed by the variation in the moves of their competitors. Hence all voices remain important—all are relational as described in Chapter 2— even if some are more or less dominant in shaping the consensus on any particular deal.

5.7.4. Relationality Between Firm and Market Cycle

This chapter provides additional insight into the relationalities behind market cycles, which we described in Chapter 2 as rippling "outwards" from an event to impact multiple risk-types. As a firm allocates capital to multiple risk-types, it does not experience the impact to its capital of an event such as the Thai floods (see Chapter 2) as a discrete "risk-type specific" event. Rather, it impacts upon the firm's portfolio as a whole and can affect how it competes in the market more broadly. Namely, capital availability within the firm generally decreases, which has an effect on all the risk-types in its portfolio (as shown in Section 5.6). Hence, the relationality between firm and risk-types underpins the pricing ripples and market cycles described in Chapter 2, showing why price fluctuations are not necessarily confined to particular deals or risk-types.

The relationality between particular firms and multiple risk-types also stabilizes the capital flows between cycles in the reinsurance market. This is a market **for** large-scale events and risk-appetite informs the firm-level response to those events from one year to the next. Variation in the risk-appetite of different firms is a stabilizing element as different reinsurers' individual portfolios are impacted in different ways by an event. Based on this variation, as some firms scale down their exposure to a particular risk-type through changing how they compete for deals, others might increase their capital because the deal meets some aspect of their risk-appetite, so ensuring continuity of supply within the overall hardening and softening of the market cycle (see also Chapter 2). In this way, the relationality between individual firm and multiple risk-types, coordinated by firm risk-appetite, is critical to "making" the cycles that characterize the reinsurance market but also in stabilizing the flow of capital within them.

5.8. FURTHER THEORIZING

This chapter also speaks to theories of **risk-appetite** (Mikes, 2011; Power, 2009), **evaluation** in making financial markets (Antal et al., 2015; Aspers, 2009;

Helgesson and Muniesa, 2013), and opportunism and restraint in relation to market stability (Baker, 1984; Abolafia, 1996). This chapter is consequently relevant to social studies of accounting (Chenhall et al., 2013; Fauré and Rouleau, 2011; Mikes, 2011; Miller and O'Leary, 2007; Whittington, 2011) as well as those interested in the practice of financial markets more generally. Furthermore, in focusing on firm as the site of practice and explaining competitive dynamics as practical enactment of risk-appetite, insights here are also of interest for those adopting a strategy-as-practice perspective (Jarzabkowski et al., 2007; Johnson et al., 2007); particularly those interested in linking micro-practices within firms to broader competitive dynamics (Jarzabkowski and Spee, 2009; Vaara and Whittington, 2012; Whittington, 2006).

In investigating the practice of firm risk-appetite, we draw from the strengths of two related but separate research areas—social studies of accounting and social studies of finance—to enable new insight into market making. The social studies of accounting literature (e.g. Ahrens and Chapman, 2007; Mikes, 2011; Power, 2009) has focused internally upon risk management and control practices in different types of firms, while social studies of finance (e.g. Beunza et al., 2006; Knorr Cetina and Preda, 2004; 2012; Millo and Mackenzie, 2009) has focused on the construction of markets but rarely on the role of "the firm" in that practice (Vollmer et al., 2009). In this chapter, we address these respective "gaps" by building greater understanding of the firm as a site for market making. Specifically, we extend social studies of finance through showing that the calculative practices involved in making markets (Callon and Muniesa, 2005) are shaped not only by general trends of marketization, but are also performed in varying ways that are particular to specific firms and their competitive positions (e.g. Mikes, 2009; 2011; Vollmer et al., 2009). By adopting this largely neglected "organizational" perspective, we have emphasized the role of competition in market-making, as it arises from the practice of varying risk-appetites in different firms. That is, our different firms all shaped the market for a particular reinsurance deal through the different risk-appetites associated with their competitive positions. Introducing the practice of firm risk-appetite (Powers, 2009) into the broader context of an individual trader's calculative practices and the social structures of markets, points to ripe opportunities for further research at this intersection between social studies of accounting and finance (Miller and O'Leary, 2007; Millo and Mackenzie, 2009; Vollmer et al., 2009).

We provide a deeper understanding of the process of evaluating risk in financial markets by showing, first, that the practice of firm risk-appetite is dynamic, involving continuous adjustments in the evaluation of a deal (Lamont, 2012; Vatin, 2013), and second, explaining variations in the way different firms define the "value" of any deal (e.g. Helgesson and Muniesa, 2013; Lamont, 2012; Zuckerman, 2012). Specifically, as Reinsurance-as-Practice examples 5D–E show, the different ways that firms in the same market evaluate the same deal is entwined with their particular risk-appetite. Further, this risk-appetite is dynamic, evolving over time (Power, 2009), and varies between firms. There might be a recognizable process (Beunza et al., 2006; Kalthoff, 2005) or commonly used tools (Millo and Mackenzie, 2009; MacKenzie, 2011) associated with evaluation in this market (Chapters 3 and 4). However, there is great variation in what is considered "valuable" as an outcome of this evaluation process. Examining evaluation through the practice of firm risk-appetite can help explain the multiple ways that firms value risk, and how this can vary, both within a firm over time, and also between firms. Our approach thus extends understanding of the evaluative dynamics of market making from the perspective of firm-level portfolios.

This chapter further addresses the notion of stability and opportunism in financial markets (Abolafia, 1996; Fligstein, 2001) that were raised in Chapter 2. While competition might be thought to exacerbate some forms of opportunism, such as escalation of price (Abolafia and Kilduff, 1988), we show the checks and balances that constitute restraint being enacted in the practice of competition. For example, the basis of competition in this market, whereby traders compete to shape the ballpark from which the consensus price will emerge restrains opportunism; the price is based on this ballpark rather than overly expensive or cheap outliers (see Figure 5.1). Similarly, variation in the risk-appetite of firms, and thus how they compete for specific deals, has a stabilizing influence on capital flows; for example, if Firm A withdraws from a deal, Firm B might still be competing to place capital on that same deal, so generating dynamic checks and balances on price fluctuations. Identifying stability as inherent in the practical enactment of competition provides a more nuanced explanation of market stability than existing studies of how restraint is enforced and monitored by structures such as regulatory institutions (Abolafia, 1996; Fligstein, 2001; Fligstein and Mara-Drita, 1996), embeddedness in social networks (Baker, 1984; Granovetter, 1985; Uzzi and Lancaster, 2004) and cultural and normative influences on appropriate behavior (Abolafia, 1996; Baker, 1984; Zaloom, 2006).

We have also developed a dynamic and processual treatment of the practice of risk-appetite, and thus risk management more broadly. This meets a call for deeper understanding of accounting practices (O'Leary and Miller, 2009), including the process of risk-appetite specifically (Power, 2009). We show risk-appetite to be variably constructed within firms as a dynamic process that is enacted in an individual's moment-by-moment engagement with the specifics of any particular risk, rather than being a largely stable property of the firm. Our approach adds three insights to an understanding of firm risk-appetite and the related concept of risk management. First, we more explicitly connect notions of risk-appetite and associated practices such as risk management and capital availability (Mikes, 2011; Power, 2009) to the practice of trading (e.g. Millo and Mackenzie, 2009). This allows us to highlight the role of traders in enacting risk-appetite. In doing so, we emphasize the importance of not conceptualizing risk management as a separate control function that is distinct from trading but rather of seeing the two as entwined, which has rarely been addressed in social studies of accounting. Second, we add to those that have highlighted variation in the way the practice of risk-appetite is managed between firms (Mikes, 2009; 2011), showing additional ways this variation can manifest, such as different beliefs in diversification, and its implications for market-making. Finally, we extend the notion of risk-appetite through developing a more multi-faceted picture of the specific practical understandings that underpin it: belief in diversification; relationship longevity, and capital availability. Drawing from this example, future research might more fully delve into the various dimensions that inform the practice of risk-appetite.

Finally, this chapter shows how underwriters, through their dynamic and continuously unfolding practice, enact the competitive positions of their firms. It consequently speaks directly to the strategy-as-practice agenda for an understanding of strategy and its practice that extends beyond top managers (Floyd and Lane, 2000; Mantere and Vaara, 2008; Rouleau and Balogun, 2011) or those specifically labeled strategists (Jarzabkowski and Spee, 2009; Whittington et al., 2003). Strategy-as-practice studies have increasingly identified middle managers (Balogun and Johnson, 2004; 2005; Mantere, 2008; Regnér, 2003), sales managers (Rouleau, 2005), and even orchestra members (Maitlis and Lawrence, 2003) and academics (Jarzabkowski, 2008) as strategic actors, whose practices are strategically consequential for their firms. This suggests that to understand "strategy" we must examine those who undertake critical actions that support the emergent enactment of a firm's strategy. This chapter provides such an illustration of underwriting or risk-trading as strategy work; showing how underwriters, as professional actors with high decision-making autonomy, enact core aspects of their firms' competitive strategies, such as how best to fulfil their firm's business portfolios, within their everyday practice. Future strategy-as-practice research can further explore the role of "traders", or other professionals such as analysts, as a specific type of strategist and examine how their strategy work shapes the competitive dynamics of markets. In so doing, our study can be built upon to address the call for studies that "zoom out" to connect localized strategy work with a larger nexus of practice (see Jarzabkowski et al., 2007; Nicolini, 2013; Vaara and Whittington, 2012; Whittington, 2006; Whittington et al., 2003).

5.9. CONCLUSION

This chapter has shown that the market consists of multiple firms with different appetites for various deals and risk-types. Firms have been shown as the site in which multiple risk-types are brought together, and the mosaic of competitive moves by those firms has emerged as critical in making this market. We have ultimately highlighted the stabilizing effect of these diverse risk-appetites for trading risks, as they stabilize the capital flows to multiple types of risks with varying profitability measures, and over pricing cycles.

This chapter again shows the careful balance, constructed within a web of relationalities, which constrain opportunism even as trading practices are shown to be competitive (Chapter 2). For example the general understanding around competing to shape the price—rather than to provide the cheapest quote—is an important feature of this market that enables the relationality inherent in collective risk-bearing. In Chapter 6, however, we explore how these densely interwoven checks and balances within the market are beginning to unravel as new players and products, unconnected to the existing relationalities, enter the market.

Summary

In this chapter we have:

- Shown how the enactment of **firm-specific risk-appetite** is a fundamental site for market making activity. We introduce this with an example of Growth Re's expanding risk-appetite (in Reinsurance-as-Practice 5A).
- Shown how the general understanding of **competing to shape the consensus price** and to attain shares of a deal, is integral to making this market.
- Shown how **variation in firms' risk-appetites,** based on their different beliefs about the benefits of diversification across multiple or few risk-types, coordinates both **how hard firms compete** for particular deals, and **which firms comprise the market** that bears collective risk upon those deals. We illustrate how risk-appetite shapes competition through an example of four different firms each competing on a different basis for a share of the GlobalInc BigCat deal (Reinsurance-as-Practice 5D–5E).
- Shown how underwriters enact the risk-appetite of their firms through the practical understandings of: **diversification, relationship longevity**, and **capital availability**, which comprise part of their evaluative practice. We illustrate this through the narrative of James and Mark, each with very different appetites for the same Polish deal (Reinsurance-as-Practice 5B); and through the story of Noah, lacking available capital with which to compete for European Property-Catastrophe deals (Reinsurance-as-Practice 5C).

6

Unraveling the Nest

From a Market for Acts of God to a
Market for Commodities

6.1. INTRODUCTION

Thus far much of this book has examined the marketization of risk—the practice through which varied risks are converted into comparable and tradable objects within a financial market—from the perspective of the reinsurers who supply their capital to cover such risks in return for premium. However, marketization of risk also covers buyers, as cedents make decisions on how much risk cover to buy and how to structure this cover into deals that they can put to the reinsurance market. Any change to cedents' reinsurance buying behavior, such as those of QBE in Reinsurance-as-Practice 6A, thus impacts on the making of a market for Acts of God.

....

REINSURANCE-AS-PRACTICE 6A
QBE Changes the Playing Field by Bundling Risk

In late 2012 a rumor spread that Berkshire Hathaway was in discussion with QBE, one of the largest global insurers in the market[1], about taking a share in QBE's global catastrophe reinsurance deal. Reinsurers with shares on this deal had recently paid out on Hurricane Sandy, so they might well have been expecting the traditional "payback" in the form of rate rises at the next renewal. Instead, Berkshire Hathaway negotiated a 15 percent share of this enormous global catastrophe deal. Given that 80 percent of the deal was already placed with three large reinsurers on a three-year basis, many of the smaller reinsurers on this deal had their renewals terminated in consequence. These smaller reinsurers were thus denied any payback from QBE for their losses on Sandy. Worse, for many, even

---

[1] McNestrie, A. 2012. "Big Cat Spenders." *Insider Quarterly*, Autumn.

losing a small share on this global deal, one of the largest in the market, meant going without a significant amount of important premium income.

In 2010, QBE had departed from the traditional way of buying reinsurance cover. Rather than the some 240 separate deals that they had been buying, each distinguished in the typical way, according to peril and territory, QBE would combine the lot into just five main deals to cover their entire global portfolio. These would include the catastrophe deal above that bundled multiple territories and perils into a single global cover, renewable every three years, rather than annually. They developed this unique, multi-year, global catastrophe deal with two of the largest reinsurers who had already been underwriting most of their separate deals around the world, and placed 80 percent of the new global deal with these two reinsurers and one other. It was a real shake-up. Indeed, apart from the three reinsurers who had taken the main shares, QBE had struggled to gain market acceptance for their new centralized approach to buying global reinsurance cover for losses from their various divisions around the world. As one underwriter stated publically the issue was "not about price, but about the global nature of cover."[2] However, by 2012 QBE was seen as at the forefront of a growing trend. Others were following, with AIG streamlining its Property per-risk coverage into a single global $1.5 billion deal for the 2013 renewal.[3]

Indeed, the demand for deals that offer global cover was increasing as cedents grew into new territories, becoming ever larger and more multinational. As industry leaders observed at the Standard & Poor Conference in London, consolidation was driving a trend towards more centralized reinsurance buying by these multinationals. QBE was just one case in point: they acquired seven insurance firms in 2010 alone, operating in countries as far ranging as Argentina, Ecuador, Colombia, Belgium, and the United States. There were many similar stories of industry consolidation and its implications at the Baden Baden Meeting in 2012. Headlines from Day One of the conference included Generali's continued drive to centralize its reinsurance spend and ACE's second significant acquisition of a Mexican firm (worth $865 million) in just over a month.[4] Throughout 2013 and 2014 the trend spread, with Mapfre signaling that for the July 1, 2014 renewals, they too would be buying global catastrophe covers.[5] It seems that these huge, global deals bought by large multinational cedents are becoming "business-as-usual" in the reinsurance industry.

....

This chapter will examine how major cedents, such as those mentioned in Reinsurance-as-Practice 6A, are altering the way that risks are calculated and traded, and thus shifting the way the reinsurance market is constituted.

---

[2] "QBE Fills Programme on One-Year Terms after Reinsurer Rejection." 2011. *Insurance Insider*, January 5.

[3] "Consolidation Fuels Centralised Reinsurance Buying Trend." 2012. *Insurance Insider*, November 28.

[4] "Baden-Baden Newsletter." 2012. *The Insurance Insider*, October 21.

[5] "Ace and Mapfre to Follow Global Cat Treaty Trend at 1 July." 2014. *Insurance Insider*, January 8.

As multinational cedents become larger and more diversified, both in terms of their geographic spread and the types of business that they insure, regulators, investors and rating agencies require them to further develop the capital models through which they calculate risk cover.[6] As one cedent explained: "In today's world the regulators are requiring insurers, from a capital standpoint, to start to think like reinsurers. One of the consequences of this shift is that in the long-term, if you understand risk capital and how it works, then you keep more of your risk yourself" (Interview, Cedent, Executive, London). In response, cedents increasingly use portfolio maximization models to calculate risk and demonstrate the adequacy of their capital reserves to cover the policies they assume worldwide.

Such changes are grounded in a pervasive belief in the marketization of risk; that it can be calculated and traded, a belief that predisposes participants to ever-greater faith in modeling as a means of trading risk in ever-more-efficient ways. That is, as cedents become larger and more diverse, they look to generate capital efficiency from the diversity of their business. Specifically, they offset much of the risk they assume around the world internally, based on the way they calculate the diversification of their portfolio. Such calculation enables diversified cedents to retain more risk on their own balance sheet, rather than transfer it to their reinsurers, while also encouraging them to be more efficient in the way that they purchase their remaining reinsurance cover.

In this chapter, we first explain three emerging trends in reinsurance buying, all grounded in a general understanding that unpredictable and uncertain reinsurance risks may be calculated and traded in an efficient way. Specifically, we will explain the increasing retention of risk by large cedents and their shift to purchasing large bundled deals such as those mentioned in Reinsurance-as-Practice 6A (see Sections 6.1.1 and 6.1.2). We will then explain how these changes are accelerating the growth of alternative products for risk transfer, which are traded outside the traditional reinsurance industry (see Section 6.1.3).

Next, we will examine how such changes are fundamentally changing the nested relationality of the reinsurance market (see Section 6.2). We argue that these changes are shifting reinsurance from a market for Acts of God to a market for financial commodities.

Finally, in Section 6.3 we emphasize that the erosion of the existing expertise and system of checks and balances in the reinsurance market is generating an overreliance on models—a reliance that downplays the volatility and unpredictability of reinsurance risk. We draw parallels to other finance sectors to explain why this could be highly dangerous.

---

[6] For example: Financial Stability Board. 2013. "Global Systemically Important Insurers (G-SIIs) and the Policy Measures That Will Apply to Them." July 18. http://www.financialstabilityboard.org/.

6.2. CHANGES IN PURCHASING
REINSURANCE COVER

6.2.1. Cedents' Retention of Risk Reduces Global
Reinsurance Premium

Large multinational cedents are increasingly able to cover their risk internally rather than transfer it to the reinsurance industry, so reducing the overall amount of reinsurance that they buy. This is known as increasing retention, meaning that large insurers retain more risk, being prepared to pay for loss claims that would have previously, or in a smaller company, been ceded into the reinsurance market. Such change is underpinned by an increasing consolidation in the global insurance industry, resulting in larger insurance firms with more diversified portfolios of risk. In managing their diversified portfolio, insurers can afford to pay for less expensive losses themselves, as Buyer's Perspective 6 shows.

Buyer's Perspective 6: Consolidation Leads Cedents to Retain Risk

---

In 2005, a small Slovenian insurance company with a portfolio of local Property, Motor, and Agriculture policies developed a strategy to grow the commercial side of its property portfolio to make the most of the ongoing growth in the Slovenian economy. However, as a small insurer it did not have the capital reserves to fund that growth, and instead depended on large quota shares with reinsurers to raise the necessary capital. Reinsurance thus enabled this cedent to grow a portfolio outside the boundaries of its own capital reserves. Further, the whole portfolio was located in Slovenia, meaning that one severe snowstorm would impact its **whole** property portfolio. Given the size of the company it would have been betting the company, literally, not to buy reinsurance cover.

In 2010, GlobalInc, a large multinational insurance company, bought this Slovenian company as part of their expansion into Eastern Europe. Suddenly, that pocket of Slovenian risk was part of a global portfolio of risk: for example, a snowstorm in Slovenia one year could be balanced by the fact that there were no events in South America. Further, any particular local event could be underpinned by GlobalInc's larger capital reserves. A snowstorm in Slovenia would have little impact on the capital reserves of the parent company, which was becoming one of the most capitalized insurance companies in the world. As Jane, the senior reinsurance buyer for the Group, explains about the new reinsurance strategy she is developing: "You look at the Group picture, before, you could just see underwriters in our new companies, such as the recent Slovenian and Puerto Rican acquisitions, buying huge amounts of unnecessary cover . . . it might have been **quota share***, it might have just been buying down too low, but against the Group appetite for the scale of business we offer they were just burning money. We can cover that on our global balance sheet."

In consultation with the Chief Risk Officer, Jane has decided that GlobalInc can be more efficient in purchasing reinsurance. From now on, all the local operating entities will transfer their reinsurance needs to the Group and Jane will then buy reinsurance for GlobalInc's global exposure. She has decided to bundle the property catastrophe component of a lot of these smaller deals they used to buy into a few large multi-region covers for catastrophe. For example, this year Jane will buy a multi-peril catastrophe deal, including windstorm, earthquake and flooding, for the whole of Europe.

Jane has also been considering the attractiveness of alternative capital, such as a **Cat bond*** available from non-traditional reinsurance suppliers, instead of relying solely on the reinsurance market. She is not sure yet how reliable they will be in the event of a big loss, but will continue to watch the development of these alternative sources of capital closely, especially in terms of price.

As Buyer's Perspective 6 shows, larger cedents are able to increase their capital reserves relative to the cost of risk assumed by their local operating units. Their centrally pooled reserves across multiple subsidiaries are proportionally greater than the reserves that that same unit would be able to generate as a stand-alone company. Furthermore cedents' diversification makes them better able to withstand shocks, as they can pay for an event in one part of their portfolio (e.g. Slovenian snowstorm) from the revenue raised in the rest of the portfolio. Growth provides a sort of "economy of scope" or capital efficiency arising from internal diversification across multiple countries and risk-types. As one cedent said, snapping his fingers dismissively at the impact of large industry events during 2011:

> If we look at the overall landscape of [our large global company], $100 million loss doesn't make a difference to anything, not even to the profit forecast. I mean we had the situation in New Zealand and Japan [the 2011 earthquakes] in the first quarter . . . That didn't change our profit forecast at all. It didn't have any impact. (Interview, Cedent, Executive, Continental Europe)

Such changes have been taking place progressively over approximately a decade but, as the QBE example shows, are now rapidly accelerating. As the reinsurance buyer at another major cedent explained in 2011: "As we've grown in size, really about two years ago we decided that we were of such a size now we could retain much more risk across the whole business rather than allowing our businesses to pick and choose [what reinsurance cover to buy], as that was inherently inefficient" (Interview, Cedent, Executive, London).

This trend towards cedents retaining more risk in-house has two consequences for the reinsurance market. First, the global reinsurance premium decreases, as the small cedents who used to buy cover are acquired by large multinationals that buy less reinsurance cover in total. As another cedent explained in 2011: "The long-term consequence is to reduce the amount of reinsurance that you place; in our case we placed a fifth less than we did just five years ago" (Interview, Cedent, Executive, London). Indeed, while insurance premiums are increasing in the primary insurance market, these increases are not transferred to the reinsurance industry. Between 2006 and

2010, insurance premium—the revenue generated by insurance companies for their policies—experienced a compound annual growth rate of 2.5 percent.[7] Yet during the same period the overall amount of global **reinsurance** premium decreased by 3.2 percent.[8] Indeed, even post the heavy loss-making year of 2011, reinsurance premium only increased by 1.1 percent[9] while the primary insurance industry grew 2.5 percent,[10] where previously the concept of "payback" would have suggested a much greater rise. Essentially, insurance companies, even as they grow their own revenue, are retaining risk rather than passing it to the reinsurance industry. Indeed, reports predict reinsurance growth to lag behind that of insurance; with an overall growth in primary insurance of 3.2 percent expected in 2015; with the corresponding real growth in reinsurance being as little as 2 percent.[11]

A shrinking pool of reinsurance premium has had a devastating effect on some reinsurance companies. As one senior manager explained in 2011: "They [large Cedent] . . . stopped ceding treaties from local operating entities. A lot of meat from the bone was gone for us; we lost 50 percent of our premium just due to this" (Interview, Reinsurer, Account Executive, Continental Europe). Furthermore, reinsurers are increasingly getting the bulk of the reinsurance income that remains from a few major global players, rather than from multiple different smaller cedents around the world. Hence, it is difficult for them to shop around to replace this lost income. The trend of decreasing reinsurance premium is decreasing profitability for reinsurers and accelerating competition for the premium that remains.

Second, the portfolio of risks for which reinsurance cover is sought is changing. As cedents are able to retain risk, they look primarily to reinsure the most volatile Property Catastrophe risks, where large events such as the World Trade Center or Hurricane Katrina can have instant and dramatic impact in losses to property, while buying less cover for other risk-types such as casualty. For example, leading global broking house Aon Benfield reported in 2012: "Workers' Compensation, general Liability, Property and Auto lines of business . . . [cedent] retentions for these segments of reinsurance have continued to increase . . . the market for reinsurance continues to become more catastrophe-centric."[12] The consequence for reinsurers is that the reinsurance premium that is available is disproportionately skewed towards Property Catastrophe risk as opposed to other risk-types, such as those discussed in Chapter 4.

[7] "Global Insurance." 2011. *Datamonitor Industry Profile*, September.

[8] "Global Reinsurance." 2011. *Datamonitor Industry Profile*, April.

[9] "Global Reinsurance." 2012. *MarketLine industry Profile*, May.

[10] "Global Insurance." 2012. *MarketLine industry Profile*, October.

[11] "Insurance Market Outlook." 2014. Munich Re, May. https://www.munichre.com/site/corporate/get/documents_E259064418/mr/assetpool.shared/Documents/0_Corporate%20Website/6_Media%20Relations/Press%20Releases/2014/Insurance-Market-Outlook-2014-en.pdf.

[12] Aon Benfield. 2012. "Reinsurance Market Outlook. Record Reinsurance Performance and Capital." September, Chicago: Aon Benfield.

6.2.2. Bundling Risk Changes the Composition of Deals

The drive for greater capital efficiency is changing the **type** of deal that cedents want to buy. Formerly, they may have put separate deals into the market to cover Property Catastrophe risks in Florida or Germany or Puerto Rico and so forth. Consolidating these risks thus creates a new deal and risk-type that spans all catastrophe covers within a cedent's entire portfolio: a global, or multi-regional, multi-peril cover that we refer to as **bundled deals***. Given their complex composition, these deals are not specific to a particular region (e.g. Florida or France) or peril (e.g. earthquake or flood), but to losses incurred above a certain threshold of incurred losses in any part of a cedent's portfolio. For example, one of the biggest cedents in the world, Allianz, buys a core Catastrophe "SuperCat" deal, which provides coverage in Western Europe, New Zealand, and Australia.[13] These bundled deals are seen as more efficient than the previous mode of buying separate deals for different localized pockets of risk because they enable the cedent to use their internal diversification to cover some localized risk, while transferring the rest to the reinsurance market in a bundled deal; "Fragmented buying is just inefficient; they're spending a lot more than if they did it smarter" (Interview, Cedent, Executive, London).

Increasingly, as shown in Buyer's Perspective 6, a peril such as "Romanian earthquake" is being bundled into a European catastrophe deal, which might also include Italian earthquake, French windstorm and German flooding, or even aggregate risks across the globe. That is, the Romanian earthquake is no longer a separately reinsured risk, but part of a multi-peril, multi-territory deal that is dissociated from the original, localized risks it comprises.[14] Bundling is generating other challenges to the traditional basis of reinsurance. Global bundles are large, technical, and complex to develop. Hence, following the bold move by QBE for a three-year global deal, other cedents are considering multi-year deals that will fix price for two to three years, rather than the current annual renewal practice (see Chapter 2). While most cedents continue to buy these bundled products on an annual renewal basis, such shifts in buying are accelerating.

New practices such as global bundling are fundamentally changing the nature of a deal and its effects on reinsurers and, hence, they affect some of the central pillars of making a market for reinsurance. First, it is affecting the way that reinsurers are able to diversify and to allocate capital within and across risk-types, as explained in Chapter 5. As bundled deals are not territory- or peril-specific, reinsurers cannot simply assemble a portfolio of deals based around their particular risk-appetite. Rather, they have to accept deals that are "pre-diversified", sometimes in regions where they do not intend to compete:

The globalization of the market is such that you cannot ignore it any more because there are clients out there that are not placing local. In the United

---

[13] "Reinsurance Buying: Changing Appetites." 2014. *Bermuda Re, Insurance + ILS*, Spring.
[14] "Axa and AIG to Buy Global Aggregate Covers." 2014. *Insurance Insider*, March 18.

Kingdom our core client base is bringing its peak exposures together and more often than not for us that's meant having [exposure in] Canada. I mean we've got three of our big deals with Canada in it now . . . It's a shift! (Interview, Reinsurer, Underwriter, London)

Second, as these deals are more complex, they are often beyond the knowledgeable calculative practice of a single underwriter as explained in Chapters 3 and 4. For example, when presented with a bundled deal that covers catastrophe risks (e.g. earthquakes and windstorms) in not only the United States but also Asia and Europe, a U.S. Catastrophe underwriter such as John in Chapter 3 would have to work in a team with other underwriters in his organization, such as Ria in Chapter 4, who are knowledgeable in these less modelable territories. The changing composition of a deal, from traditional (single peril, single territory) to bundled (multiple perils across territories), has consequences for the practical understandings required to evaluate such deals. As an underwriter explained to us, when faced with such a deal: "I can use these RMS models, but I do it at a maximum when two or three countries are involved. But if there are too many for me . . . the same storms could also happen in different countries . . . We don't have anyone who can calculate super catastrophe" (Interview, Reinsurer, Underwriter, Continental Europe). Many reinsurers thus have to shift their approach to deal appraisal, both in terms of evaluating a deal, and in calculating how to sell their capital to it. Such changes call for new calculative practices that are still being developed within the market. As such deals began to appear, we observed reinsurers struggling to deal with the challenges they posed:

And we're not ready [for the renewal] . . . it's taken us a week and a half to get all the rough edges smoothed off one particular deal . . . we need to start bringing our pricing into one. They've [the client] ultra-complicated it this year by bringing in a lot of other territories into one big deal. (Interview, Reinsurer, Account Executive, London)

Due to the continuously shrinking pool of global reinsurance premium, reinsurers feel compelled to get a share of these bundled deals despite a lack of practical understanding about how to evaluate them. As one reinsurance manager explained: "These products are there and they are growing more and more. More of what was previously local goes in to these big pots. So unless you write yourself out of the market, you have to be on them [these bundled deals]" (Interview, Reinsurer, Executive, Continental Europe). Hence, the relationality between deal and market is changing. In Section 6.3 we unpack how such changes have fundamentally altered practical understandings about technicalization, contextualization, and risk-appetite, through which the relationality between deal, firm and market has previously been coordinated.

6.2.3. Growth of Alternative Risk Transfer (ART) Products

These trends in the ways cedents buy reinsurance risk cover have exacerbated the growth of **alternative risk transfer (ART)*** products that increasingly compete with the traditional deals on which the general reinsurance industry is founded (Cummins and Trainar, 2009). ART includes a range of **Insurance Linked Securities (ILS)***, such as **Industry Loss Warranties (ILW)*** and **Catastrophe bonds*** (Cat bonds) that are an alternative means of providing capital to cover risk. In a similar way to reinsurance deals, cedents typically issue these products as a means of transferring their risk of a loss to a third party. However ART products are not the same as traditional reinsurance products in at least three critical ways.[15] First, while the various ART products each differ slightly, most do not trigger on the basis of a loss to the cedent's specific portfolio of risks, but on the basis of a particular type of industry loss. For example, an ILW triggers only if the insurance industry **as a whole** loses more than a specified amount, due to a specified catastrophe. Similarly while Cat bonds can be tied specifically to and triggered by a predefined loss to a cedent's portfolio, they may also be triggered by a specified industry loss, or by the magnitude of a particular event, such as an earthquake of a particular magnitude within a specified radius of a particular region, such as Tokyo or San Francisco. Hence, unlike reinsurance deals, which are tied specifically to the exposures in the cedent's portfolio, and so require deep knowledge of the cedent, different types of ART are tied predominantly to modeled probabilities of events and losses within the industry.

Second, the capital for ART—particularly Cat bonds—is not generally offered by reinsurers but by parties in the wider financial market, typically pension funds or hedge funds.[16] These parties invest in the Cat bond, which, in combination with the premium paid by the cedent, is managed in a special purpose vehicle in order to generate money market returns. Should there be none of the identified losses, such as peril of a particular magnitude, or an industry loss to a specified amount, the investors receive quarterly returns as well as the principal back on maturity. However, if the Cat bond is triggered, all or part of the principal is paid to the insurance company. These products arose in the reinsurance market post-Hurricane Andrew in 1992, when there was a shortfall of reinsurance capital and insurance companies looked for alternative solutions to provide risk transfer that was not dependent on reinsurance capital (Borscheid et al., 2013). Hence, the fact that traditional

---

[15] Our intention in this chapter is not to go into exhaustive detail on the various nuances of ART products, each of which has slightly different points about how it is issued and what triggers loss. Rather, we aim to illustrate why this general class of products operates on a different basis to the traditional reinsurance products explained in this book.

[16] Fedorova, A. 2012. "European Consultants Pitch Insurance-Linked Securities." *Global Money Management*, January 30.

reinsurers are **not** the source of this capital is frequently identified by cedents as being central to the merits of these alternative products. That is, they provide a diversified access to capital should reinsurance companies either collapse or their capital become very expensive in the hard market following a major event:

> We have been issuing catastrophe bonds since 200[X] . . . we have had around four or five of them. We are committed to the use of capital markets in our entire reinsurance portfolio in getting catastrophe bond protection. We like it because it's a diversified source of protection because it's not only traditional reinsurers but a lot of investors who are not traditional reinsurers . . . it's multi-year. It's very hard in this marketplace to get multi-year coverage and we do like to have multi-year protection. (Interview, Cedent, Executive, United States)

Third, ART products do not operate on the typical annual renewal basis of traditional reinsurance deals. While ILW are often annual, they can in fact be issued specifically in advance of an event—for example, when there is a hurricane approaching that may or may not hit shore and cause insurance damage, or even after an event, while the industry is still working out what the losses will be, while Cat bonds are typically issued on a three-year basis. These differences to the annual renewal of traditional reinsurance deals (see Chapter 2) make them attractive to cedents for either locking in price on some parts of their risk cover, to offset possible fluctuations in reinsurance cycles, or allowing them to buy specific spot covers for particular events where they might feel exposed.

ART products were initially a complementary product that operated outside the traditional reinsurance industry, providing risk cover during hard market cycles when reinsurance capital was scarce. However, in the past two to three years their importance as a substitute for traditional reinsurance has increased,[17] capturing about 11 percent of the global Property Catastrophe market with a capacity of $45 billion in 2013.[18] Specifically, since 1996, the Cat bond market has seen US$44 billion of cumulative reinsurance issuance.[19] While Cat bonds, together with the hedge funds, mutual funds, and pension funds that write them, took a hit in the financial crisis, they have since bounced back and, by 2012, reached their highest level for new issuances in four years offering $19 billion in cover.[20]

---

[17] "Bonds that Pay Out When Catastrophe Strikes are Rising in Popularity." 2013. The Economist, October 5. http://www.economist.com/news/finance-and-economics/21587229-bonds-pay-out-when-catastrophe-strikes-are-rising-popularity-perilous-paper.

[18] "Global Insurance Review 2013 and Outlook 2014/2015." 2013. *Swiss Re Sigma*.

[19] Aon Benfield. 2012. "Reinsurance Market Outlook." September, Chicago: Aon Benfield.

[20] AonBenfield. "Insurance-Linked Securities: Evolving Strength." 2012. Chicago: Aon-Benfield; "Confronting New Market Realities." 2012. PWC. http://www.pwc.com/gx/en/insurance/reinsurance-rendezvous/assets/pwc-confronting-the-new-market-realities.pdf; "Global Insurance Review 2013 and Outlook 2014/2015." 2013. *Swiss Re Sigma*.

There are two reasons for the popularity and growth of ART products. First, from the supply side they are an attractive product for investors outside the reinsurance industry, such as pension funds, because they are not correlated with other financial products and markets. This attractiveness has increased during a period of relatively low returns on most investments since 2008. Hence, external capital providers are flocking to the reinsurance industry, which previously operated in a more discrete space, separate from and largely "ignored" by other financial markets. As these capital providers are not part of the collective risk-bearing reinsurance market, they and their products work on different general and practical understandings from the traditional reinsurance industry described in this book. Thus, they undermine some of these central pillars that sustain the market-making practices of the reinsurance industry. For example, the issuance of a Cat bond does not involve a quoting process or the establishment of a consensus price (as illustrated in Chapter 2). Furthermore, on ART products there is no expectation of renewal with the same panel of investors. The products simply inhere and expire at set contractual dates, which undermines both renewal business (see Chapter 2) and the longevity of reinsurance relationships (see Chapter 5).

Second, as large global cedents increasingly base their reinsurance spend on assumptions of capital efficiency, ART products have become attractive parts of their suite of risk-transfer solutions. This is because they cover catastrophe risk that remains the main part of the portfolio for which cedents still wish to gain most cover (Section 6.1.1). Hence they fill a need in the changed risk portfolio of cedents. They are also sold on a favorable cost-of-capital basis with traditional reinsurance products, particularly in the areas of peak exposure, such as U.S. Property Catastrophe, which is also the area where traditional reinsurance is most expensive. Their lower price is based on two factors. First, ILW are typically cheaper because they are simple products where price is based on modeled assumptions, while the alternative capital on which these and Cat bonds are based has become cheaper due to a period of low return on investment in many asset classes.

As the CEO of leading insurance company, Allianz's, reinsurance buying division (called Allianz Re) explained to the media, ART products have become a key component of sourcing reinsurance cover: "About one tenth of our overall natural catastrophe protection comes from cat bonds. In conjunction with our protection against U.S. natural catastrophe risks, the share of cat bonds is considerably higher, about one third."[21] Given the size of Allianz, listed as one of nine systemic insurers in the world,[22] sourcing of a third of

[21] Ahmed, A. 2013. "Emergency Relief is 'Only the Second Best Solution.'" Allianz, June 12. https://www.allianz.com/en/press/news/business/insurance/news_2013-06-12.html.
[22] Financial Stability Board. 2013. "Global Systemically Important Insurers (G-SIIs) and the Policy Measures That Will Apply to Them." July 18. http://www.financialstabilityboard.org/.

their coverage for U.S. catastrophe from Cat bonds contributes significantly to the continuous decline in global reinsurance premium. In addition, products classified as ART are growing in popularity for other regions. For example, when asked about their relevance outside the United States, the CEO continued that the application of ART products was increasing to wider sections of the market:

> Yes. For example, Allianz Re has issued a cat bond with European storm risks. In 2007, we covered flood risks in the United Kingdom with one of our first Cat bonds. So the potential is there, and investors are interested. They're also looking for diversification. In the market we have also seen Australian risks and a liability portfolio. So there is movement in that regard.[23]

Third, beyond arguments for capital efficiency, ART also exemplifies the seduction of marketization for many insurers. As insurers become large enough to consider a Cat bond as cover, entering the ART market allows them to make a statement in a way that just buying reinsurance does not: "There's a level of disclosure that goes on with Cat bonds, you know, it's sort of beyond a reinsurance transaction, it's sort of a public relations move to say to the world 'look, I'm sophisticated, I bought a Cat bond'" (Interview, Cedent, Executive, United States). That is, cedents are signaling that they want to tap into new capital from the wider financial market, so that their risk will be borne at least partially outside the relatively closed traditional reinsurance industry.

The implications are grim for the traditional reinsurance market, with its heritage of long-term relationships that coordinate capital supply across market cycles. Increasingly, reinsurers see their core buyers shift to these new products for at least part of their reinsurance spend, and this trend is not confined only to large multinationals. For example, 2013 saw Citizens Property Insurance (Florida) issue the largest Cat bond for a first-time buyer at a level of $750 million. This was a company that many thought would never tap the Cat bond market. However, Citizen's CFO reportedly stated that the Cat bond "came in at a lower rate than what Citizens paid in the reinsurance market last year."[24] Indeed, even though the number of Cat bonds has increased, their issuance is still insufficient to meet investors' demands,[25] a further indication that these products are likely to grow in size and volume and remain price-competitive.

[23] Ahmed, A. 2013. "Emergency Relief is "Only the Second Best Solution." Allianz, June 12. https://www.allianz.com/en/press/news/business/insurance/news_2013-06-12.html.
[24] "Everglades Re Catastrophe Bond was Cheaper than Reinsurance for Citizens." 2012. *Artemis*, June 7. http://www.artemis.bm/blog/2012/06/07/everglades-re-catastrophe-bond-was-cheaper-than-reinsurance-for-citizens/; http://www.bloomberg.com/news/2012-05-23/florida-outperforms-as-hurricane-forecast-improves-muni-credit.html.
[25] Swift, J. 2012. "Willis: Cat Bonds Hit a New High in 2012 With 37% Increase." *Insurance Insight*, January.

ART products are growing in popularity but their efficacy in providing for reinsurance loss is yet to be thoroughly proven. While the traditional reinsurance market has demonstrated that it is robust in the face of shocks such as the World Trade Center, earthquakes, tsunamis, and hurricanes, no event of such magnitude has yet tested whether ART products will be able to respond effectively in terms of both agreeing on losses to be paid, and ensuring rapid payment. In particular, for those that are triggered by levels of industry loss, such levels may take some time to establish post-event, as illustrated by the Japanese earthquake and tsunami and Thai floods in Chapter 2.

The effect on reinsurers is that part of cedents' spend on risk cover is going to ART products that operate outside the collective risk-bearing and consensus pricing of the traditional reinsurance market (see Chapter 2). The abundant supply of new capital flowing into ART products is thus a source of competition that is reducing prices for traditional reinsurance. Indeed, it was noteworthy at Monte Carlo in 2013, where industry players met to talk the market up or down, that the growth of ART was the single hammer driving the market down.[26] By contrast, there was no counter-force pushing the market up. Reinsurers thus face greater competition, and yet the principles on which the market has been based to date are irrelevant for this class of products. Hence, reinsurers face an erosion of their existing understandings about market function, and must scrabble to find new ones, even as other players come into their market on a different basis.

6.3. PRESSURES ON NESTED RELATIONALITIES

My personal belief is that the insurance and reinsurance **industries** are going through a process that will require a certain shift in mindset from the insurance and reinsurance **companies**. If margins are huge we can always play the relationship game because both of us will win, right? The insurance companies have enough margin and the reinsurers have enough margin. One year you might have a loss but you will make it up in three or four years, so we just stick together. If margins get thin, the result will become more volatile and companies . . . will become more opportunistic on the insurance but also on the reinsurance side. And that will have to be accepted, because if you don't get the margins you need, you can't make too many exceptions anymore—because

[26] Zulli, R. 2013. "Convergence takes Center Stage at Monte Carlo's Rendez-Vous." *The Royal Gazette*, 23 September. http://www.royalgazette.com/article/20130923/BUSINESS03/130929916; Collins, S. 2013. "Alternative Capital Causing Stir in Risk Transfer Market." *Commercial Risk Europe*, 28 September. http://www.commercialriskeurope.com/cre/2674/134/Alternative-capital-causing-stir-in-risk-transfer-market/; "Old Meets New as Alternative Reinsurance Capital Grows Share." 2013. *Artemis*, September 7. http://www.artemis.bm/blog/2013/09/07/old-meets-new-as-alternative-reinsurance-capital-grows-share/.

there's not enough margin there just to basically say yes, yes, it's OK, in a few years we'll all be in the black again . . . It's not going to happen. (Interview, Reinsurer, Executive, Continental Europe)

As this reflective comment suggests, these changes in reinsurance buying are already altering many of the principles on which the nested relationality of the reinsurance market is based. When one connection within the nexus of general understandings, sites and practical understandings that make up the distributed nature of the reinsurance market shifts, all others shift in relation to it (Nicolini, 2013; Schatzki, 2001). Hence, such shifts must be seen in light of their fundamental reconfiguration of the market itself. We now explain the specific ways that the changes outlined above alter the various relationalities that we have developed in each chapter. We begin by explaining how these changes are altering the sites of market-making practice.

6.3.1. Altering Sites of Market-Making

As explained in Chapter 1, there are multiple sites of interaction within which aspects of the market are made. In Chapters 2 and 3, we examined the deal as one key site in which distributed individuals interact to shape the market. Specifically, in Chapter 2 we examined the quoting process on deals, through which consensus pricing is established at particular points in the market cycle, while in Chapter 3 we examined the calculative practices that render deals comparable for the purposes of capital allocation. The shift to bundled deals that contain multi-territory, multi-peril Property Catastrophe risks (see Section 6.1.2) constitutes a fundamental shift in the deal as a site. The size of these deals mean that fewer parties have the knowledge or capital resources to have a significant impact on the consensus pricing process, while their multi-territory, multi-peril nature shifts the calculative practice involved in their evaluation towards technicalizing at the expense of contextualizing, as further explained below.

In Chapter 4 we examined risk-type as site, noting enormous variation between risk-types in their quality of information and the extent to which they could be standardized for the purposes of evaluation. We showed that underwriters on different risk-types participate in quite different epistemic cultures with distinct and specialist calculative practices that are attuned to evaluating deals within their specific risk-type. However, in the shift towards bundled deals that cover multiple risks, issues of information quality and standardization are collapsed into a single deal. The nature of the underlying risk is conflated, creating a complex deal that is no longer attached to a specific territory or peril, or to a specific object such as a dwelling, crop, or vessel. For example, a bundled deal can contain both frontier risk, such as those arising from property in territories such as Romania, India, and so forth, in the same deal as highly modelable risk, such as property in Florida. At the same time, many large insurers also retain more of their specialist risk, so depleting the stock of such risks within the market (see Section 6.1.1). Together, these deals that bundle risk, and the retention that removes some risk from the market, mean that particular risk-types and the associated calculative practices within epistemic cultures become less relevant as specific sites for market practice, whilst deals of a new "multi-risk" type emerge.

In Chapter 5 we examined the firm as the site in which risk is actually borne, showing how reinsurers compete for, allocate capital to, and assume risk on different deals according to their risk-appetite. Hence, the collective risk-bearing function of the market is actually enacted by those firms that allocate capital to particular deals and risks according to their specific portfolio diversification. Yet when risk is bundled within a particular deal, the ability for firms to select only those deals that most suit their risk-appetite is altered. For example, a reinsurer that dealt primarily in the most modelable US, Western European, and Australian risk will now have to also accept other types of risk that are bundled in the deal, if it wishes to remain in the market. This means the firm will have to reconfigure the diversity of its underwriting teams to match the range of risk within bundled deals, even as it reconfigures its capital allocation to wider pools of risk, albeit without the ability to pick and choose how it selects the risk within its portfolio.

At the same time new types of organization—the hedge funds, mutual funds and pension funds that are investing in ART products, such as Cat bonds—are becoming more prevalent in the market (Section 6.1.3). These organizations compete indirectly with the traditional reinsurers to supply capital to cedents, so eroding reinsurance firms' centrality as the sites for bearing risk within the market.

6.3.2. Eroding Consensus Pricing and Altering the Basis of Competition

In Chapter 2, we examined the general understanding of consensus pricing that underpins collective risk-bearing within the reinsurance market, and how this is enacted through practical understandings about renewing business on a specific date within a well-established and very consistent quoting process. In Chapter 5 we demonstrated how reinsurance firms compete to shape this consensus price, as part of competing for their share of the deal. However, bundled deals erode the current general understandings underlying consensus pricing and its association with competition.

Because bundled deals are complex, multi-peril, multi-territory, and sometimes multi-year products, they require different forms of calculative practice and allocation of considerable amounts of capital that are beyond most reinsurance companies. Hence, competition over consensus pricing is increasingly concentrated in those few reinsurers that have sufficient capital available to be significant partners for cedents. For example, the headline deal by QBE in Reinsurance-as-Practice 6A was actually developed in conjunction with only two key reinsurers, Munich Re and Swiss Re, who took 75 percent of the deal on a three-year basis in 2010. Due to its complexity, development of the deal took some six months of work with these two major incumbents, with SCOR then taking an additional five percent on the same basis. Only twenty percent of the deal remained on an annual quoting basis, making another big share ripe for the picking by a large player such as Berkshire Hathaway in 2012. Even where deals are placed amongst a panel of reinsurers, only those biggest reinsurers capable of taking a large share of such huge deals are significant in quoting and shaping the price.

Hence, the general understanding of consensus pricing, and the associated practical understanding of quoting through which it is enacted, is being altered. In the process, much of the relationality between firms on a deal is eroded (see Chapter 2, Figure 2.2), since only a few key players have a significant impact on the consensus pricing of bundled deals. Indeed, the very concept of competition changes, as only the largest players can genuinely compete on such deals, as this CEO of a smaller firm noted: "If we talk about the ten biggest insurers; if you look at their deals it's going to be a worldwide Cat XL: $2 billion of capacity. What can we do? How can we be with them? We just haven't got the modeling and also capital and capacity to be a meaningful partner to them" (Interview, Reinsurer, Executive, Continental Europe).

6.3.3. Eroding Market Cycles

A multi-year deal such as the QBE one alters the way that quoting is coordinated around a renewal date. The renewal date ceases to be a meaningful point at which the value of any particular deal can be established in relation to the market cycle, if 80 percent of the deal is no longer dependent upon an annual pricing point. While not all deals are traded in such a way, some deals that command the largest revenue in the industry can no longer be enacted on the basis of a practical understanding of quoting to a renewal date, which has been central in establishing the **hard*** and **soft market*** cycle in reinsurance. The general understanding of market cycles has arisen to ensure stability of capital over the long duration, so that reinsurers can accumulate capital during a loss-free period, albeit at a lower rate because of the softness of the cycle, and can rely on payback for excessive losses in order to renew their capital reserves following a severe loss (see Chapter 2, Section 2.2.2). However, multi-year products flatten the cycle because payback is not triggered on a particular renewal date each year, so altering yet another general understanding about market cycles. Hence, the relationality between deal and consensus price at a point in the market cycle is shifting.

The erosion of consensus pricing, market cycles and competition to establish a consensus price, is compounded by the presence of ART products, and helps to accelerate their growth. Specifically, ART products operate outside the consensus market; there is no quoting process, as ILW and Cat bonds are issued to investors at a set price. ART products may be multi-year and, unlike reinsurance deals, do not work on a renewal basis, either in terms of a specified renewal date or a renewing panel of investors. Hence, they further erode the general understanding of market cycles. Furthermore, because there is ample alternative capital available, most of it not connected to traditional reinsurance, the (traditional) market cycle flattens even further because there is no need for payback; the cedent can simply shop around for better priced capital offered by ART products. Hence, the very notion of reciprocity that underpins the practice of renewing business is changing (see Chapter 2, Section 2.4.1). Renewing business has been based on a practical understanding between cedents and reinsurers that neither will act opportunistically in maximizing their own position at any point in the cycle, but rather will enact reciprocal obligations in order to ensure stability of capital flows across hard and soft cycles. When the buyer no longer needs that reciprocity because capital can be gained from new entrants who do not operate on that understanding, it breaks down. Hence, the temporal coordination of pricing across the market cycle that is currently enacted through quoting upon and renewing business annually on a specific date is being eroded.

6.3.4. Technicalizing Is Strengthened at the Expense of Contextualizing

In Chapters 3 and 4 we showed the role of calculative devices, such as statistical models, within the deal appraisal process. Such devices are grounded in a general understanding about the marketization of unpredictable risks of uncertain value. That is, that they may be rendered calculable, comparable and tradable as financial objects (Çalışkan & Callon, 2009; 2010). At the same time, we illustrated that these models are essentially flawed, even for evaluating the most modelable risk-type, U.S. Property Catastrophe, let alone on risks where there is little standardizable or high quality information available for calculating risk. Thus, we clarified that models do not predict or value the risk, but rather provide the basis for coordination of pricing efforts alongside other knowledgeable practices within the market. Specifically, we showed that marketization is enacted within the practical understandings of "technicalizing" deals through calculative devices such as models. However, we also showed how the inadequacy of the models is tempered by importing deep professional knowledge into the calculation of unpredictable risk. Such "contextualizing" includes evoking knowledge of the physical properties of the risk, knowledge of the client, and knowledge of the market cycle (see Chapters 3 and 4).

The changes in reinsurance buying highlighted in Section 6.2 have been brought about by increasing marketization of reinsurance risk by cedents, which is, unsurprisingly, exacerbating the marketization of risk by reinsurers. Specifically, bundling risk is weighting the appraisal of deals further towards technicalizing and a dependence on models.

First, bundled products decrease both the possibility and also the value of contextualizing as part of calculative practice. As shown with the various examples from U.S. Property Catastrophe to Indian **bouquet deals*** in Chapters 3 and 4, contextualizing involves deep local knowledge of a risk-type. However, bundled deals are not specific to any particular territory or risk; rather, multiple risks are bundled into a more commoditized product that makes catastrophic risk homogenous and generic across vastly different territories and perils. Hence, they have no particular context that may be evoked in their pricing. For example, in Chapter 3, we witnessed U.S. Property Catastrophe underwriter John, factoring features of loss containment around bushfire damage in Californian company BlingCo into his evaluation while on another company FloTex, he invoked his contextual knowledge of physical features, such as the location of trees and pool screens within particular wind-exposed areas into his pricing. In a bundled deal that contains not only California and Florida, but also multiple other territories around the world, there is no specific context in which the deal is based. While different underwriters might apply their contextual knowledge to evaluating different parts of the deal, these various understandings of context are not easily aligned within pricing because of the great underlying variation in risk (see Chapter 4). Hence, increasingly the technical aspects of the deal dominate any contextual practice.

Second and relatedly, a single underwriter, operating as a member of an epistemic culture for a particular risk-type, cannot evaluate the bundled product. As Figure 4.1 in Chapter 4 showed, even for Property Catastrophe risk there is considerable variation in the quality of information underpinning any particular deal, according to its territory of origin. Hence, different underwriters belong to different epistemic cultures that are specific to a risk-type, and from which they gain the particular contextualizing and, indeed, technicalizing practice that is germane to their risk-type. However, a bundled deal is not specific to any particular epistemic culture, but rather requires a team of underwriters to evaluate its different elements, so that Ria writing Indian and Pakistani risk in Chapter 4, and John writing U.S. Property Catastrophe risk in Chapter 3 must bring together their calculative practice on bundled deals. Such risks are barely comparable and so these varying forms of calculative practice are difficult to combine. As one senior reinsurance manager noted of

Making a Market for Acts of God

these bundled deals that were beginning to emerge: "I see a series of the same things from clients; pushing in remote earthquake covers . . . Multi-territory covers expose us to multiple perils. We can't know every little exposure the client has" (Reinsurer, Observation, Executive, Continental Europe). While bundled deals are just as "risky" as the former stand alone deals, containing risk for which contextual knowledge is salient—that is, they still contain the Italian earthquake, French windstorm and Thai flood—the relevant contextualizing practice for those risks is marginalized.

Third, while contextualizing is marginalized, technicalizing is strengthened during the evaluation of bundled deals. Bundling risks deepens the marketization of risk that has firmly established technicalizing and its associated calculative devices as the appropriate way to evaluate risk (see Chapters 3 and 4). These deals are essentially technical, aggregating mathematical probabilities of risk on various different dimensions in order to enable the bundling of risk. As they become more complex in their modeling, they are also more remote and abstracted from the underlying localized aspects of risk, such as factories in Thailand, residential properties in Australia and New Zealand, commercial properties in the United States and Canada, and heavy industrial plant in Europe. They thus lend themselves to technicalizing at the expense of other forms of knowledge and expertise about how different property types respond to different perils under different contextual conditions, which factors are increasingly reduced to modeled outputs that can be technically evaluated. Furthermore, because such complex deals are typically developed over several months with a few key reinsurers who will be the main partners, as with the QBE deal (Reinsurance-as-Practice 6A), the analysis on which they are based is known primarily to those reinsurers and will be a "black box" to other reinsurers who have neither the time nor analytic resource to unpack their assumptions and hence are reduced to accepting the modeled results. This reinforces the general understanding about marketization: that the most volatile of reinsurance risks—Catastrophe—is increasingly perceived to be analyzable via sophisticated calculative devices. Thus, a basic premise of this industry, that such risks are to some extent un-modelable and hence need to be both contextualized and also hedged through the collective risk-bearing practices described in Chapter 2, is being replaced by greater reliance on calculating and trading them as financial objects.

Finally, by overriding the natural variation within risk-types (see Chapter 4), bundled products increase the perception that reinsurance risk can be commoditized. Bundled deals render local variation invisible by drawing out the homogeneous elements of risk and presenting them in a standardized form, so also eroding the expertise through which variation is understood. In doing so, they erode the specific knowledgeable practices that enable the evaluation of vastly different risk-types. While the variation in the underlying risk remains within a bundled deal, consideration of such variation during the deal evaluation is obscured and the perception of com-moditization is strengthened; that this is a bundle of catastrophic risk, all sufficiently similar to be purchased in a single deal as a financial commodity for which no localized risk-specific knowledge is necessary.

6.3.5. Altering Risk-Appetite

In Chapter 5 we examined how reinsurers attempt to ensure both survival and profitability when trading unpredictable and uncertain risks through the way they assemble a portfolio of risk, known as their risk-appetite. This involves varying practical understandings about what constitutes desirable diversification and how to allocate capital to different risk-types and in differ-ent territories. That is, while diversification is central to a reinsurance firm's ability to withstand exposure to risk, the enactment of that diversification is unique to each firm.

However, as we have shown in Section 6.1.1, retention of risk is reducing the variation in risk being ceded, as cedents increasingly retain many types of risk—liability for example—whilst concentrating the risk they transfer into the reinsurance market into a single risk-type—Property Catastrophe. Diversification is becoming increasingly difficult for those reinsurers that base their risk-appetite on a spread across all types of risk (see Chapter 4, Figure 4.1), as fewer of the non-catastrophe risks that reduce the volatility of their portfolio are ceded into the market.

Enactment of risk-appetite is further constrained by bundled deals, which encompass significant territorial diversification that must be taken as a whole package by any reinsurer. That is, in the past a reinsurer could diver-sify through allocating capital in isolation to particular territories, such as French windstorm and German flood, to offset their risk in other territories, such as Australian bushfire. However, on bundled deals, reinsurers must be willing to take the diversification inherent in the deal, regardless of its fit with their specific risk-appetite. Yet many reinsurers lack the epistemic diversity to adequately appraise the full range of risk in a bundled deal. For example, few firms have the expertise in all the territories necessary to evaluate the QBE global deal and indeed, few firms would have written risk in all of those territories. Hence, such firms increasingly rely on the modeling provided by the cedent, further placing their faith in the "black box" of calculative practices through which such deals are developed and hoping that they will not blow their own portfolios. As one reinsurer explained of the QBE deal:

> I don't think we could really analyze it, I don't know if we'd have confidence in it even if we put twenty people on it . . . We could put some actuaries on it and have two teams and have two completely different answers. Our ability to analyze it

is none. So you don't even try. We just have to focus more on the relationship. (Observation, Executive, Continental Europe)

As a result, reinsurers run the risk of over-exposure in certain territories with which they may be unfamiliar. Losses might thus come as a surprise, as occurred with many firms during the Thai floods (see Chapter 2).

6.4. WAYS FORWARD: COMMODITIZING REINSURANCE COVER

Reinsurers, brokers and analysts alike agree on the changing tides facing the traditional reinsurance market, which are being triggered by changes in cedents' reinsurance purchasing behavior. A recent article in the *Insurance Journal* summarizes:

> It's become apparent, however, that this market, for a number of reasons, has seen changes that have set it on new paths and perhaps into uncharted waters. Analyzing why this has occurred is complicated, as each factor involved impends on all the others. While the increase in alternative capital is the most talked about, stronger balance sheets, greater retentions, technology, more sophisticated Cat models, interest in emerging markets, new regulations, rating agency criteria, M&A activity, as well as a benign hurricane season in 2013, have all combined to produce changes for reinsurers that in all likelihood have forever altered the way they will do business in future years.[27]

Understanding market-making in terms of nested relationalities offers some insights into what lies ahead for the traditional reinsurance market and the implications for the cover of reinsurance risks. While the nested relationalities that we uncovered in previous chapters show how the reinsurance industry works as a market for Acts of God, recent trends treat reinsurance risk as a commodity. We speculate below on the implications for future nested relationalities by drawing on insights from the history of related financial markets, such as derivatives, and from alarmed voices within the current reinsurance industry.

6.4.1. Bundling Risks: Losing a Sense of Reality?

The shifting composition of deals—away from the traditional types that were strongly connected to their underlying risk and territory, and towards

---

[27] Boyle, C. 2014. "Reinsurance at Crossroads as New Factors Sweep Away Old Habits." *Insurance Journal*, January 23.

bundled deals—has ramifications for general and practical understandings that have been central pillars of market-making practices in reinsurance. Bundled deals obscure the underlying risks on which they are based. As a result, there is a displacement of the knowledgeable practice of underwriting professionals in evaluating risk. The evaluation of such a bundled deal almost becomes a gamble around the likelihood of a cedent's incurred losses across its portfolio reaching a set threshold. As we have seen in Chapters 3 and 4, it is very hard to assess either the probability of an event, or the size and value of a potential loss to specific territories, necessitating considerable professional expertise to supplement modeling. What happens to this valuable expertise that cannot easily be applied to bundled deals? What rules of thumb or "guestimates" might take the place of this deep contextual knowledge in evaluating the modeling of such deals?

Such shifts in the underlying basis of a deal bear resemblance to changes that were linked to the subprime mortgage crisis of 2008 (MacKenzie, 2011). Specifically, asset-based securities (ABS) were introduced as the basis for collateralized debt obligations (CDOs); while these products were initially evaluated and traded separately, an opportunity for arbitrage emerged when ABS were taken as the basis for CDOs. MacKenzie's work uncovered that the calculative practices used to evaluate CDOs shifted the basis for understanding risk from those professionals who were experienced in potential subprime mortgage default. As CDOs became more remote and abstracted from their underlying assets, they were evaluated by a different group of actors who did not understand the underlying risk, while the models that they used vastly underestimated the probability for default across an entire market (MacKenzie, 2011). This shift was fatal as a systemic collapse showed a much higher correlation in the risk of default than that incorporated in the models, contributing to the collapse of the market for subprime mortgages.

So what can be learnt? Reinsurance is a smaller market and the bundled deals may not be as opaque as CDOs, at least to those large reinsurers that develop them. Yet some parallels exist; reinsurance risk like the earlier subprime mortgage market, has also been built on a principle of avoiding correlation of risk through diversification into varied risk-types, each closely connected to its own territory of origin and each evaluated by a risk professional in that type and territory. By contrast, bundled deals abstract from the underlying risk, make mathematical assumptions about the correlation of these risks, and remove judgment from the hands of the professionals who understand them. That is, bundled reinsurance deals are following the path of abstraction from risk followed in the development of CDOs. Hence, evaluating bundled deals as if they were simply a form of a traditional reinsurance deal is becoming the same act of faith seen in other financial markets, where those who lacked knowledge of the underlying risk vastly underestimated probabilities and exposures. Losing a handle on the underlying risk has to be taken seriously. Bundled reinsurance deals should thus be accepted as a new risk-type requiring new practices and new expertise.

6.4.2. Taking Catastrophe Modeling too Seriously?

Bundled deals also pose the danger of an overreliance on calculative devices such as vendor models. This trend is being reinforced through strengthened partnerships between broking firms and analytics firms.[28] Thus far, even in the most modeled areas of risk, U.S. Property Catastrophe, deal evaluation is complemented with calculative practices that contextualize the deal in relation to client features and market dynamics (see Chapter 3). Yet, these important supplementary calculative practices will rapidly become extinct as they can no longer be developed and applied to bundled deals. Furthermore, bundled deals often contain elements of risk that have previously been considered un-modelable (see Frontier and Specialized risk-types, Chapter 4) and which are heavily reliant on these contextual calculative practices. Yet bundled deals are prone primarily to modeling in the absence of any valid contextualization.

While some cautionary voices amongst reinsurers show skepticism about the increasing reliance on modeling,[29] it is doubtful that the current prominence of vendor models or internally-developed analytic techniques will be diminished in the deal-evaluation process. Experience in related financial markets paints a grim outlook. For instance, MacKenzie and Millo's (2003; Millo & MacKenzie, 2009) study into the 1987 crisis demonstrated that the wide acceptance of the Black-Scholes-Merton (BSM) model amongst traders and in the clearing house had disastrous effects when the model's assumptions proved wrong. Trading had to be discontinued for several days! While doubts about BSM surfaced when initially introduced, these were swept away by the ease and innovation of the results it had generated.

So what can be learnt? An overreliance on models can be disastrous when the results are taken as valid truths rather than as benchmarks, particularly as the ever-increasing dominance of models is accompanied by the diminishing value placed on contextual knowledge. Might contextualizing be a skill of the past? If so, what is the professional knowledge for a reinsurance underwriter going to be? An appraisal developed on a purely modeled basis? An overreliance on models even for less-modelable risk-types disrupts the way calculative practices have been formed within epistemic cultures. As contextualizing

---

[28] "RMS and AonBenfield." 2009. Aon Media Room, June 17. http://aon.mediaroom.com/index.php?s=25776&item=63577; Hemenway, C. 2013. "RMS New Risk Management Platform." *Property Casualty 360*, May 9. http://www.propertycasualty360.com/2013/05/09/rms-ceo-new-risk-management-platform-to-crush-late.

[29] "Cat Model Flaws might be Systemic Risk." 2014. *Reactions*, February 10.

and the soft skills that substitute for the lack of modelability get sidelined in the evaluation of bundled deals, what will happen to these epistemic cultures? Who are the rising stars,[30] and what is going to be the professional basis of the next generation of reinsurance underwriters as contextual knowledge becomes irrelevant?

6.4.3. What Is the Purpose of Reinsurance?

The purpose of the reinsurance market has been to provide capital rapidly to pay insurance losses, which is critical in getting societies and economies back on their feet after a major and often unpredictable disaster. Thus far the market, with its complex relationalities, has worked to provide such cover. Yet, as this chapter has demonstrated, the critical general understandings about collective risk-bearing across market cycles that have sustained the reinsurance market are being displaced. What effects might an increasing focus on achieving capital efficiency through bundled products, retained risk, and cheaper sourcing of reinsurance cover have on the sustainability of this market? A reducing pool of reinsurance premium, increasing competition from new capital offered through ART, and more complex deals constrain the collective risk-bearing nature of the market. These factors skew the reinsurance market towards a few reinsurers with very large capital resources. Thus far, given the difficulty of valuing something as unpredictable and uncertain as reinsurance risk, cedents have benefited from multiple independent evaluations of the same deal across the reinsurance market. Who will cedents turn to when only a handful of reinsurers are left?

The displacement of the market cycle is also a cause for concern. Market cycles and the notion of "payback" have traditionally stabilized capital flows between cedents and reinsurers as long-term partners in risk transfer (see Chapter 2). What will determine the price for a complex deal—and thus how much capital is available to cover these deals—when the basis for the evaluation is no longer connected to market cycles that account for gains and losses over the life of the deal?[31] While the relationship model might have been dominant in the past, the recent trend of reinsurance purchasing behavior marginalizes relationships, as cedents maximize their capital efficiency. While calculation on return periods and payback may be altered to correspond with such a shift from relationship longevity to short-termism, the capacity for catastrophic events to cause capital shocks does not change. After such events,

[30] "The Insurance Industry's Rising Stars." 2014. *Reactions*, January 7.
[31] "Convergence Capital's Impact on the Reinsurance Market." 2013. *GC Capital Ideas*, October 2. http://www.gccapitalideas.com/2013/10/02/convergence-capitals-impact-on-the-reinsurance-market/print/.

what will happen to the flow of capital, previously stabilized by these tacit general understandings of market cycles? Furthermore, what potential ripple effects have not yet been factored into the equation when this new capital from ART is called upon to pay for catastrophic losses? What happens if several Cat bonds are triggered simultaneously to cover losses incurred around the world? Whose capital, which will hopefully be sufficiently liquid to enable rapid payment, is at stake? Will pensions in Europe have to cover losses in the United States (or vice versa)?

6.5. CONCLUSION

This chapter has illustrated how the growing marketization of reinsurance risk is changing the way that reinsurance is purchased. We argue that these changes are shifting the nature of the market from one that is able to financially trade within the "randomness" of Acts of God, which can never be accurately predicted or valued, to one that views risk as a commodity that may be relatively precisely valued and traded. The nested relationality of this market grew around the need to collectively bear risk for events that, over and over again, have demonstrated both their sheer unpredictability and their capacity to cause devastation. Hence, this unwitting shift towards commoditization, with its overreliance on models and its undervaluing of professional knowledge about risk, is a dangerous development for the industry. As other financial industries have collapsed (MacKenzie, 2011), in part through their reliance on inaccurate models (MacKenzie & Millo, 2003; Millo & MacKenzie, 2009), so too, reinsurance places itself at risk of collapse through the marginalization of those homegrown practices, carefully honed over years of bearing risk. These have allowed the industry to survive so far and to provide its critical function, paying rapidly for losses that allow societies to function again in the wake of devastating loss.

The changes we have discussed in this chapter, defining a particular industry at a particular point in time, are conceptually "timeless" in two ways. First, we show how the nexus of market relations is both complex and fragile. As we have shown, a shift in one practice can cause the entire nexus to fragment and reconfigure into new patterns. The discussion of current change therefore substantiates our development of the concept of nested relationality, in which all the relations are intertwined.

Second, our empirical exploration of these still emerging changes provides insight into issues related to managing risk in increasingly technological and model-driven times. It also gives further insights into instances of financial crisis or the **mis**management of financial risk. Such lessons are important not only for understanding current trends, but also more broadly for addressing risk mismanagement in the twenty-first century. We provide a new lens into questions of risk mismanagement through the financial sector of reinsurance, which has largely avoided the excess (and resultant pitfalls) of adjacent sectors such as investment banking. Nonetheless, we characterize this sector as one experiencing trends of marketization that are related to those already experienced in other finance sectors, and sound an important note of caution. We have developed unique insights in the preceding chapters, which show how nested relationality enables an industry to survive and to stabilize capital flows. These insights suggest that it is important to value the practices associated with a specific context and body of professional knowledge; perhaps they can yet be preserved in this industry, and also examined and instated, or perhaps reinstated in other industries.

Third, we argue that the continued stability of the reinsurance sector has never been more important than it is now. The trends we outlined, which we argue have the potential to destabilize the industry, are set in the context of rising costs of natural disasters. For example, 2011 was the costliest year on record for natural catastrophe.[32] As we enter 2014, the United Kingdom is experiencing unprecedented flooding that is rewriting history, while the United States is undergoing its worst winter storms in decades, and Australia is experiencing its hottest year on record. Such trends are set to continue as the Intergovernmental Panel on Climate Change (IPCC) confirms that natural disasters will be ever more prevalent.[33] The reinsurance industry will continue to be required to provide stability in the context of changing weather patterns, increased global connectedness of risk, and the rising need to provide coverage in emerging markets. The stakes involved in modifying the rules of the reinsurance game have never been higher.

[32] "2011: The Year of the Cats." 2011. *The Insider Quarterly*, Winter; "Sigma—preliminary estimates for 2011." 2011. Swiss Re, December 15. http://www.swissre.com/media/news_releases/nr_20111215_preliminary_estimates_2011.html; "Swiss Re Says 2011 Natural Disasters Cost Insurers $110 Billion." 2012. *Bloomberg News*, March 28. http://www.bloomberg.com/news/2012-03-28/swiss-re-says-2011-natural-disasters-cost-insurers-110-billion.html.

[33] "Climate Change 2014: Mitigation of Climate Change." 2014. Intergovernmental Panel on Climate Change (IPCC), March. http://mitigation2014.org/report/final-draft/.

Summary

In this chapter we have:

- Shown how the shift to buying bundled reinsurance deals marginalizes the process of consensus pricing and flattens market cycles, so eroding the collective risk-bearing nature of the reinsurance market.
- Explored how bundling catastrophic risk into single deals increases the **technicalizing** of risk at the expense of **contextualizing** during deal evaluation. Such shifts towards technicalizing tend to emphasize the financial commodification of reinsurance risk rather than its essential unpredictability and associated uncertainty about potential loss.
- Demonstrated that the selective diversification through which reinsurance firms hedged for unpredictable and uncertain risk is being eroded and replaced by the pre-existing diversification incorporated in large bundled deals. This reduces reinsurers' ability to balance the exposure in their portfolio, potentially leading to collapse from over-concentration of particular territories or perils.
- Argued that these changes are fundamentally altering the collective risk-bearing nature of the reinsurance market—which has enabled it to function as a market for unpredictable Acts of God—and shifting it to a market for financial commodities, with potentially disastrous effects for both the market and the provision of risk cover.

7

Addressing "Big Questions"

Advancing a Practice Theory of the Market

7.1. INTRODUCTION

Our aim in this book has been to make the collective **practice*** of a global market visible through our ethnographic tales of the field (Van Mannen, 2011). Through our many examples of Reinsurance-as-Practice on risks as diverse as credit default in Spain, flooding in Thailand, Motor Liability in India, hurricane in the Gulf of Mexico, and earthquake in Japan, we have taken readers on a world tour of how this important and unique market works. In doing so, we have developed a theory of the market as a nested set of **relationalities***, showing, chapter-by-chapter, how different practices come together within interconnected **sites*** to form the market. In this chapter, we further elaborate this theory, explaining how the nexus of practices that is the market is enacted through the **relational presence*** amongst actors. While these actors are geographically dispersed and very diverse in the **risk-types*** they evaluate and trade, they are relationally present with each other in the collective practice of making this market for **Acts of God***. We will explain this concept of relational presence as an extension to current theorizations of the market.

This book demonstrates that a practice approach can answer "big questions" of importance to society, such as how a critical financial market is able to function. As financial collapse has shown us that the practice of markets is flawed, people seek ever more detailed explanations of how markets function and who or what to blame for their failure. Explanations include criticisms of the models used for trading, or point to the physiological characteristics of the traders themselves, such as their cortisol stress hormone levels, or the testosterone that might predispose risk-taking. Our theory shows that such answers are too atomized to account for the collective practice that perpetuates a market, or to help pinpoint its potential failures. Instead, practice theory helps us to approach the deeply systemic nature of market practice in a detailed fashion, as we will explain in the final section of this chapter.

7.2. THE THEORY OF MAKING A MARKET

Our book is ambitious, seeking to explain the collective practice of a global market for Acts of God based on a global ethnographic dataset collected over a number of years. While economic sociologists and social studies of finance scholars have long accepted that financial markets are socially constructed, the question of how people's actions are coordinated to make a market has remained an enduring puzzle. Scholars have advanced various theories about how people's actions are coordinated to collectively construct a market through social networks (e.g. Baker, 1984; Granovetter, 1985); the use of common models, tools and technologies (Beunza and Stark, 2012; Millo and Mackenzie, 2009); cultural diffusion of trading norms (Abolafia, 1996; Zaloom, 2006); and microstructures of interaction (Knorr Cetina and Bruegger, 2002a). While all of these theories proved illuminating, this puzzle of coordination was particularly perplexing in our market because actors are globally dispersed and yet bear risk collectively, without the benefits of real-time interaction to enable their practice. We now flesh out the three concepts that provide our answer to this puzzle: relationality, nested relationality, and relational presence. This theoretical and methodological framework that we develop is useful for practice theorists generally (e.g. Jarzabkowski, 2004; Nicolini, 2013; Vaara and Whittington, 2012) and those interested in studying market and field dynamics specifically (e.g. Beunza et al., 2006; Knorr Cetina and Preda, 2004; 2012; Zilber, 2014).

First, each chapter developed a concept of relationality as it occured between actors, their practices and the collective practice of the market in any particular site. This concept of relationality is grounded in a practice theory approach to the world as a nexus of connections (Nicolini, 2013; Schatzki, 2002). We defined **site*** through social practice theory, not as a particular geographic location, but in terms of a particular market-making activity that we were making visible. Specifically, we looked at quoting on deals (Chapter 2), evaluating deals (Chapter 3), different evaluative practices enacted within risk-types (Chapter 4), and enacting the firm's risk-appetite (Chapter 5) as different sites of market making.[1] Each of these sites constitutes particular

---

[1] Naturally, the sites examined in this book are not exhaustive but, rather, are those most pertinent to our examination of how underwriting practice shapes the market. Other studies might examine the relationality within other sites, such as that of regulatory activity, adding to our understanding the densely interwoven nested relationality that comprises a market.

sets of relationalities between individual actors' practices and the collective practice of the market.

These relationalities are grounded within specific **general understandings***. This is a social practice theory term referring to a common sense among members of a community, such as a the reinsurance market, about how to participate in the **practices*** of that community, such as **consensus pricing*** of deals (Chapter 2) (Schatzki, 2002: 86). These general understandings are enacted within **practical understandings***. These are market actors' complex know-how about the specific practices for participating in the market, such as how to use and to contextualize models in the evaluation of a deal (Chapter 3). In this book, we have carefully untangled some of these general and practical understandings, chapter by chapter, in order to show the nexus of connections—the relationalities—within which they come together (e.g. Nicolini, 2013; Schatzki, 2002).[2] For example, in Chapter 2 we showed how the general understanding of consensus price is enacted within the relationality between any particular underwriter quoting a deal and other underwriters also quoting upon that same deal, while the general understanding of **market cycle*** is enacted in the relationality between underwriters on that deal and other underwriters quoting different deals for a specific **renewal date***. We illustrated this through the Reinsurance-as-Practice 2B example of fluctuations in the market cycle following the Thai floods in 2011. Our book thus identified relationality as the central dynamic inherent in market-making.

Second, the practice of market-making within these sites is not discrete or separate but, rather, is connected in **nested relationality***, which we explained in Chapter 6. As we have shown, the practice of a global market is interdependent, coordinating different actors from different geographic locations and in different firms, writing different types of risk, using different calculative practices, into a coherent pattern. The practices involved in these multiple sites of market-making are thus all nested within each other. For this reason we used the metaphor of a kaleidoscope (Knorr Cetina, 1999), turning the lens in each chapter in order to reflect those practices enacted within different sites, while the book as a whole shows the nested relationality of practices among sites. This enables us to theorize the practice of any specific underwriter at the nexus of multiple connected relationalities (Nicolini, 2013). That is, when we explained the practices of John, a U.S. Property Catastrophe underwriter in Bermuda (Chapter 3), he acted within the relationality of evaluating a U.S. Property Catastrophe deal and yet his practices were also at the

---

[2] While we made analytical distinctions between general understandings and practical understandings in order to tease them apart and make them visible for readers, in the many empirical tales of the field we showed how these understandings come together in practice. In doing so, we provide a unique methodological approach for applying social practice theory to studying collective phenomena, such as the practice of a market.

nexus of practices in other sites of market-making activity. An example is enacting his firm's risk-appetite (Chapter 5) as part of a collective process for quoting on deals (Chapter 2). As we showed in Chapter 6, when the practices of actors in one site are modified, so, relationally are the practices of others. Thus, we showed how the changed practice by multinational cedents to bundling risk within reinsurance deals is, relationally, altering the practice of evaluating deals, with far-reaching ramifications for practices in other sites, such as the erosion of the practices that underpin the market cycle. That is, nested relationality is a continuously unfolding dynamic within which the market is always being constructed and reconstructed amongst sites.

To further elaborate upon how people's practice is enacted at the nexus of multiple relationalities, we now develop our final concept, **relational presence***, which is generated from our prior theorizing about relationality and nested relationality. Relational presence is grounded in the profoundly social nature of practice, in which actors can only act with consideration of others, through the social resources that are recognizable by those others (e.g. Schatzki, 2001; Wenger, 1998). Such resources in our market comprise the specific general and practical understandings through which the practices of any individual actor are relationally present with those of other actors, even where they are not connected in time (for example, through a computer screen) or space (for example, being present together on a trading floor). Such relational presence explains the connectivity of actors within sites. For example, John in Bermuda is relationally present with U.S. Property Catastrophe underwriters in Lloyd's, Zurich, Paris, and Munich, as they all engage in, construct and embed the practice of evaluating and trading deals, including the similar models used (Chapter 3), and the consistent practice for quoting (Chapter 2). Hence, underwriters are relationally present with each other through their common practice.

Yet relational presence goes beyond specific sites to explain connectivity amongst sites. When Stan in Chapter 4 underwrites a Credit & Surety deal, his practice is relationally present with other underwriters on that deal; other underwriters on other deals within the Credit & Surety risk-type; and other underwriters in his own firm and the wider market who write different risk-types. For example, Stan is relationally present with John in Bermuda doing U.S. Property Catastrophe deals (Chapter 3); Ria in Singapore doing Pakistani bouquet deals (Chapter 4); and with Christina and Jim acting in and for their respective firms Mega Re and Property Re (Chapter 5); even as each of these actors is individually quoting to shape the consensus price on their own deals in ways that will ultimately shape the overall market cycle (Chapter 2). This relational presence can be seen through the practice of underwriting their very different deals, during which these underwriters engage in the same broad process of technicalizing and contextualizing, including the same calculative practice of using a rating sheet, to derive a **rate of return*** for their various deals. Indeed, through that relational presence these rates of return on different risk-types, while very different as absolute measures as we saw with Ria's negative equity in Chapter 4, can also be made comparable and brought together as a single portfolio of reinsurance deals within a firm (Chapter 5). This relational presence between globally distributed actors' practices comprises the collective practice of the market.

Our concept of relational presence goes beyond existing theories of market-making that examine how actors interact to make financial markets. Early theories examined embodied presence as it played out in open outcry trading floors and was reinforced through social networks. Here, traders could physically observe each other's bodily signals as they quoted prices within a confined space—the flailing arms, raised voices, and physical gestures that indicated traders' varied influence in shaping the market (e.g. Abolafia, 1996; Baker, 1984; Zaloom, 2006). Later theories examined the **response presence** of traders with one another when trading prices on a computer screen in real time (Knorr Cetina and Bruegger, 2002a; 2002b; Preda, 2009a). These theories showed that electronic markets are also social, constructed in direct interactions between actors who are physically dispersed. Both embodied presence and response presence involved a theory of markets as socially constructed within direct interaction (Goffman, 1967). By contrast, our concept of relational presence is underpinned by a theory of markets as continuously constructed within the nested relationality between multiple sites of interaction (Cooper, 2005; Nicolini, 2013; Schatzki, 2002).

7.3. PRACTICE THEORY—ANSWERING BIG QUESTIONS

The reinsurance market is vital to the economic and social well-being of an increasing number of people globally. Insured losses have increased dramatically in the past two decades[3] and this trend is set to continue. Reinsurance supports insurance companies in paying for these losses during times of crisis, when rapid payment of claims is critical for people to rebuild homes, businesses, and infrastructure. The stability and functioning of the reinsurance market thus matters to us all, especially in the context of climate change and

---

[3] Wharton Risk Management and Decision Processes Center. 2008. "Managing Large-Scale Risks in a New Era of Catastrophes: Insuring, Mitigating and Financing Recovery from Natural Disasters in the United States." Philadelphia, PA: The Wharton School, University of Pennsylvania; Swiss Re. 2012. "Natural catastrophes and man-made disasters in 2011: historic losses surface from record earthquakes and floods." Sigma Report, February.

the projected increase in natural catastrophes.[4] By showing how the reinsurance market performs its critical function at the nexus of underwriters' everyday activities, our book emphasizes the value of practice theory in moving beyond purely descriptive detail, to addressing big questions of global importance (Jarzabkowski and Spee, 2009; Knorr Cetina et al., 2000; Nicolini, 2013; Vaara and Whittington, 2012; Whittington et al., 2003).

As we have shown, through the nested relationality of practices the reinsurance market has been able to withstand the shocks of unpredictable risks, and support payment of claims on most of the major disasters of the last century, even as their costs escalate each year. Critically, our theory of nested relationality points to the collective practice of the market, as it inheres in many small, taken-for-granted practices performed by underwriters in their everyday work. Thus, the ability of a market to function is not a result of some grand input or structure, but rather of mundane, densely interwoven (or nested) practice.

As we suggest in Chapter 6, drawing parallels to the collapse of the subprime mortgage market, when changing practices disturb this nested relationality, market failure can occur. For instance, the practice of trading on subprime mortgages shifted from the initial traders whose practices were connected to the risk, to others who traded them as a new class of asset-backed security—a collateralized debt obligation. Along the way, the probability of mortgage default—particularly the systemic probability that it could occur in multiple contexts simultaneously—was vastly underestimated (Mackenzie, 2011). These changes in practice escalated different understandings about the quality of risk being traded, leading to the 2008 financial crisis. We pointed to evidence that in the reinsurance market similar mistakes may be made when the nested relationalities are altered, as cedents shift to buying **bundled deals***, and new players such as hedge funds and pension funds enter the market to trade in **alternative risk transfer*** products. These changes have increased the reliance on models, whilst downplaying the expertise of underwriters or the social norms governing long-term trading relationships. When these relationalities shift, the tentative balance by which a market works is altered and may collapse. Collapse thus happens in a systemic way as small changes escalate, fundamentally reconfiguring the practice of a market.

As market failure causes the demise of pensioners' and savers' funds, common scapegoats are often identified: the flaws of the algorithmic models or the failings of the traders. Our findings show that these are overly atomized approaches that neglect the fundamental relationality of practices and their

---

[4] European Parliament. 2006. "Climate Change and Natural Disasters: Scientific Evidence of a Possible Relation between Recent Natural Disasters and Climate Change." Brussels: European Parliament; "Climate Change 2014: Mitigation of Climate Change." 2014. *Intergovernmental Panel on Climate Change* (I.P.C.C.), March. http://mitigation2014.org/report/final-draft/.

nestedness through which markets work. With the surge of algorithmic trading and automated trading platforms in other financial markets, the reliance on mathematical models has significantly altered trading (Beunza and Stark, 2004; MacKenzie, 2006). Yet these models are only ever based on simulated assumptions that infer particular behavior within a market. A market, and the models that are developed to trade within it, is still made up of people and is guided by their motivations and interests (Beunza and Millo, 2013). Hence, to attribute market failure to the flaws of models neglects the densely nested relationality that places models at the heart of trading—a relationality that perpetuates their use, even where their flaws are acknowledged (Millo and MacKenzie, 2009). As long as models are considered to be the problem, we will continuously seek a better model, as if some perfect one might be attainable, rather than examining and improving the practice within which the model is situated.

Another common approach to explain market failure is to blame the trader. Typically, traders' behavior has been portrayed as greedy, driven to maximize personal gains, and influenced by adrenalin rushes, oversupply of testosterone, and other substances. Indeed, increasingly a body of research into the neuroscience of markets links financial collapse to physiological characteristics of traders that predispose irrational exuberance (Coates and Herbert, 2008; Coates et al., 2009). Such studies are just one more way to locate market failure in managerial hubris, albeit grounded in the physiology of traders, rather than examining how the systemic practice within which such exuberance—and its accompanying release of stress hormones—occurs and is legitimized as the everyday practice of working within a market. While undoubtedly in any social order there can be mavericks and deliberate fraudsters, our practice approach highlights that such fraudulent practice is only the most extreme enactment of collective practices that are shared amongst a group of traders. In ordinary situations, these practices are deemed "typical" and have generated millions for those banks that reward and incentivize such practices. Thus, we argue that it is not a single trader that brings down a bank or a single bank that causes the collapse of a global financial system. Rather, it is the taken-for-granted assumptions that shape traders' practices and through which they enact the collective practice of markets.

Rather than placing emphasis on one facet of a market, such as the models or technologies (Colander et al., 2009; Lewis, 2014), traders (Coates et al., 2010; Geddes, 2009; McDowell, 2010),[5] or particular firms (Erkens, Hung, and Matos, 2012), the theorizing in our book cuts across firms and individuals' behavior and the use of models, to show how practices are connected

[5] Adams, T. 2011. "Testosterone and High Finance do not Mix: So Bring on the Women." *The Guardian*, June 19. http://www.theguardian.com/world/2011/jun/19/neuroeconomics-women-city-financial-crash.

across a global market. Our theory of nested relationality sheds light on the mundane practices through which models become accepted, hubris constitutes the norm, stress is celebrated, and traders become entangled in a dense relationality of miscalculation. We show that these everyday practices constitute the collective practice of the market and, hence, are the crux of systemic health—or systemic risk—within markets.

Our theorizing constitutes a call to arms about the potential threats arising from the current changes in the reinsurance market. As we showed in Chapter 6, rapidly escalating changes in the collective practice of the reinsurance market—such as the shift to purchasing bundled reinsurance deals by global cedents, or the growth of alternative risk transfer products—disturbs the current nested relationality. These shifts are potentially dangerous, not just for a capital market, but also for the society that depends upon that market to work.

Speculating on the implications of these changes, we provide a cautionary note about the potential for the collapse of this market. First, cedents and reinsurers may find that they have insufficient cover for the risk they carry, as probabilities about the correlation between these risks are underestimated, obscured, or skewed within **bundled deals**. Second, reinsurance cover for such deals is increasingly concentrated in the hands of only a select few of the (largest) traditional players, which marginalizes the collective bearing of risk that has served the market so well in withstanding shocks. Third, new parties provide cover through **alternative risk transfer** products which remain untested as a form of reliable cover against large-scale disasters of multiple kinds. These products are not based on reinsurance market assumptions about relationships and payback and will result in an increasingly price-driven and contractual market that will likely leave some players without the risk cover or capital reserves they need (see Chapter 6 for a detailed discussion of these points). These changes are occurring at a time of increasing frequency and severity of natural disasters, as well as threats from new, unanticipated sources of damage such as cyber-risk and political risk. Thus far, the reinsurance market has worked through the complex practices it has developed to ensure collective risk- bearing that protects reinsurers, whilst ensuring that cedents are paid, even after disasters as unexpected at the World Trade Center, Hurricane Katrina, and the Tōhoku earthquake. Reinsurance is a market for Acts of God—those unpredictable events that result in enormous personal and financial loss. As yet we remain skeptical that these new practices will be able to meet the fallout from such events. If they cannot, the systemic implications, socially and economically, will be profound.

Methodology Appendix

A global ethnography. This book is based on a global ethnography, with data collected for over three years (mid-2009 to mid-2012) around the world.[1] Methodologically, this study is at the forefront of ethnographies that seek to follow practices globally (Çalışkan, 2010; Falzon, 2009; Jarzabkowski et al., 2014; Marcus, 1995; Smets et al., 2014; Zilber, 2014). Initial access to field sites was gained through the Insurance Intellectual Capital Initiative, a group of senior executives in reinsurance firms and broking houses. They opened doors within reinsurers operating in Lloyd's of London, Bermuda and Continental Europe (Zurich, Munich and Paris predominantly). These three regions constitute the oldest and largest reinsurance trading hubs, with the vast majority of reinsurance business flowing through these trading hubs regardless of where it might originate. As the fieldwork progressed, we also included the Asia-Pacific region through fieldwork in Hong Kong, Japan, Singapore, and Australia. This region became particularly important in rounding out our understanding of global practice, as events such as the New Zealand earthquake, Australian and Thailand floods, and Japanese earthquake and tsunami began to have significant impact on the market. It also gave us a greater sense of emerging and less traditional markets and trading hubs.

Our unprecedented access to this financial market spanned sixty subsidiary sites in twenty-two reinsurance firms and three brokerage houses across fifteen countries. These firms ranged from the largest reinsurers in the market to start-ups with small teams. We also conducted interviews in an additional thirty-five insurance firms (**cedents***), which spanned seventeen countries from Germany, to America, to Pakistan, and differed dramatically in their size and reinsurance needs.

The ethnographic object. The ethnographic object we were following (Czarniawska, 2007; Falzon, 2009; Marcus, 1995) through our access to these firms was the global practice of trading risks, from the perspective of the reinsurance firms that supply their capital to underwrite these risks, and the underwriters who make everyday decisions about trading these risks. Our initial interviews indicated some of the factors that shape industry trading. We were thus aware of a series of common dates at which all **deals*** are renewed. As these constitute the natural trading rhythms of the industry, we chose to focus our observations around the build-up to these dates and the way that underwriters made decisions on risks at these dates across the annual cycle; that is, to follow their own naturally occurring cyclical behavior. In total, we followed three annual cycles across their multiple renewal dates, which enabled us to

---

[1] Aspects of our methodology, such as following a global practice and conducting ethnography within a team, are detailed in: Jarzabkowski, Bednarek and Cabantous (2014) "Conducting global team-based ethnography: Methodological challenges and practical methods." *Human Relations*; Smets, M., Burke, G., Jarzabkowski, P., and Spee, A. P. 2014. "Charting new territory for organizational ethnography: Insights from a team-based video ethnography." *Journal of Organizational Ethnography*, 3(1): 10–26.

observe the highs and lows of risk-trading, and reactions to events as they occurred, such as Windstorm Xynthia in Europe, floods in Australia, the Chilean earthquake in 2010, the New Zealand earthquake, the Japanese earthquake and tsunami, and the Thai floods in 2011. We were also able to observe the industry in relatively calm times, such as 2009, when no major events affected the renewals.

Data collection. As we identified the practice of underwriting as the basis of reinsurance trading, we shadowed underwriters trading reinsurance deals (Czarniawska, 2007). We immersed ourselves in the practice of underwriting by sitting beside underwriters during their everyday practices, including receiving, appraising, quoting, and placing capital on deals. We furthered our understanding of their actions and interactions by listening to their phone calls, noting their work-related emails, and shadowing them to their team, client, and broker meetings, as well as to their main conferences (of which we attended four in Europe, America, and Singapore). In addition, we sometimes shadowed brokers in their interactions and meetings with and about reinsurance underwriters. Often after a period of shadowing, a participant might spend a few minutes talking about their day with us, or even meet us for a coffee or drink after work, all of which added to our understanding and the richness of our interpretations.

During all of this shadowing, we took notes in real time and also audio-recorded interactions, as well as video-recording some interactions. We made five- to ten-minute time markers in our fieldnotes so that we could revisit the audio and video recordings during analysis, going over specific sections that related to our fieldnotes in order to check impressions and deepen our insights. Each episode of shadowing and associated fieldnotes resulted in one "observation" for the data set. An observation means a meeting (either internal, with a broker or a client), or a period of shadowing individual underwriters at their desk; or a period of shadowing a specific person at a conference. Hence, an observation involved any continuous single period of shadowing by a researcher of a specific individual or a specific activity and may range from some thirty minutes to a whole day, but is typically half a day. This remained the primary basis of our observational data for the lifespan of the project. In total, we collected **935 observational field notes** (see Table A.1).

As part of our engagement with the field we also attended numerous social events and engaged in many informal interactions with participants. These included dinners with participants (both formal and informal), Christmas parties in different cities, lunches (from schnitzel in Vienna to noodles in Singapore), social trips up mountains or to lakes, conference cabaret parties and bus trips to "corporate away days". In these instances, it was often impossible to make recordings or take notes in real time, but we made "reflective notes" soon after the interaction, and also entered them into our database. In total, we maintained a record of **146 work related social interactions** (see Table A.1).

In addition to our primary corpus of ethnographic fieldwork, we engaged in multiple interviews (Watson, 2011). We interviewed everyone from CEOs, brokers, analysts, and Chief Risk Officers to, of course, underwriters. These ethnographic interviews focused on asking people about their practice (Nicolini, 2009) as well as their reflections on their market and how it worked. The interviews typically focused on getting underwriters to describe in detail how they underwrote particular deals and managed particular clients; interviewees would sometimes go so far as to bring out specific files and talk us through their trading practices, including their stage-by-stage thinking on particular deals. More broadly these interviews focused on increasing our understanding about the role of things such as consensus pricing and models, providing us with greater insight into and context about the everyday work we were

Table A.1. Data Summary

	Countries	Subsidiaries in Firms	Work observations (field notes)	Additional field interactions	Interviews
Reinsurers & brokers	15 Data collection focused on the main trading hubs of London, Bermuda, Zurich, Paris and Munich, as well as Singapore. Additional data-collection was conducted in Australia, Belgium, Canada, Hong Kong, Italy, Japan, Netherlands, Spain and U.S.	51 subsidiaries; plus additional 7 via video conference, across 25 firms	935	146 (e.g. social events)	382
Cedents	17 Austria, Australia, India, Indonesia, Israel, Japan, Germany, France, Netherlands, Pakistan, Philippines, Poland, Singapore, Spain, Switzerland, U.K. and U.S.	35 firms	n/a	n/a	49

observing. In order to gain a perspective on the buyers' side of the market we also engaged in a number of interviews with cedents regarding the practice of purchasing reinsurance. We interviewed whoever was responsible for reinsurance buying in the cedent firm, which was usually someone with a designated "reinsurance buyer" role and/or the CEO. In total, across the entire dataset, we conducted 431 interviews, sometimes with multiple interviewees simultaneously; 382 of them in reinsurance and brokerage firms and forty-nine interviews with cedents (see Table A.1). These interviews were usually one hour in length but sometimes as long as three hours.

The research team. A team was required in order to collect, manage, and code this breadth of data across multiple individuals, firms, and countries. The scope of the project demanded much energy and investment from all data-collecting team members for extended periods. This included time away from home, friends and family (including at the key renewal time over Christmas); multiple flights (including dealing with cancelations and delays as well as 3:00 a.m. taxis); late nights; and all the variation in interactions and emotions (from the stressful to the enjoyable) that fieldwork entails. At the same time, much methodical, rigorous and yet also creative work was required in conducting the coding and analysis across all team members.

Initially, the project began with a single researcher, the Project Lead, Paula Jarzabkowski. However, it rapidly expanded to a team of three researchers as Paul Spee and Michael Smets joined the team in 2009, and later to a team of five with Rebecca Bednarek and Laure Cabantous joining in 2011. We needed a multi-lingual team to enable us to collect data in Germany and France (two important trading hubs in Europe) and our team encompassed native speakers for this purose. This team of five, who engaged in fieldwork, were assisted with data management and analysis by Adriana Allocato, Gary Burke, and Stella Luig at different times throughout the project.

In conducting the fieldwork we struck a balance in terms of "division of labor". We needed to divide and conquer, at least to a degree, in order to cover the many research contexts; but tried to ensure that at least two researchers were familiar with the majority of organizational subsidiaries and countries. This enabled us to ensure there were overlapping experiences between team members to facilitate information sharing and add layers to our observation and interpretation in each context (Jarzabkowski et al., 2014; Mauthner and Coucet, 2008). It was also ideal that one team member was familiar first-hand with the vast majority of companies, trading hubs and subsidiaries. Ultimately, the first author, Paula, fulfilled that (demanding) role, negotiating the various points of access to research contexts and introducing the different team members to those contexts, then acting as a conduit for the different parts of the ethnography carried out by multiple team members, while also being deeply immersed in the field herself for extended periods (see Table A.2).

Managing the data. We developed and implemented protocols to establish a clear record of all our data and engagement with the field. These protocols facilitated sharing of data amongst team members, and ensured that searches for data during analysis were easy and comparable. Our labeling system allowed any one of us to search for and find a particular piece of data within our database based on when it was recorded, which firm, which geographic location, what type of data, what was observed, the content of the data, and the researcher. This ensured that all of our individual data was shared, could be identified individually, and yet become part of the collective database. Such labeling also enabled careful auditing for consistency of the database, which is a critical element in the trustworthiness of qualitative analysis

Table A.2. Summary of Firm Subsidiaries (Reinsurers and Brokers) and Researchers

	Subsidiaries					Total orgs. [subsidiaries]
1	U.K. PJ & APS	Bermuda PJ & APS	C. Europe 2 countries PJ & MS	Asia-Pacific 3 countries PJ	U.S. PJ	25 [53; plus additional 7 through video calls]
2	Switzerland PJ & RB	France PJ	U.K. PJ & RB	Singapore PJ	Various (video calls) PJ & RB	
3	Spain PJ	Germany MS & PJ	Belgium LC & PJ	France LC & PJ		PJ [Research Lead]: 25 [49; plus calls]
4	France LC & PJ	Switzerland RB & PJ	Singapore PJ	Bermuda PJ		APS: 10 [12]
5	Bermuda PJ, MS, APS	Switzerland RB & PJ	France LC			MS: 10 [12]
6	Germany APS, PJ, MS	Singapore PJ	U.S. PJ			RB: 8 [9, plus 2 calls]
7	U.K. APS & PJ	Bermuda PJ, APS, MS	Switzerland PJ & RB			LC: 3 [4]
10	UK PJ & MS	Bermuda PJ, APS, MS	U.S. PJ			
8	Switzerland RB & PJ	U.K. RB				
9	U.K. MS, PJ, RB	Bermuda PJ & MS				
11	Singapore PJ & RB	Hong Kong PJ				
12	U.K. PJ	Japan PJ				

Firms (anonymized 1–25); data collection was often conducted across multiple subsidiaries

(continued)

Table A.2. (Continued)

	Subsidiaries	Total orgs. [subsidiaries]
13	U.S. PJ	
14	Japan PJ	
15	Switzerland RB & PJ	
16	U.K. PJ & APS	
17	U.K. APS & PJ	
18	U.K. MS & PJ	
19	U.K. APS & PJ	
20	Bermuda PJ & MS	
21	Bermuda PJ, MS, ASP	
22	Bermuda PJ, APS, MS	
23	Bermuda PJ	
24	Bermuda PJ	
25	Bermuda PJ	

Firms (anonymized 1–25); data collection was often conducted across multiple subsidiaries

Key: Main regions

U.K.	Bermuda
Continental Europe 6 countries	Asia-Pacific 4 countries
U.S. and other (1 country plus video calls [2 additional countries])	

Key: Researchers at each subsidiary and firm

Each set of initials refers to the specific ethnographer in that context.

Bold indicates the main person at subsidiary collected data.

No bold indicates that fieldwork was shared equally.

(Lincoln and Guba, 1985). We also developed a data-mastersheet, in which we carefully recorded every piece of data collected along a number of dimensions, and established a password-protected server as a shared depository for all our data. We then developed a coding schema that we could all access and work on, particularly as the coding evolved and continues to evolve based around specific academic concepts, such as those developed for this book. NVivo, which is a qualitative data software program with sophisticated search functions, was the database used for this coding schema. Strict protocols were developed to enable data to be indexed and sourced by anyone in the team.

Developing a coding framework. The coding schema for our analysis was developed collaboratively as a team, beginning with concepts generated and shared in the field. These were then formalized into more tightly defined categories as the fieldwork progressed, and even after fieldwork had stopped. During the most active phase of coding, while the schema was being developed, fortnightly Skype meetings were held between team members, including those members taken on specifically to support coding. In these meetings we discussed any issues, changes or ideas, and checked that we had consistent definitions of codes and categorization of data cross team members. This broader coding structure became the starting point for refining our understanding of particular themes such as "information quality" or "calculation" (Chapter 3–4) that we had experienced in the field. We often broke these open to develop more fine-grained understanding as required. For instance, the coding around the Thai floods initially involved deeper analysis of the "Thailand" and "disasters" codes, but these were then combined with searches in other codes, such as those to do with market cycles and quoting. With this finer-grained coding, we could isolate and examine pieces of data that related specifically to how people were quoting deals in relation to the Thai floods. We also often developed understanding of central concepts in this book by bringing multiple empirical codes together. For instance, developing an understanding of "risk-appetite" involved bringing together multiple codes such as "diversification", "capital availability", and "relationships".

Trustworthiness of analysis. Our experience of being immersed in the field engendered a deep understanding of this market that underpins all of the theorizing in this book (Cunlifffe, 2010; Van Maanen, 2011). In this sense, while this book draws from the systematic thematic coding in NVivo, the primary basis for theorizing was the authors' holistic and deep understanding of "what makes this market work", established through long hours in the field over three years, and through constant reflection and discussion as a team. Theorizing through and from such immersion is central to establishing the trustworthiness and authenticity of ethnographic data (Guba and Lincoln, 1985; Watson, 2011). Our subsequent detailed thematic coding (Miles and Huberman, 1994) supported and refined, rather than established, our understanding.

Constant interaction with and feedback from industry participants also informed our understanding (Lincoln and Guba, 1984; Hammersley and Atkinson, 2007). Over a number of years, both during and following the fieldwork, Paula held monthly meetings with a Steering Group Committee with whom we shared emerging interpretations and were given feedback and further insights into the industry. We also presented the work at industry events and within particular organizations, engaging in rigorous question-and-answer sessions at each presentation. In addition, we received feedback from industry practitioners on specific chapters of this book. This practice joined the evident triangulation between multiple researchers, participants, organizations and types of data (Denzin, 1989; Denzin and Lincoln, 2005; Hammersley and Atkinson, 2007; Miles and Huberman, 1994) on which our analysis is based, and which helps ensure its trustworthiness.

Writing this book. This book draws from the whole corpus of our data. Our aim was to theorize about the field through the vivid and readable accounts we provide (Cunliffe, 2010; Golden-Biddle and Locke, 1993; Van Maanen, 2011). In this endeavor, we use data in two ways. First, we use direct excerpts from our data (whether interview, documents, or observation) to illustrate particular points throughout the book. Second, the rich Reinsurance-as-Practice empirical illustrations provide more fully developed accounts that take the reader into the particular aspects of market-making about which we are theorizing. While drawing directly from our field experiences, these illustrations are composites, drawing from multiple incidents within our data to develop a story that can illustrate underwriters' collective work practices in a comprehensible, reader-friendly way. Throughout these illustrations we have also taken care to protect the anonymity of individual participants (Humphreys and Watson, 2009). For example, while these composite narratives are presented as being the experience of "Ria" or "John" they are established from our engagement with multiple underwriters in that particular risk-type, rather than referring to a specific individual (e.g. see Chapters 3–4).

This book is a result of a collective writing process under the first author, Paula's, leadership. Each chapter was crafted between all of us and written through multiple iterations between us. While one person might have taken responsibility for developing the first draft, we discussed and edited each chapter collectively as a means of advancing each draft. We relied on both face-to-face meetings—especially when theorizing and planning the book, where we spent a week away together to focus solely on it—and then frequent, often long Skype calls as each chapter was developed and redeveloped. During this process we took on board feedback and received a great deal of help in refining and reworking our various drafts from many colleagues, whom we mention in the acknowledgements.

Given the scope of our study, we have more data and potentially interesting themes than could be included in a single book. For this book, we thus focused on those themes that were central to understanding the supply side of market-making, specifically the practice of reinsurance underwriting. This does mean that we foreground the practice of underwriters and leave the practices of other actors such as brokers, analysts, executives and cedents in the background, despite the fact that we know much about them. We have shown their presence implicitly; including, for instance, the Chief Risk Officer in Chapter 5; the analysts (modelers and actuaries) in Chapters 3 and 4; and the cedent throughout our "Buyers' Perspective" text boxes. Future papers and books may bring out elements of these actors' practice more thoroughly as we continue to work with our extensive data set.

Glossary

Account manager/executive. A manager in a reinsurance firm who, rather than underwriting a specific deal, looks after the overall relationship with an important cedent. This role is especially useful when a reinsurer is underwriting multiple deals with a cedent.

Act of God. A legal term defined as an extraordinary event that could have been neither predicted nor prevented. In this book, "Acts of God" are categorized as "man-made" or "natural" disasters—or events—that are inherently unpredictable. "Natural" would include events such as earthquakes, flooding, or windstorms; "man-made" would include terror attacks, political risks, liability for asbestos, or damages to oil rigs (e.g. the Deepwater Horizon disaster of 2009).

Actuary. See **Analyst**.

Agriculture. A risk-type comprised of reinsurance cover for damage to agricultural property, including crop, livestock, bloodstock, forestry and greenhouses.

Alternative Risk Transfer. See **ART**.

Analyst. A person working for a reinsurer, broker or cedent who is responsible for the analytical assessment of a risk. These are usually either actuaries, specializing in pricing techniques for various types of risk (Chapter 4) or modelers, specializing in running vendor models for Property Catastrophe risk (Chapter 3).

ART or Alternative Risk Transfer. Various insurance-linked securities (ILS), such as Catastrophe Bonds that are an alternative to traditional reinsurance deals. These products are typically collateralized, meaning that the capital from investors is held in an account as collateral against any loss. They attract investment from additional capital markets, outside the reinsurance market, such as hedge funds and pension funds (see Chapter 6).

Attachment point. A specified dollar amount on a reinsurance deal at which the reinsurance cover begins to apply. While an insurance company will use its own capital to pay for any losses below this point, it seeks reinsurance to cover any losses above this attachment point. For example, in Property Catastrophe reinsurance, when the insurance company has a loss that exceeds the attachment point, it triggers a reinsurance payout.

Bouquet deal. A deal that comprises multiple lines of business, which is in contrast to a stand alone deal and a bundled deal. For example, a bouquet might cover Property Catastrophe, Marine and Casualty risks in one deal. Small insurance firms and those within developing markets typically issue bouquet deals (see Chapter 4).

Broker. A person working for a broking firm, who is engaged by cedents to advise on the appropriate structure of a deal, distribute the deal to a reinsurance panel, help with negotiations, and facilitate the establishment of a consensus price from the range of quotes for a deal. For their service, they receive a commission of a percentage of the overall premium of the reinsurance deal.

Bundled deal. A deal that comprises multiple perils and spans multiple geographies within a single risk-type, in contrast to a stand alone deal or a bouquet deal. Typically, bundled deals involve Property Catastrophe risk across territories, and are issued by large multinational insurance firms. Some such deals may even be global, bundling one risk-type across all the territories in the cedent's portfolio (see Chapter 6).

Burning cost. See experience pricing.

Casualty. A risk-type comprised of workers' compensation, vehicle insurance, various forms of malpractice, and any other liabilities. The largest payout on Casualty risk has been the set of liability claims for asbestos-related disease (see Chapter 1).

Capacity. The volume of capital a reinsurer has available to place on a deal or number of deals. Risk-appetite shapes the way a reinsurer allocates and places its capital.

Cat(astrophe) Bond (see ART). This collateralized financial product is one of the most common ILS products. It is issued by a cedent. Cat bonds can be triggered by a predefined loss to a cedent's portfolio. They may also be triggered by a specified industry loss, or by the magnitude of a particular event, such as an earthquake of a particular magnitude within a specified radius of a particular region. If no catastrophe occurs, the investors make quarterly returns from their investment, and get the principal back on maturity. However, if a loss does occur, the cedent uses the money in the collateralized account to pay their claims (see Chapter 6).

Cedent. An insurance company that buys reinsurance. An insurance company gathers premium from its policyholders and has an obligation to pay their claims for loss. To protect itself against the vast payouts that would arise from either a high severity event, such as a hurricane or frequent smaller events, such as multiple motor accidents, it buys reinsurance that enables the insurance company to "cede" part of its risk to the reinsurer in return for premium.

Chief Risk Officer (CRO). An executive in an insurance or reinsurance company who is responsible for identifying and mitigating risks, typically at the level of an oversight on the firm's portfolio of risk-types and risk-appetite (see Chapter 5).

Chief Underwriting Officer (CUO). A person working for an insurer or reinsurer who is responsible for overseeing the evaluation and placement of capital on deals; often across risk-types. The CUO leads a group of underwriters, and reports to the Chief Risk Officer.

Combined ratio. A measure of profitability that takes the sum of incurred losses and expenses and divides them by earned premium. It is one way to measure rate of return.

Consensus price. The common price at which any particular deal is traded in the market to all reinsurers on the panel.

Credit & Surety. A risk-type comprised of different financial lines. Surety insurance kicks in to pay the insured if another fails to fulfil the obligation of a contract. They are very common in construction to protect the project's owner and ensure that a general contractor will abide by the contract. Credit insurance pays the insured if there is a default on receivables owed to them (often used in retail and shipping). For example, it will protect a firm's account receivable from loss due to protracted default or bankruptcy. There are then a variety of slightly different Credit & Surety products that also need to be treated differently (or avoided), such as financial guarantees (Alwis and Steinbach, 2003) (See Chapter 4).

Deal. A contract between a cedent and those reinsurers who agree to bear its risk at a set price, typically for the duration of twelve months. A typical reinsurance deal specifies the risk-type (e.g. Property Catastrophe), the territory (e.g. Florida) and defines the peril (e.g. earthquake). There may also be bouquet deals, which include multiple risk-types, and bundled deals, which include multiple perils and territories. Deals involve two main ways of providing reinsurance cover: non-proportional and proportional.

Epistemic culture. A term originating in social practice theory that comprises "how we know what we know" (Knorr Cetina, 1999: 1). In Chapter 4 we show how epistemic culture shapes the way underwriters evaluate different risk-types (see Chapter 4).

Evaluation. Refers to an underwriter's activity to calculate a deal. Evaluation occurs through technicalizing and contextualizing (see Chapters 3 and 4).

Event. The occurrence of a man-made or natural disaster. An event is defined by a date of occurrence and can be assessed in terms of severity of caused damages. In relation to models, an event refers to the likely occurrence of a specific disaster predicted to happen within a defined period, e.g. an earthquake with the magnitude of six is assumed to occur every 150 years. These "modeled" events are based on assumptions and predictions from past events.

Excess-of-loss. See non-proportional reinsurance.

Experience Pricing. Pricing calculations based on experience (that is, on past losses). A burning cost analysis is the most common of these. This is an underwriter's manual calculation of the accumulated losses paid out by reinsurers, as a ratio to the cedent's premium within the same period. The ratio provides an indication of the past reinsurance experience, and can be used to project a cedent's potential reinsurance losses in the future.

Exposure Pricing. Determining a price based on an analysis of the exposure within a deal rather than the losses experienced in the past.

Full placement/coverage. A deal reaches full placement if the entire amount of capital that is required to cover the deal has been provided by several reinsurers (cf. short fall).

General understanding. A social practice theory term referring to a common sense understanding among members of a community, such as a religious order, about how to participate in and enact the practices of that community; for example, a church service (Schatzki, 2002: 86). We use this term throughout the book to refer to general understandings that are specific to the reinsurance community and the ways of participating in its practices, such as consensus pricing in Chapter 2.

Hard market. This refers to a period where deals renew at a consensus price that is significantly higher than the previous years (cf. soft market; market cycle). Typically, a hard market is triggered by significant losses that affect several reinsurers and deplete the total amount of capital available to cover deals within a risk-type.

Hazard. See **Peril**.

ILS or Insurance-linked Security. An alternative to traditional reinsurance covers. ILS are a means of transferring risk to the capital market based on loss events triggered by catastrophes (see ART). These products include Industry Loss Warranties (ILW) and catastrophe bonds (see Chapter 6).

ILW or Industry Loss Warranty. Issued by a cedent, this is a collateralized financial product to provide cover if the total losses to the insurance industry exceed a pre-defined threshold (see **ART** and **ILS**).

Layer. An excess-of-loss deal is structured in layers that specify the particular range of loss for which cover is sought—for example, a layer of $100–$150 million would mean the cedent has purchased cover within that layer for any losses exceeding $100 million and up to $150 million. Any reinsurer who placed capital on this layer will share the payout for such losses. The lowest figure in each layer is the attachment point while the upper figure is the limit above which losses are not covered by that layer. The top layer defines the ceiling of a deal, at which any cedent's loss is capped (see Chapters 1 and 3).

Liability (re)insurance. Protects the insurer from the risks of liabilities imposed by lawsuits and similar claims. Litigation related to asbestos claims provides an example.

Life. A risk-type comprised of reinsurance cover to cover the potential of death and various associated health risks. Not covered in this book, which is focused on the non-life segment of the market.

Limit. Part of a non-proportional reinsurance cover, it denotes the largest amount of loss to be covered by reinsurers on a deal (or on a particular layer of a deal).

Line of business. The type of reinsurance, such as Property Catastrophe, Liability, Marine, or Agriculture.

Long-tail risk. Refers to the relatively long time it takes to determine the size of loss on Casualty risks, and thus for reinsurers to settle claims after an event occurs. While the loss occurs in the year covered by a deal, the actual claims may only become apparent and determine the size of a loss after many years (cf. short-tail risk). An example is asbestos where claims continue to occur decades after the event (see Chapter 4).

Loss. A loss is triggered by the occurrence of an event and is sustained by an insurer's policyholders/customers. It also refers to the size of a cedent's claim made against reinsurers. The length of time it takes to determine the amount of a loss is distinguished by short-tail and long-tail risk.

Loss history. A cedent's losses that have accumulated over a number of years. There are two ways to show a cedent's loss history. First, it is illustrated in the form of a total sum of sustained losses. Second, it is shown as a ratio of losses and gross written premium.

Loss Event. The total losses to the ceding company or to the reinsurer resulting from a single cause such as a windstorm.

Loss-ratio. The ratio of incurred losses to earned premiums, expressed as a percentage. The loss-ratio provides a number that can be used for some types of reinsurance pricing (see Chapter 4).

Marine. A risk-type comprised of reinsurance cover for loss of vessels, cargo, terminals and any transport of cargo by which property is transferred, acquired, or held between the points of origin and final destination (see Chapter 4).

Market cycle. Refers to the flow of capital in the reinsurance industry. The market cycle shifts between hard market and soft market on the basis of the cost of capital available in the market. As severe losses, such as the World Trade Center (2001) deplete reinsurers' capital reserves, the cost of capital increases and rates rise on reinsurance deals, shifting the market cycle from a soft market (capital oversupply) to a hard market (limited capital) (see Chapter 2).

Marketization. A term originating in social practice theory (Çalışkan & Callon, 2010). It forms a general understanding that risks can be defined, evaluated and traded in order to generate a return (see **Rate of return**).

Market-maker. A firm with the capacity to set or strongly influence the eventual price, and usually one who can then get the share on a deal they want. These are usually the largest players in the market (such as Munich Re and Swiss Re) or long-term dominant players on a particular deal or particular territory (see Chapters 2 and 5).

Model. Refers to an analytical approach to assessing risk that has been formulated within a relatively standardized set of statistical parameters. See also **Vendor model**.

Modeler. See **Analyst**.

Motor Liability. A risk-type comprised of reinsurance cover for injuries, loss of life and damages to road vehicle from traffic collisions and against liability that may arise from these accidents (see Chapter 4).

Nested relationality. A theoretical construct we develop in this book, building on social practice theory. It refers to the nexus amongst relationalities of practices across sites that comprise the global market. (See Chapter 6 for an empirical demonstration, and Chapter 7 for a theoretical discussion of this concept).

Non-proportional reinsurance. A type of reinsurance cover in which payment is triggered if an insurer suffers cumulative losses (within a given period) that exceed the specific amount in the attachment point, up to a specified limit (above which losses are no longer covered). The most common form of such a deal is excess-of-loss reinsurance (see Chapters 1 and 3) (cf. proportional reinsurance).

Panel. A selection of reinsurers who are invited by the cedent or their brokers to quote on a deal, and a selection of reinsurers who eventually place capital on that deal.

Peril. Refers to the causes of possible loss in the property field, such as Fire, Windstorm, Collision, Hail, etc. In certain lines of business, such as Casualty, the term "Hazard" is more frequently used.

Portfolio. The specific balance of risk-types that a reinsurance firm underwrites. This balance is set at the firm level by how much capital is allocated to each risk-type, which determines how many deals an underwriter can accept within that risk-type. The portfolio is a reflection of the specific risk-appetite of a firm (see Chapter 5).

Practical understanding. A term originating in social practice theory that means complexes of know-hows regarding the actions that make up a practice (Schatzki, 2006: 1,864). We use this theoretical term throughout this book to denote the specific practices through which people enact aspects of the market—such as the practical understanding of how to calculate deals technically (see Chapters 3 and 4).

Practice(s). A term originating in social practice theory. A practice refers to a pattern of activities that is recognizable, for instance as "evaluating a deal" (see practical understandings) and is governed by general understandings. As a practice is rarely singular, "practices" refers to multiple patterns of activities. A practice is a collective phenomenon, enacted by multiple people. For a practice to have a consequence—for example to establish a quote for a deal—it needs to be enacted by people drawing on materials and tools, such as evaluating a reinsurance deal using models and maps. For the purpose of this book, the nexus of practices is defined in terms of relationality and nested relationality.

Premium. The money paid by the buyer for insurance and reinsurance cover. In reinsurance this is a cost to the cedent (insurer) and revenue to the reinsurer.

Premium ceded. The premium an insurer cedes to reinsurers in return for the reinsurance cover. Global premium ceded refers to the total amount that insurance companies across the globe cede to reinsurers.

Premium written. The "writers" of the premium here are the reinsurance firms. The premium is that which has been ceded by insurers and effectively forms the reinsurer's revenue. Gross premium written is therefore equivalent to the premium ceded by insurance firms to that particular reinsurer. Net premium written is the difference of gross written premium after deducting reinsurance costs.

Price. In reinsurance, "price" may be differentiated as quoted price, which is the price that any individual reinsurer provides on a deal, and consensus price, which is the overall market price at which that deal is eventually traded to all reinsurers who take a share. A price in reinsurance is often called a rate.

Property Catastrophe. A risk-type comprised of reinsurance covers against natural catastrophes such as earthquakes, floods, windstorms, and man-made disasters such as terrorist attacks.

Proportional reinsurance. A type of reinsurance cover where the reinsurer takes a proportional share in the cedent's entire portfolio at a specified rate, so sharing in that cedent's profits and losses. For instance, a reinsurer might carry 40 percent of any gains and losses on every policy underwritten by a cedent. Proportional reinsurance deals are often called quota share or pro rata deals (cf. non-proportional).

Quota share. See **Proportional reinsurance**.

Quote/Quoted price. A quoted price provides a legally binding price indication on a deal at which the quoting reinsurer would sell its capital. These quotes are submitted by a selected group of reinsurers, the reinsurance panel. Quotes from multiple reinsurers provide the basis to set the consensus price. Quoting reinsurers are legally bound to honor their quoted price if it is selected as the consensus price.

Rate of return. Refers to a measure of profitability on which to select a deal for the purpose of capital placement. The actual measure is firm-specific, for instance measuring a deal's return in terms of return on equity. The actual number that is derived from measuring the rate of return ought to be seen as relative to the other deals that a reinsurer is currently evaluating within a particular risk-type.

Rate on line (RoL). A measure of the premium required for a deal relative to the risk limit. It shows how much premium a reinsurer is getting as a percentage of the risk being carried. For example, a $10 million catastrophe cover with a premium of $2 million would have a RoL of 20 percent, which provides a higher premium volume to the reinsurer than a premium of $1 million, which would be expressed as a RoL of 10 percent.

Rate. The percentage applied to the cedent's premium to determine the reinsurance premiums to be paid to the reinsurer. This rate is effectively the price for reinsurance, hence the use of the term rating sheet.

Rating sheet. A spreadsheet used by an underwriter to evaluate a deal (see Chapters 3 and 4).

Reinsurance cover. There are two types of reinsurance cover: proportional (e.g. quota shares) and non-proportional (e.g. excess-of-loss).

Reinsurer. A firm that supplies capital to pay for potential losses on a cedent's deal. The cedent transfers the risk of a loss to the reinsurer, who holds capital in reserve to pay for such losses, in return for which the reinsurer receives a premium from the cedent.

Relationality. A term originating in social practice theory. For the purpose of this book, we define relationality as a relation amongst practices (patterns of activities) that construct a facet of the market. The relationality amongst practices is identified within each chapter according to the specific site of activity examined in that chapter.

Relational presence. A theoretical construct we develop in this book, building on social practice theory. It refers to the way a market is brought into existence because the practices of underwriters are relational to one another; showing how the market can be coordinated through practice, despite market actors not being connected in time or space.

Renewal date. Reinsurance deals are typically annual, and renew each year. There are five major dates when deals renew for another year: January 1 (1/1); April 1 (4/1); June 1 (6/1); July 1 (7/1); October 1 (10/1).

Return on equity (RoE). Provides a specific measure for a reinsurer to calculate the success of capital allocation per risk-type. It takes the operating profit (premium less claims) of a single risk-type, e.g. Property Cat and divides it by the equity allocated to the specific risk-type.

Return on risk-adjusted capital (RoRAC). A rate of return whereby deals judged to carry a greater risk of payout are adjusted based on the capital at risk, making it easier to compare and contrast the financial returns on deals with different risk profiles.

Return period. The number of years at a given premium level necessary to accumulate the premiums received by a reinsurer to equal a payout. It is calculated for deals according to an excess-of-loss cover.

Risks. A term used to denote the physical units of property at risk or the object of insurance protection. The word is also defined as "chance of loss" or "uncertainty of loss".

Risk-appetite. Refers to: i) a reinsurer's optimum diversity of risk-types carried within its portfolio; ii) the value they attribute to the longevity of business relationships; and, iii) fluctuations in their capital availability.

Risk-bearing. The reinsurance market is based on collective risk-bearing as competing reinsurers take shares in a deal, which means they share the risk of a loss and any subsequent payouts to a cedent.

Risk-type. Reinsurance risk is differentiated according to its underlying peril (see Figures 1.2 and 4.1). For the purposes of this book, we distinguish the following risk-types: Property Catastrophe, Credit & Surety Marine, Agriculture, and Liability, amongst others.

RoE. See **Return on equity**.

RoL. See **Rate on line**.

Security rating. An evaluation by a rating company, such as Standard & Poor's, of the credit-worthiness of any reinsurer.

Shortfall. A deal has a shortfall if reinsurers have provided only a part of the required amount of capital that is necessary to cover the deal. To attract further capital to cover a cedent against potential losses, typically an additional deal is designed which tends to be priced higher than the original deal (cf. full placement).

Short-tail risk. A category of risk in which it takes a relatively short time to determine the size of loss, and thus for reinsurers to settle claims after the occurrence of an event for particular risk-types. After the occurrence of a loss, claims are made shortly following the event, enabling a quick determination of the size of a loss (cf. long-tail risk). An example: Property Catastrophe where one can tell almost immediately after the hurricane which houses have been damaged and how badly.

Site. A term originating in social practice theory, and referring to a focus of social activity. It goes beyond a mere physical location or a cultural background that may bound activities. More importantly, a site is not separate from any practice, but a practice enacts the site as an activity is accomplished. The identity of practices is tied to a particular site. For the purpose of developing a theory of a market, this book identifies and distinguishes four sites of market-making activity: quoting a deal (see Chapter 2), evaluating a deal (see Chapter 3); different evaluative practices enacted within different risk-type (see Chapter 4) and enacting risk-appetite within firms (see Chapter 5). These sites are not exhaustive and others may also be identified to further illuminate the practice of the reinsurance market.

Soft market. A sustained period of time in which deals renew at a consensus price lower than the previous year's (cf. hard market). A soft market usually occurs during a period of insignificant losses in which reinsurers' capital reserves are untouched.

Underwriter(reinsurance). The person who is at the heart of market-making in this book. A reinsurance underwriter works for a reinsurer and is responsible for evaluating reinsurance deals in order to select those that will make best use of the reinsurer's capital.

Vendor model. A statistical package based on a set of parameters and formulae devised from meteorological, geological, engineering and actuarial science. These models estimate probability by reconstructing past events. For example, they build on information about the most destructive hurricanes, such as Andrew, Katrina, and Wilma, to determine probable hurricane paths and their potential damages. They can then run several thousand scenarios in order to identify what might happen for any particular deal, based on statistical extrapolations from these past events. Firms that specialize in risk analysis, such as Risk Management Solutions (RMS) and AIR, license these models and their updates to cedents, reinsurers and brokers. These models thus provide a common industry basis for evaluating deals; particularly Property Catastrophe deals (see Chapter 3).

Whole-account. An approach to trading risks where a reinsurer takes a holistic view of the profitability of the entire relationship with a cedent (their whole-account of deals), rather than the profitability of any particular deal in isolation. A whole-account approach might mean accepting some deals with a lower rate of return because of the advantages this gives that reinsurer on higher-return deals from that cedent, whereas a reinsurer who does not take a whole-account approach will consider each deal separately for its rate of return (see Chapter 5).

References

Abolafia, M. 1996, *Making Markets: Opportunism and Restraint on Wall Street*, Cambridge: Harvard University Press.

Abolafia, M. Y. 2010a, "Can Speculative Bubbles Be Managed? An Institutional Approach", *Strategic Organization* 8(1): 93–100.

Abolafia, M. Y. 2010b, "The Institutional Embeddedness of Market Failure: Why Speculative Bubbles Still Occur", *Research in the Sociology of Organizations* 30: 177–200.

Abolafia, M. Y. and Kilduff, M. 1988, "Enacting Market Crisis: The Social Construction of a Speculative Bubble", *Administrative Science Quarterly* 33(2): 177–193.

Ahrens, T. and Chapman, C. S. 2007, "Management Accounting as Practice", *Accounting, Organizations and Society* 32(1): 1–27.

Alwis, A. and Steinbach, C. M. 2003, "Credit & Surety Pricing and the Effects of Financial Market Convergence", *Casualty Actuarial Society Forum* Winter: 139–159.

Amin, A. and Roberts, J. 2008, "Knowing in Action: Beyond Communities of Practice", *Research Policy* 37(2): 353–369.

Antal, A. B., Hutter, M., and Stark, D. (eds.). 2015, *Moments of Valuation: Exploring Sites of Dissonance*, Oxford University Press: Oxford, U.K.

Aspers, P. 2009, "Knowledge and Valuation in Markets", *Theory and Society* 38(2): 111–131.

Baker, W. E. 1984, "The Social Structure of a National Securities Market", *American Journal of Sociology* 89(4): 775–811.

Balogun, J. and Johnson, G. 2004, "Organizational Restructuring and Middle Manager Sensemaking", *Academy of Management Journal* 47(4): 523–549.

Balogun, J. and Johnson, G. 2005, "From Intended Strategies to Unintended Outcomes: The Impact of Change Recipient Sensemaking", *Organization Studies* 26(11): 1573–1601.

Beckert, J. 2009, "The Social Order of Markets", *Theory and Society* 38(3): 245–269.

Beunza, D., Hardie, I., and MacKenzie D. 2006, "A Price Is a Social Thing: Towards a Material Sociology of Arbitrage", *Organization Studies* 27(5): 721–745.

Beunza, D. and Stark, D. 2004, "Tools of the Trade: The Socio-Technology of Arbitrage in a Wall Street Trading Room", *Industrial and Corporate Change* 13(2): 369–400.

Beunza, D. and Stark, D. 2012, "From Dissonance to Resonance: Cognitive Interdependence in Quantitative Finance", *Economy and Society* 41(3): 383–417.

Beunza, D. and Millo, Y. 2013, "Folding: Integrating Algorithms into the Floor of the New York Stock Exchange", Working paper series, Social Science Research Network (S.S.R.N.), London, U.K.

Borch, K. 1962, "Equilibrium in a Reinsurance Market", *Econometrica* 30: 424–444.

Borscheid, P., Gugerli, D., and Straumann, T. 2013, *The Value of Risk: Swiss Re and the History of Reinsurance*, Oxford: Oxford University Press.

Boyer, M. M. and Nyce, C. M. 2013, "An Industrial Organization Theory of Risk Sharing", *North American Actuarial Journal* 17(4): 283–296.

Brown, J. S. and Duguid, P. 2001, "Knowledge and Organization: A Social-Practice Perspective", *Organization Science* 12(2): 198–213.

Cabantous, L. 2007, "Ambiguity Aversion in the Field of Insurance: Insurers' Attitude to Imprecise and Conflicting Probability Estimates", *Theory and Decision* 62(3): 219–240.

Cabantous, L., Hilton, D., Kunreuther, H., and Michel-Kerjan, E. 2011, "Is Imprecise Knowledge Better Than Conflicting Expertise? Evidence from Insurers' Decisions in the United States", *Journal of Risk and Uncertainty* 42(3): 211–232.

Çalışkan, K. 2010, *Market Threads: How Cotton Farmers and Traders Create a Global Commodity*, New Jersey: Princeton University Press.

Çalışkan, K. and Callon, M. 2009, "Economization, Part 1: Shifting Attention from the Economy Towards Processes of Economization", *Economy and Society* 38(3): 369–398.

Çalışkan, K. and Callon, M. 2010, "Economization, Part 2: A Research Programme for the Study of Markets", *Economy and Society* 39(1): 1–32.

Callon, M. (ed.). 1998, *Laws of the Market*, London: Blackwell Publishers.

Callon, M. and Muniesa, F. 2005, "Economic Markets as Calculative Collective Devices", *Organization Studies* 26(8): 1229–1250.

Carruthers, B. G. and Stinchcombe, A. L. 1999, "The Social Structure of Liquidity: Flexibility, Markets, and States", *Theory and Society* 28(3): 353–382.

Chenhall, R. H., Hall, M., and Smith, D. 2013, "Performance Measurement, Modes of Evaluation and the Development of Compromising Accounts", *Accounting, Organizations and Society* 38(4): 268–287.

Chia, R. and Holt, R. 2006, "Strategy as Practical Coping: A Heideggerian Perspective", *Organization Studies* 27(5): 635–655.

Coates, J. M., Gurnell, M. and Sarnyai, Z. 2010, "From Molecule to Market: Steroid Hormones and Financial Risk-Taking", *Philosophical Transactions of the Royal Society B: Biological Sciences* 365(1538): 331–343.

Coates, J. M. and Herbert, J. 2008, "Endogenous Steroids and Financial Risk Taking on a London Trading Floor", *Proceedings of the National Academy of Sciences* 105(16): 6167–6172.

Colander, D., Goldberg, M., Haas, A., Juselius, K., Kirman, A., Lux, T., and Sloth, B. 2009, "The Financial Crisis and the Systemic Failure of the Economics Profession", *Critical Review* 21(2-3): 249–267.

Cooper, R. 2005, "Peripheral Vision Relationality", *Organization Studies* 26(11): 1689–1710.

Cummins, J. D. 2007, "Reinsurance for Natural and Man–Made Catastrophes in the United States: Current State of the Market and Regulatory Reforms", *Risk Management and Insurance Review* 10(2): 179–220.

Cummins, J. D., and Outreville, J. F. 1987, "An International Analysis of Underwriting Cycles in Property-Liability Insurance", *Journal of Risk and Insurance* 54(2): 246–262.

Cummins, J. D. and Trainar, P. 2009, "Securitization, Insurance, and Reinsurance", *Journal of Risk and Insurance* 76(3): 463–492.

Cunliffe, A. L. 2010, "Retelling Tales of the Field: In Search of Organizational Ethnography 20 Years On", *Organizational Research Methods* 13(2): 224–239.

Czarniawska, B. 2007, *Shadowing: And Other Techniques for Doing Fieldwork in Modern Societies*, Copenhagen: Copenhagen Business School Press DK.

Denzin, N. 1989, *The Research Act*, Englewood Cliffs: Prentice Hall.

Denzin, N. K. and Lincoln, Y. S. 2005, "Introduction: The Discipline and Practice of Qualitative Research", in *The Sage Handbook of Qualitative Research*, edited by Denzin, N. K. and Lincoln, Y.S., pp. 1–32. 3rd ed. Thousand Oaks: Sage Publications.

Diers, D. 2011, "Management Strategies in Multi-Year Enterprise Risk Management", *The Geneva Papers on Risk and Insurance-Issues and Practice* 36(1): 107–125.

Dupont-Courtade, T. 2013, *Perceptions Et Couvertures Des Risques Extrêmes En Présence D'incertitudes Sur Les Marchés De L'assurance Et De La Réassurance*. Ph.D., Paris School of Economics, Université Paris.

Elango, B., Ma, Y. L., and Pope, N. 2008, "An Investigation into the Diversification–Performance Relationship in the U.S. Property–Liability Insurance Industry", *Journal of Risk and Insurance* 75(3): 567–591.

Erkens, D. H., Hung, M., and Matos, P. 2012, "Corporate Governance in the 2007–2008 Financial Crisis: Evidence from Financial Institutions Worldwide", *Journal of Corporate Finance* 18(2): 389–411.

Espeland, W. N. and Stevens, M. L. 1998, "Commensuration as a Social Process", *Annual Review of Sociology* 24(1): 313–343.

Falzon, M.-A. 2009, *Multi-Sited Ethnography: Theory, Praxis and Locality in Contemporary Social Research*, Surrey: Ashgate Publishing.

Fauré, B. and Rouleau, L. 2011, "The Strategic Competence of Accountants and Middle Managers in Budget Making", *Accounting, Organizations and Society* 36(3): 167–182.

Feldman, M. S. and Orlikowski, W. J. 2011, "Theorizing Practice and Practicing Theory", *Organization Science* 22(5): 1240–1253.

Fligstein, N. 1996, "Markets as Politics: A Political-Cultural Approach to Market Institutions", *American Sociological Review* 61(4): 656–673.

Fligstein, N. 2001, *The Architecture of Markets: An Economic Sociology of Twenty-First-Century Capitalist Societies*, Princeton, PA: Princeton University Press.

Fligstein, N. and Goldstein, A. 2010, "The Anatomy of the Mortgage Securitization Crisis", *Research in the Sociology of Organizations* 30: 29–70.

Fligstein, N. and Mara-Drita, I. 1996, "How to Make a Market: Reflections on the Attempt to Create a Single Market in the European Union", *American Journal of Sociology* 102(1): 1–33.

Floyd, S. W. and Lane, P. J. 2000, "Strategizing Throughout the Organization: Managing Role Conflict in Strategic Renewal", *Academy of Management Review* 25(1): 154–177.

Geddes, L. 2009, "Financial Traders Are Born, Not Made", *New Scientist* 201(2691): 11.

Goffman, E. 1967/2005, *Interaction Ritual: Essays on Face-to-Face Behaviour*, New Brunswick, New Jersey: Transaction Publishers.

Golden-Biddle, K. and Locke, K. 1993, "Appealing Work: An Investigation of How Ethnographic Texts Convince", *Organization Science* 4(4): 595–616.

Granovetter, M. 1985, "Economic Action and Social Structure: The Problem of Embeddedness", *American Journal of Sociology* 91(3): 481–510.

Grossi, P. and Kunreuther, H. (eds.). 2005, *Catastrophe Modeling: A New Approach to Managing Risk*, New York: Springer.

Gurenko, E. N. 2004, *Catastrophe Risk and Reinsurance: A Country Risk Management Perspective*, Washington, D.C.: World Bank Publications.

Hallak, I. and Schure, P. 2011, "Why Larger Lenders Obtain Higher Returns: Evidence from Sovereign Syndicated Loans", *Financial Management* 40(2): 427–453.

Hammersley, M. and Atkinson, P. 2007, *Ethnography: Principles in Practice,* London: Routledge.

Hardie, I. and MacKenzie, D. 2007, "Constructing the Market Frame: Distributed Cognition and Distributed Framing in Financial Markets", *New Political Economy* 12(3): 389–403.

Helgesson, C.-F. and Muniesa, F. 2013, "For What It's Worth: An Introduction to Valuation Studies", *Valuation Studies* 1(1): 1–10.

Hennion, A. 2015, "Paying Attention. What Is Tasting Wine About?" in *Moments of Valuation: Exploring Sites of Dissonance*, edited by Antal, A. B., Hutter, M., and Stark, D., Chapter 3, Oxford: Oxford University Press.

Herschaft, J. A. 2005, "Not Your Average Coffee Shop: Lloyd's of London—a Twenty-First-Century Primer on the History, Structure, and Future of the Backbone of Marine Insurance", *Tulane Maritime Law Journal* 29(2): 169–185.

Heuts, F. and Mol, A. 2013, "What Is a Good Tomato? A Case of Valuing in Practice", *Valuation Studies* 1(2): 125–146.

Ho, K. 2009, *Liquidated: An Ethnography of Wall Street*, Durham, North Carolina: Duke University Press.

Hopwood, A. G. and Miller, P. 1994, *Accounting as Social and Institutional Practice*, Cambridge: Cambridge University Press.

Huault, I. and Rainelli-Weiss, H. 2011, "A Market for Weather Risk? Conflicting Metrics, Attempts at Compromise, and Limits to Commensuration", *Organization Studies* 32(10): 1395–1419.

Humphreys, M. and Watson, T. J. 2009, "Ethnographic Practices: From 'Writing-up Ethnographic Research' to 'Writing Ethnography'", in *Organizational Ethnography: Studying the Complexities of Everyday Organizational Life*, edited by Ybema, S., Yanow, D., Wels H. and Kamsteeg, F., pp. 40–55, London: Sage.

Jaffee, D. M. and Russell, T. 1997, "Catastrophe Insurance, Capital Markets, and Uninsurable Risks", *Journal of Risk and Insurance* 64(2): 205–230.

Jarzabkowski, P. 2004, "Strategy as Practice: Recursive, Adaptive and Practices-in-Use", *Organization Studies* 25(4): 529–560.

Jarzabkowski, P. 2005, *Strategy as Practice: An Activity-Based Approach*, London: Sage.

Jarzabkowski, P. 2008, "Shaping Strategy as a Structuration Process", *Academy of Management Journal* 51(4): 621–650.

Jarzabkowski, P., Balogun, J., and Seidl, D. 2007, "Strategizing: The Challenges of a Practice Perspective", *Human Relations* 60(1): 5–27.

Jarzabkowski, P., Bednarek. R., and Cabantous, L. 2014, "Conducting Global Team-Based Ethnography: Methodological Challenges and Practical Methods", *Human Relations*. Online First.

Jarzabkowski, P. and Spee, P. 2009, "Strategy–as–Practice: A Review and Future Directions for the Field", *International Journal of Management Reviews* 11(1): 69–95.

Jarzabkowski, P. A., Lê, J. K., and Feldman, M. S. 2012, "Toward a Theory of Coordinating: Creating Coordinating Mechanisms in Practice", *Organization Science* 23(4): 907–927.

John, A. H. 1958, "The London Assurance Company and the Marine Insurance Market of the Eighteenth Century", *Economica* 25(98): 126–141.

Johnson, G., Langley. A., Melin, L., and Whittington, R. 2007, *Strategy as Practice: Research Directions and Resources*, Cambridge: Cambridge University Press.

Johnson, G., Melin, L. and Whittington, R. 2003, "Micro-Strategy and Strategizing: Guest Editors' Introduction", *Journal of Management Studies* 40(1): 3–22.

Kalthoff, H. 2005, "Practices of Calculation", *Theory, Culture & Society* 22(2): 69–97.

Kiln, R. and Kiln, S. 2001, *Reinsurance in Practice*, London: Routledge.

Knorr Cetina, K. 1999, *Epistemic Cultures: How the Sciences Make Knowledge*, Cambridge, MA: Harvard University Press.

Knorr Cetina, K. and Bruegger, U. 2000, "The Market as an Object of Attachment: Exploring Postsocial Relations in Financial Markets", *Canadian Journal of Sociology* 25(2): 141–168.

Knorr Cetina, K. and Bruegger U. 2002a, "Global Microstructures: The Virtual Societies of Financial Markets", *American Journal of Sociology* 107(4): 905–950.

Knorr Cetina, K. and Bruegger, U. 2002b, "Traders' Engagement with Markets a Postsocial Relationship", *Theory, Culture & Society* 19(5-6): 161–185.

Knorr Cetina, K. and Preda, A. 2001, "The Epistemization of Economic Transactions", *Current Sociology* 49(4): 27–44.

Knorr Cetina, K. and Preda, A. 2004, *The Sociology of Financial Markets*, Oxford: Oxford University Press.

Knorr Cetina, K. and Preda, A. 2007, "The Temporalization of Financial Markets: From Network Markets to Flow Markets", *Theory, Culture and Society* 22(7-8): 213–234.

Knorr Cetina, K. and Preda, A. 2012, *The Oxford Handbook of the Sociology of Finance*, Oxford: Oxford University Press.

Knorr Cetina, K., Schatzki, T. R., and Von Savigny, E. (eds.). 2000, *The Practice Turn in Contemporary Theory*, New York: Routledge.

Kopf, E. W. 1929, "The Origin and Development of Reinsurance", *Proceedings of the Actuarial Society* 16(33): 22–91.

Ladoucette, S. A. and Teugels, J. L. 2006, "Analysis of Risk Measures for Reinsurance Layers", *Insurance: Mathematics and Economics* 38(3): 630–639.

Lamont, M. 2012, "Toward a Comparative Sociology of Valuation and Evaluation", *Sociology* 38(1): 201–221.

Leonardi, P. M. and Barley, S. R. 2010, "What's under Construction Here? Social Action, Materiality, and Power in Constructivist Studies of Technology and Organizing", *The Academy of Management Annals* 4(1): 1–51.

Lewis, M. 2014, *Flash Boys,* Penguin U.K.

Lincoln, Y. S. and Guba, E. G. 1985, "But Is It Rigorous? Trustworthiness and Authenticity in Naturalistic Evaluation", in *Naturalistic Evaluation* (edited by Williams, D. D., San Francisco: Jossey-Bass.

MacKenzie, D. 2004, "Social Connectivities in Global Financial Markets", *Environment and Planning D* 22(1): 83–102.

MacKenzie, D. 2006, *An Engine, Not a Camera: How Financial Models Shape Markets.* Cambridge, MA: MIT Press.

MacKenzie, D. 2009, "Making Things the Same: Gases, Emission Rights and the Politics of Carbon Markets", *Accounting, Organizations and Society* 34(3): 440–455.

MacKenzie, D. 2011, "The Credit Crisis as a Problem in the Sociology of Knowledge", *American Journal of Sociology* 116(6): 1778–1841.

MacKenzie, D. 2012, "Knowledge Production in Financial Markets: Credit Default Swaps, the ABX and the Subprime Crisis", *Economy and Society* 41(3): 335–359.

MacKenzie, D. and Millo, Y. 2003, "Constructing a Market, Performing Theory: The Historical Sociology of a Financial Derivatives Exchange", *American Journal of Sociology* 109(1): 107–145.

Maitlis, S. and Lawrence, T. B. 2003, "Orchestral Manoeuvres in the Dark: Understanding Failure in Organizational Strategizing", *Journal of Management Studies* 40(1): 109–139.

Mantere, S. 2008, "Role Expectations and Middle Manager Strategic Agency", *Journal of Management Studies* 45(2): 294–316.

Mantere, S. and Vaara, E. 2008, "On the Problem of Participation in Strategy: A Critical Discursive Perspective", *Organization Science* 19(2): 341–358.

Marcus, G. E. 1995, "Ethnography in/of the World System: The Emergence of Multi-Sited Ethnography", *Annual Review of Anthropology*: 95–117.

Markowitz, H. 1952, "Portfolio Selection", *The Journal of Finance* 7(1): 77–91.

Mauthner, N. S. and Doucet A. 2008, "Knowledge Once Divided Can Be Hard to Put Together Again: An Epistemological Critique of Collaborative and Team-Based Research Practices", *Sociology* 42(5): 971–985.

McDowell, L. 2010, "Capital Culture Revisited: Sex, Testosterone and the City", *International Journal of Urban and Regional Research* 34(3): 652–658.

McFall, L. 2011, "A 'Good, Average Man': Calculation and the Limits of Statistics in Enrolling Insurance Customers", *The Sociological Review* 59(4): 661–684.

Mikes, A. 2009, "Risk Management and Calculative Cultures", *Management Accounting Research* 20(1): 18–40.

Mikes, A. 2011, "From Counting Risk to Making Risk Count: Boundary-Work in Risk Management", *Accounting, Organizations and Society* 36: 226–245.

Miles, M. B. and Huberman, A. M. 1994, *Qualitative Data Analysis: An Expanded Sourcebook*, Thousand Oaks, CA: Sage.

Miller, P. 2008, "Calculating Economic Life", *Journal of Cultural Economy and Society* 1(1): 51–64.

Miller, P. and O'Leary, T. 2007, "Mediating Instruments and Making Markets: Capital Budgeting, Science and the Economy", *Accounting, Organizations and Society* 32(7): 701–734.

Millo, Y. and MacKenzie, D. 2009, "The Usefulness of Inaccurate Models: Towards an Understanding of the Emergence of Financial Risk Management", *Accounting, Organizations and Society* 34(5): 638–653.

Miyazaki, H. 2003, "The Temporalities of the Market", *American Anthropologist* 105(2): 255–265.

Muniesa, F., Millo, Y., and Callon, M. 2007, "An Introduction to Market Devices", *The Sociological Review* 55: 1–12.

Nicolini, D. 2009a, "Articulating Practice through the Interview to the Double", *Management Learning* 40(2): 195–212.

Nicolini, D. 2009b, "Zooming in and Out: Studying Practices by Switching Theoretical Lenses and Trailing Connections", *Organization Studies* 30(12): 1391–1418.

Nicolini, D. 2013, *Practice Theory, Work and Organization*, Oxford: Oxford University Press.

Niehaus, G. and Terry, A. 1993, "Evidence on the Time Series Properties of Insurance Premium and Cause of the Underwriting Cycle: New Support for the Capital Market Imperfection Hypothesis", *Journal of Risk and Insurance* 60(3): 466–479.

Orlikowski, W. 2001, "Using Technology and Constituting Structures: A Practice Lens for Studying Technology in Organizations", *Organization Science* 11(4): 404–428.

Orlikowski, W. J. 2007, "Sociomaterial Practices: Exploring Technology at Work", *Organization Studies* 28(9): 1435–1448.

Orlikowski, W. J. and Scott, S. V. 2008, "Sociomateriality: Challenging the Separation of Technology, Work and Organization", *Academy of Management Annals* 2(1): 433–474.

Pettigrew, A. M. 1990, "Longitudinal Field Research on Change: Theory and Practice", *Organization Science* 1(3): 267–292.

Pickering, A. 1995, *The Mangle of Practice: Time, Agency, and Science*, Chicago: University of Chicago Press.

Pinch, T. 2015, "Moments in the Valuation of Sound: The Early History of Synthesizers", In *Moments of Valuation. Exploring Sites of Dissonance*, edited by Antal, A. B., Hutter M. and Stark, D, Chapter 2, Oxford: Oxford University Press.

Pinch, T. and Swedberg R. (eds.). 2008, *Living in a Material World: Economic Sociology Meets Science and Technology Studies*. Cambridge, MA: The MIT Press.

Power, M. 2009, "The Risk Management of Nothing", *Accounting, Organizations and Society* 34(6): 849–855.

Preda, A. 2006, "Socio-Technical Agency in Financial Markets the Case of the Stock Ticker", *Social Studies of Science* 36(5): 753–782.

Preda, A. 2007, "The Sociological Approach to Financial Markets", *Journal of Economic Surveys* 21(3): 506–528.

Preda, A. 2009a, "Brief Encounters: Calculation and the Interaction Order of Anonymous Electronic Markets", *Accounting, Organizations and Society* 34(5): 675–693.

Preda, A. 2009b, *Framing Finance: The Boundaries of Markets and Modern Capitalism*, Chicago: University of Chicago Press.

Raim, D. M. and Langford, J. L. 2008, "Understanding Reinsurance" in *New Appleman Insurance Law Practice Guide*, pp. 40–131, Los Angeles, CA: LexisNexis.

Reckwitz, A. 2002, "Toward a Theory of Social Practices a Development in Culturalist Theorizing", *European Journal of Social Theory* 5(2): 243–263.

Regnér, P. 2003, "Strategy Creation in the Periphery: Inductive Versus Deductive Strategy Making", *Journal of Management Studies* 40(1): 57–82.

Robertson, M., Scarbrough, H., and Swan, J. 2003, "Knowledge Creation in Professional Service Firms: Institutional Effects", *Organization Studies* 24(6): 831–857.

Rouleau, L. 2005, "Micro-Practices of Strategic Sensemaking and Sensegiving: How Middle Managers Interpret and Sell Change Every Day", *Journal of Management Studies* 42(7): 1413–1441.

Rouleau, L. and Balogun, J. 2011, "Middle Managers, Strategic Sensemaking and Discursive Competence", *Journal of Management Studies* 48(5): 953–983.

Salamat, A. and Burton, C. 2008, "Current Issues in the Subscription Market", *Mealey's Litigation Report* 18(24): 1–14.

Schatzki, T. 2001, "Introduction: Practice Theory" in *The Practice Turn in Contemporary Theory*, edited by Schatzki, T. R., Knorr-Cetina, K., and Savigny, E. V., pp. 1–14. London: Routledge.

Schatzki, T. 2002, *The Site of the Social: A Philosophical Account of the Constitution of Social Life and Change*, Pennsylvania, PA: Penn State University Press.

Schatzki, T. 2005, "Peripheral Vision the Sites of Organizations", *Organization Studies* 26(3): 465–484.

Schatzki, T. 2006, "On Organizations as They Happen", *Organization Studies* 27(12): 1863–1873.

Smets, M., Burke, G., Jarzabkowski, P. and Spee, P. 2014, "Charting New Territory for Organizational Ethnography: Insights from a Team-Based Video Ethnography", *Journal of Organizational Ethnography* 3(1): 10–26.

Smets, M., Jarzabkowski, P., Spee, P. and Burke, G. 2014, "Reinsurance Trading in Lloyd's of London: Balancing Conflicting-yet-Complementary Logics in Practice", *Academy of Management Journal*. In Press.

Stark, D. 2009, *The Sense of Dissonance: Accounts of Worth in Economic Life*, Princeton, NJ: Princeton University Press.

Swedberg, R. 1994, "Markets as Social Structures", in *Handbook of Economic Sociology*, edited by Smelser, N. and Swedberg, R., pp. 255–282. New York, Princeton: Princeton University Press.

Uzzi, B. and Lancaster, R. 2004, "Embeddedness and Price Formation in the Corporate Law Market", *American Sociological Review* 69(3): 319–344

Vaara, E. and Whittington, R. 2012, "Strategy-as-Practice: Taking Social Practices Seriously", *The Academy of Management Annals* 6(1): 285–336.

Van Maanen, J. 2011, *Tales of the Field: On Writing Ethnography*, Chicago: University of Chicago Press.

Vatin, F. 2013, "Valuation as Evaluating and Valorizing", *Valuation Studies* 1(1): 31–50.

Vergara, O., Zuba, G., Doggett, T., and Seaquist, J. 2008, "Modeling the Potential Impact of Catastrophic Weather on Crop Insurance Industry Portfolio Losses", *American Journal of Agricultural Economics* 90(5): 1256–1262.

Vollmer, H., Mennicken, A. and Preda, A. 2009, "Tracking the Numbers: Across Accounting and Finance, Organizations and Markets", *Accounting, Organizations and Society* 34(5): 619–637.

Watson, T. J. 2011, "Ethnography, Reality, and Truth: The Vital Need for Studies of 'How Things Work' in Organizations and Management", *Journal of Management Studies* 48(1): 202–217.

Weber, M. 1922/1968, *Economy and Society*, New York: Bedminster Press Inc.

Weick, K. E. 2001, *Making Sense of the Organization*, Oxford: Blackwell

Wenger, E. 1998, *Communities of Practice: Learning, Meaning and Identity.* Cambridge: Cambridge University Press.

White, H. C. 1981, "Where Do Markets Come From?", *American Journal of Sociology* 87: 517–547.

White, H. C. 2001, *Markets from Networks, Socioeconomic Models of Production.* Princeton, New Jersey: Princeton University Press.

Whittington, R. 2006, "Completing the Practice Turn in Strategy Research", *Organization Studies* 27(5): 613–634.

Whittington, R. 2011, "The Practice Turn in Organization Research: Towards a Disciplined Transdisciplinarity", *Accounting, Organizations and Society* 36(3): 183–186.

Whittington, R., Jarzabkowski, P., Mayer, M., Mounoud, E., Nahapiet, J., and Rouleau, L. 2003, "Taking Strategy Seriously Responsibility and Reform for an Important Social Practice", *Journal of Management Inquiry* 12(4): 396–409.

Zaloom, C. 2003, "Ambiguous Numbers: Trading Technologies and Interpretation in Financial Markets", *American Ethnologist* 30(2): 258–272.

Zaloom, C. 2006, *Out of the Pits: Traders and Technology from Chicago to London*, Chicago: University of Chicago Press.

Zilber, T. B. 2014, "Beyond a Single Organization: Challenges and Opportunities in Doing Field Level Ethnography", *Journal of Organizational Ethnography* 3(1): 96–113.

Zuckerman, E. W. 2010. "What If We Had Been in Charge? The Sociologist as Builder of Rational Institutions". *Research in the Sociology of Organizations* 30: 359–378.

Zuckerman, E. W. 2012. "Construction, Concentration, and (Dis)Continuities in Social Valuations". *Annual Review of Sociology* 38: 223–245.

Index

Printed and bound by CPI Group (UK) Ltd, Croydon, CR0 4YY